GOD WHO ARE YOU ANYWAY?

GOD
WHO ARE
YOU
ANYWAY?

I AM BIGGER
THAN YOU THINK

BILL BRIGHT
WITH BRAD BRIGHT

NASHVILLE

NEW YORK • LONDON • MELBOURNE • VANCOUVER

GOD WHO ARE YOU ANYWAY?
I AM BIGGER THAN YOU THINK

© 2019 **Bright Media Foundation**

Published in New York, New York, by Morgan James Publishing. Morgan James is a trademark of Morgan James, LLC. www.MorganJamesPublishing.com

Unless otherwise indicated, Scripture quotations are from the *New Living Translation*, © 1996 by Tyndale Charitable Trust. Scripture quotations designated NIV are from the New International Version, © 1973, 1978, 1984 by the International Bible Society. Published by Zondervan Bible Publishers, Grand Rapids, Michigan. Scripture quotations designated TLB are from The Living Bible, © 1971 by Tyndale House Publishers, Wheaton, Illinois. Scripture quotations designated NKJV are from the New King James Version, © 1979, 1980, 1982 by Thomas Nelson Inc., Publishers, Nashville, Tennessee. Scripture quotations designated NASB are from The New American Standard Bible, © 1960, 1962, 1963, 1968, 1971, 1972, 1973, 1975, 1977 by the Lockman Foundation, La Habra, California.

ISBN 978-1-63047-869-8 paperback
ISBN 978-1-63047-870-4 eBook
Library of Congress Control Number: 2015918105

Edited by:
Joette Whims and Lynn Copeland.

Cover Design by:
Rachel Lopez
www.r2cdesign.com

Interior Design by:
Bonnie Bushman
The Whole Caboodle Graphic Design

I AM

GodWhoRU.com

I AM Personal –John 15:15
God, because You are personal I will seek a deep relationship with You.

I AM All-Powerful –Jeremiah 32:17
God, because You are all-powerful I know You can help me with anything.

I AM Love –John 3:16
God, because You are love I know You are unconditionally committed to my well-being.

I AM Holy –Isaiah 6:3
God, because You are holy I will devote myself to You in purity, worship and service.

I AM Everywhere All the Time –Hebrews 13:5
God, because You are everywhere all the time I know You are always with me.

I AM Merciful –Ephesians 2:4-5
God, because You are merciful I know that through Christ all my sins are forgiven.

I AM Absolute Truth –John 14:6
God, because You are absolute truth I will believe what You say and live accordingly.

I AM All-Knowing –Colossians 2:3
God, because You know everything
I will come to You with all my questions, concerns and worries.

I AM Just –Deuteronomy 32:4
God, because You are just I know Your justice will prevail.

I AM Faithful –Hebrews 10:23
God, because You are faithful I will trust You to always keep Your promises.

I AM Sovereign –1 Timothy 1:17
God, because You are sovereign I will joyfully submit to Your will.

I AM Righteous –Psalm 119:137
God, because You are righteous I will live by Your standards.

I AM Unchanging - James 1:17
God, because You never change I know my future is secure and eternal.

Contents

Leader's Guide material may be found at GodWhoRU.com

Who Was Bill Bright...Really?

Bill Bright grew up on a ranch in rural Oklahoma. Like his father and grandfather before him, he did not see God as relevant to his life. The only thing that mattered was money and success. He moved to Hollywood as a young man and was well on his way to making his millions. However, one day a businessman he greatly admired said something that startled him: "Making money is great, but the most important thing in my life is Jesus Christ." Intrigued, Bill started studying the life of Jesus. A few months later, convinced Jesus was who He claimed to be, he became an ardent follower.

Over the next 50 years, Bill Bright's resume grew into a testament of what God can do through one person who commits to following Jesus, holding nothing back. In 1951 at UCLA, he launched Campus Crusade for Christ, which became the largest missionary organization in the 20th century (27,000 full-time staff, 250,000 trained volunteers in every country on earth). He wrote *The Four Spiritual Laws*, an evangelistic booklet with over two billion copies in print worldwide. He was the impetus behind the creation of the JESUS film, which has been translated into over 1,500 languages and viewed by an estimated three billion people in every nation around the globe. The Guinness Book of World Records says it is the most translated film in history.

What most people do not know about Bill Bright is what occurred behind the scenes revealing his character, humility, integrity, and compassion. Although he traveled 80 percent of the time for 40 years, he almost always flew economy class in order to be a faithful steward of God's money. For the last 50 years of his life, he never owned the home he lived in. He was never alone with a woman who was not his wife. He gave away all his retirement savings to help tell the Russian people about Jesus Christ. He won the $1 million Templeton Prize for Progress in Religion and gave it all away 30 minutes later. For years he quietly fasted one day each week and gave away the money he saved from fasting to help the poor.

In 2003 he died at the age of 81 after a four-year battle with lung disease. In his final days, when asked how he was feeling, Bill always sincerely responded, "I'm rejoicing in the Lord!" His self-chosen epitaph on his grave sums up his life the best: "A slave of Jesus by choice."

What was the real genius of Bill Bright? It cannot be found in his accomplishments or character, though they are impressive. The genius of Bill Bright was his view of God. It is what enabled him not just to talk about Jesus, but to model what it looks like to be a true follower of Jesus.

Your Focus Is Everything

Bill Bright was my dad. Before my eyes, day after day, I watched him live out what you are about to read. His gut-level understanding of God, and belief in who God is, enabled him to do what eludes so many of us:

- He experienced peace when all he had worked for appeared to be crumbling.
- He experienced joy in the midst of great sorrow.
- He treated people who hurt, attacked or betrayed him with love and grace.
- He gave thanks even in his deepest disappointments.
- He consistently achieved what others said was impossible.
- He stayed humble in the midst of receiving worldwide accolades.
- He rejoiced when doctors informed him he would suffer a horrible death.

I saw my dad filled with joy and peace to the end. How? After reading these pages, you will understand. Apply what you learn and you can experience it for yourself.

Jesus *promised* us His peace. He said, "Peace I leave with you, My peace I give to you" (John 14:27, NKJV). If you are a follower of Jesus, would you say that is your normal daily experience? If not, then either Jesus lied or you missed something. Which do you think it is?

Dad clearly recognized the root of the problem: "We can trace all our human problems to our view of God." If that is true, then the most important question in life is, "God, who are You anyway?"

The reality is, you can't fix yourself (I know, I've tried), but you *can* fix your view of God. That's the point of this book. You have to change your focus. Then, as your view of God deepens you will change in response.

Change your focus, change your life. Are you ready?

Yours for making GOD the issue,
Brad Bright

P.S. I updated this book for small discussion groups. If you want to read it on your own, that's fine. However, if you can think of a few friends you could ask to read it along with you and talk about it (either face-to-face or online), you should find it an even richer experience.

CHAPTER 1

Is Your God Too Small?

W ho am I to write a book about God? Yet, that is the task I found I must undertake.

How can we as mere human beings fully grasp any facet of our gloriously incomprehensible God? Have you ever felt like I do about understanding and knowing our great God? So why would I attempt to undertake such a seemingly impossible task? More importantly, why should any of us try to understand who God is?

Renowned theologian and Bible translator J. B. Phillips once wrote, "Your God is too small."[1]

You may naturally ask, "How do I know if my God is too small?" Great question! Let me turn the question back to you: Do *you* think your God is big enough? Consider the following. In John 14:27, Jesus promised us His peace—a "peace of mind and heart." In Galatians 5:22, Paul said the fruit of the Spirit is "love, joy, peace..." Is peace of mind and heart your daily, moment-by-moment experience? If not, then either Jesus and Paul lied or you missed something. Which do you think it is? Here is the bottom line: peace is the result of trust. Trust is a result of how you view God.

Truthfully, none of us can completely grasp the width, depth, complexity, or immensity of any part of God's nature. But if we merely have a small, human-centered view of God, we limit ourselves to only what we can accomplish through our self-efforts. Or we may think He is just a little more intelligent, powerful, or wise than we are. Such inadequate views of God rob us of an intimate life-changing relationship with our awe-inspiring Creator.

> Everything else in the universe had a beginning, except God.

God has given us minds that can see farther than our own human limitations. For example, we can discover the intricacies of the DNA molecule, which no one has ever seen. We can study about places we have never visited, such as the underwater world of deep-sea creatures. We use cell phones with the knowledge that the signals may be coming to us from as far away as telecommunication satellites orbiting in space. These concepts extend our thinking beyond what we can observe with our eyes. In the following pages, let us put aside our tendency to be superficial in our understanding of God and stretch our minds to get a clearer idea of His magnificent nature.

God's Most Profound Name: I AM

One of the biblical concepts that help establish God's unlimited nature is His most important name. When God commanded Moses to lead the Israelites out of Egyptian slavery, Moses wondered what to tell them if they should ask the name of this God, because in ancient cultures, names reflected deeper meanings. In His short reply, the Lord spoke some of the most profound and revealing words recorded in the entire Bible. He said, "I AM WHO I AM. This is what you are to say to the Israelites: 'I AM has sent me to you'" (Exodus 3:14, NIV).

The Israelites immediately understood that the Hebrew word for I AM identified God as the only self-existent, eternal, personal Supreme Being. They clearly realized who had given Moses the message. It was God Himself! In the very next verse, God said to Moses:

"Say to the Israelites, 'The LORD, the God of your fathers—the God of Abraham, the God of Isaac, and the God of Jacob—has sent me to you.' This is My name forever, the name by which I am to be remembered from generation to generation." (Exodus 3:15, NIV)

The word "LORD" is written in all capital letters in many Bible versions to distinguish this name from other references to God. It is translated from the Hebrew YHWH, which means God's personal name. Other Bible versions translate it as Jehovah. In Isaiah 42:8, God clearly says, "I am the LORD [YHWH]; that is My name!" This name was so sacred and holy that the ancient rabbis would not allow anyone to say it aloud for fear someone would inadvertently use it wrongly. When reading Scriptures that contained this name, the rabbis substituted Adonai (LORD) instead of reading aloud the most holy name. Consequently, the exact pronunciation of YHWH was lost. Today, scholars believe it was pronounced Yahweh.

Because I AM contains no adjective or qualifier that describes or limits its meaning, it signifies that God is complete. He has no beginning, no end, needs no help, no counsel. Everything He is and does is perfect, not lacking in anything.

The Splendor of God

As king of Israel, David composed many lyrical psalms expressing God's grandeur. In Psalm 145, he writes:

I will praise You, my God and King, and bless Your name each day and forever. Great is Jehovah [YHWH]! Greatly praise Him! His greatness is beyond discovery! Let each generation tell its children what glorious things He does. I will meditate about Your glory, splendor, majesty, and miracles. Your awe-inspiring deeds shall be on every tongue; I will proclaim Your greatness. Everyone will tell about how good You are and sing about Your righteousness. (Psalm 145:1–7, TLB)

> What misconceptions prevent you from trusting God completely?

Many other biblical writers also wrote of God's splendor. In the New Testament, Paul describes Him as "the King eternal, immortal, invisible, who alone is wise, be honor and glory forever and ever" (1 Timothy 1:17, NKJV). The apostle John described what happened when he glimpsed God the Son during a vision. "When I saw Him, I fell at His feet as though dead. Then He placed His right hand on me and said: 'Do not be afraid. I am the First and the Last. I am the Living One'" (Revelation 1:17,18, NIV).

Our God is so gloriously incomprehensible that our minds just cannot grasp the whole nature of God. Yet we must find some human way to understand God's characteristics—at least in part.

Four basic qualities of God are integral to each of His other attributes: His infinity, self-existence, eternal nature, and self-sufficiency.

God is infinite; He has no limits.

One day, Augustine, a leader in the early Church, was walking along the ocean shore pondering God's nature when he noticed a small boy playing in the sand. The child scooped a hole in the sand with a seashell, then ran down to the water's edge and dipped his shell full of seawater. Immediately, he ran back and dumped the water into the hole he had made in the sand. Of course, the water just leaked out through the sand.

Augustine asked the boy, "What are you doing?"

The boy confidently replied, "I am going to pour the sea into that hole."

"Ah," Augustine later reflected, "that is what I have been trying to do. Standing at the ocean of infinity, I have attempted to grasp it with my finite mind."[2]

Who can understand God's infinity? The prophet Isaiah writes, "Who has measured the waters in the hollow of His hand, and marked off the heavens by the span, and calculated the dust of the earth by the measure, and weighed the mountains in a balance, and the hills in a pair of scales? Who has directed the Spirit of the LORD, or as His counselor has informed Him?" (Isaiah 40:12,13, NASB).

God's infinity means that He has no limits, boundaries, or end. God cannot be compared to any finite standard. Everything within our world is finite; even the universe, as vast as it is, has a limit. God and only God is infinite. Since His infinite nature relates to all of His attributes, God's love, holiness, mercy, and all other qualities are unlimited in their scope and expression.

God is self-existent; He has no creator.

As humans, we use the word "create" differently than God does. When we "create" a work of art, we start with a material, such as sculptor's clay, and mold it into a different shape. Our "creation" is actually something reshaped, rearranged, combined, or invented. Mankind has never made something out of nothing. Not so with God. When He created the world, He made it out of nothing. We cannot really comprehend what that means. We have never seen "nothing."

We cannot even use the word "created" to describe God. God was not created. Everything else in the universe had a beginning, except God. Because He is the Creator, He exists outside of the created order. He is different from and independent of His creation, dwelling in pure existence far above everything He has made.

God is also the force or cosmic glue that holds everything together (Colossians 1:17; Hebrews 1:3). Without Him, everything that He created would disintegrate.

God is eternal; He is not bound by space and time.

Imagine that you want to discover what is going on in a room filled with people, but the door is locked. You peer through the keyhole, trying to piece together what each person in the room is doing. People move about, coming into view, then disappearing out of sight. What a frustration! If only you could open the door and walk into the room to see what is going on!

That is how time and space are to us. We look at events through a keyhole, and all we know is what we can see happening right now. For us, time defines boundaries. We mark the point in time of our birth and death. We count history by years and ages. As a human being, I cannot even begin to imagine what it must be like to live outside the boundary of time.

But God is not bound by the dimensions of time. Before He spoke the first word of creation, time did not exist. He created time as a temporary context for His creation.

It baffles my mind to realize that God experiences all past, present, and future events simultaneously. Everything that has ever happened or will ever happen has already occurred within His awareness. God sees the beginning of the parade of life; He sees its end. All history is but a little speck within the spectrum of eternity. Our God encompasses all of eternity!

God is self-sufficient; He is dependent on nothing.

Every living thing on earth needs food, water, and air. Without a constant supply of these, all living things die.

Although God is a living being, He has no needs. He is dependent upon nothing outside Himself. All creation relies upon God for existence and the maintenance of life. God has no need for anything and is not vulnerable in any way. He does not need our help. Yet He offers us the privilege of being involved with Him in the fulfillment of His purposes as His friends.

We will never be able to fully understand God's magnificence. In fact, His infinity, self-existence, eternal nature, and self-sufficiency are incomprehensible. But are you not glad that God is so far beyond our human abilities? We can have complete confidence in a God who is greater than us and any of our problems.

Applying God's Qualities to His Character

One important principle about God's nature is that all the attributes of God are interactive and completely interrelated. With our human limitations, we dissect God's nature into parts or attributes so we can understand them, but that is not how they exist in God's character. Each attribute is perfectly complete and fully a part of God's personality. As we study these attributes, keep in mind that if we exalt one of God's qualities over another, we can get a distorted view of God's character. In fact, overemphasizing any one of God's attributes to the exclusion of others can lead to heresy. For example, teaching only about God's mercy and neglecting His role as a judge will prevent people from understanding God's hatred of sin and the future punishment for wrongdoing. Therefore, as we study each quality individually, we must remember that it is only one aspect of God's magnificent nature.

Since God's attributes are so interlinked, we cannot understand one without the others. God's attributes relate to each other; they are all part of the whole of God's nature.

> If we emphasize one of God's attributes over another, we will get a distorted view of God.

Let me apply the principle of God's unified nature to the four basic qualities we just covered. One of the attributes we will examine is God's love. God is not just a huge bundle of love; His love has all four basic qualities.

God's love is *infinite*. There is no limit to His love; it is beyond measure.

God's love is *self-existent*. It did not come to Him from somewhere else. It has always been a part of His character. God's love did not begin at some point; it has always existed in the heart of God.

God's love is *eternal*. It never had a beginning and will last forever. His love is never less or more. It always exists without the limitations of time or amount.

God's love is *self-sufficient*. He does not need love to make Him what He already is. He is not dependent on love to make Him happy or more fulfilled.

Throughout the rest of this book, keep these four qualities in mind and apply them to each of the attributes we will learn about.

Applying New Insights to Your Life

As you read, I urge you to consider what might be keeping you from hungering after God. Do you have misconceptions about God that might be preventing you from trusting Him completely?

If so, take heart. Because of God's love, He has provided the way for us to better understand what He is like, what He is up to, and how He can help us change our lives completely.

My prayer is that the Holy Spirit will mightily use this book to reveal to you the amazing and wonderful character of our glorious Creator God and Savior. If you read this book with prayerful sincerity, asking God to help you see Him for who He really is, you will find your life changing in response.

Please understand that this magnificent God wants a personal relationship with you! It is not enough to simply know who God is on an intellectual level, because He is not an impersonal force. He is a personal Being who wants you to know Him. So in Chapter 2 we will start with one of the most important questions anyone can ask.

Talk About It: Is Your God Too Small?

"Great is the LORD! He is most worthy of praise!
No one can measure His greatness."
(Psalm 145:3)

1. If someone saw a film of your life from the past month, how big would they say your God is? What are some examples that would lead them to that conclusion? Why do you think you see God this way?

2. Do you think your view of God is big enough? Why or why not? For example, do you question if He is really big enough to handle your problems?

3. As your view of God grows, what impact do you hope that has on your daily life?

4. Although God is knowable, our human brains can't possibly comprehend all there is to know about Him. Why is that important for us to keep in mind as we seek to know Him better?

5. What do you think God is conveying about Himself when He tells Moses His name is "I AM" in Exodus 3:14? How does that make you feel (secure, fearful, small, grateful, etc.)?

6. Many religions reject the idea that God is truly infinite. They believe God was created in time and space just like us. Why is it so important for us to recognize that God has no beginning and no end? Why is it impossible for something finite to become infinite?

7. How does the fact that God is infinite, self-existent, eternal and self-sufficient influence the way you see His love?

8. As you look back over your life what is one event that had a major impact in shaping who you are today? How did it shape your view of God?

FOCUS ON GOD

The next time a major challenge comes your way, ask yourself, "Do I believe God is big enough to handle this?" Are you facing one of those challenges now?

This coming week, create a timeline of your life focusing on the events and times that have shaped who you are. Keep your timeline with this book so you can refer back to it as you consider who God is and how your view of God has affected your life.

CHAPTER 2

I Am Personal

Have you ever considered one of the most important questions anyone could ask? *Is it possible for a mere human, less than a tiny speck on a pebble of a planet in the midst of a vast galaxy, to know the great God who created everything?* If so, can we know God well enough to trust Him with the most sensitive areas in our lives? Even more, *do* we know God well enough to love and obey Him in whatever He asks of us? Although fully understanding God is impossible, the quest to know, love, and serve God is the greatest adventure in life!

To put this in perspective, let's consider the size of the universe. Scientists estimate that the universe is at least 156 billion light-years wide.[3] Hurtling through that span of space whirl billions of galaxies that contain billions of stars. No one has ever seen the edge of the universe. This is mind-boggling. The immensity of the universe is so beyond our comprehension that we don't even have adequate words to grasp it.

Yet the Bible tells us that God rules over the entire universe. Isaiah writes: "This is what the LORD says: 'Heaven is My throne, and the earth is My footstool. Could you ever build Me a temple as good as that? Could you build a dwelling place for Me? My hands have made both heaven and earth, and they are Mine.

I, the LORD, have spoken!'" (Isaiah 66:1,2). In Ephesians, the apostle Paul writes of Jesus, "The same one who came down is the one who ascended higher than all the heavens, so that His rule might fill the entire universe" (Ephesians 4:10).

As I set forth to write about our glorious and mighty God I faced an overwhelming predicament—how to describe this God, infinitely greater than even our own universe. He lives in indescribable splendor beyond my wildest imagination. His character is far above the limited scope of my human understanding.

Why Is It So Important to Know God?

My desire to write a book about God began many years ago when Dr. James Montgomery Boice of the "Bible Hour" radio program interviewed me. One of the first questions Dr. Boice asked me was, "What is the most important truth to teach any follower of Christ?"

What an incredible question! No one had ever asked me that before, so I was not prepared to answer it. For a brief moment, I was speechless. But then I am convinced that God's Holy Spirit gave me the answer: "The attributes of God."

I have had years to think about that question and my answer. Today I am more convinced than ever that there is nothing more important to teach another believer than who God is, what He is like, and why or how He does what He does. These attributes of God can be referred to as His character, nature, qualities, or personality.

Yet one of the most tragic trends I have noticed in our churches today is the way believers view God. Renowned author A. W. Tozer writes in his book *The Knowledge of the Holy:*

> The low view of God entertained almost universally among Christians is the cause of a hundred lesser evils everywhere among us. With our loss of the sense of majesty has come the further loss of religious awe and the consciousness of the divine presence... It is impossible to keep our moral practices sound and our inward attitudes right while our idea of God is erroneous or inadequate. If we would bring back spiritual power to our lives, we must begin to think of God more nearly as He is.[4]

In fact, everything about our lives—our attitudes, motives, desires, actions, and even our words—is influenced by our view of God. Whether our problems are financial, moral, or emotional, whether we are tempted by lust, worry, anger, or insecurity, our behavior reflects our beliefs about God. What we believe to be true about God's character affects our friendships, our work and leisure activities, the types of literature we read, and even the music to which we listen. If the majority of believers do not have the right view of God, how can our society even begin to see Him as He is? Because of the wrong view of God that predominates in all areas of our culture today, our society is in moral turmoil, and we are in danger of losing our moral soul.

We can trace all our human problems to our view of God. A contrast in two lives from history illustrates the different outcomes that result from a wrong and a right view of God.

The first example is Karl Marx, who was born in Trier, Germany, in 1818. Educated in German universities, he became the editor of a Cologne newspaper. Marx denied the existence of God, believing that man, not God, is the highest form of being. Instead of God being in control, he felt that people make themselves what they are by their own efforts. Society, therefore, is the supreme agent for achieving success and fulfillment.

In *Economic and Philosophic Manuscripts of 1844,* he wrote, "All that is called history is nothing else than the process of creating man through human labour, the becoming of nature for man. Man has thus evident and irrefutable proof of his own creation by himself... For man, man is the supreme being."[5]

Since Marx believed that man was, in effect, a god, he concluded that society, composed of the common man, should rule and overthrow the reigning government by force. He and Friedrich Engels collaborated on defining philosophical ideals that eventually formed the basis for communism.

In the early 20th century, Vladimir Lenin revived Marx's ideas, accomplishing the overthrow of the czarist rule in Russia. Stalin followed Lenin as Communist leader of the Soviet Union. Under their reigns and the Communist rulers who followed them, tens of millions of Russians were slaughtered by the state. The loss of life resulted because these Communist leaders believed that there was no God, that the individual had no inherent value, and that the state was of supreme importance. Today, Marx's ideas still form the basis for totalitarian government in many countries, including North Korea, Cuba, and China.

Contrast the life of Marx with the life of Martin Luther. He too was a revolutionary. He was born in 1483 in Eisleben, Germany, only a couple of hundred miles from where Marx would later begin his life. Martin Luther was also educated in German universities.

Like Marx, the young Luther struggled with ideals of authority, morality, and ethics. Although he tried to serve God as a monk, he grew increasingly terrified of God's wrath. Then he was drawn to Romans 1:17, "The righteous shall live by faith." This simple concept changed his view of God. Luther wrote:

> At last, meditating day and night and by the mercy of God, I...began to understand that the righteousness of God is that through which the righteous live by a gift of God, namely by faith... Here I felt as if I were entirely born again and had entered paradise itself through gates that had been flung open.[6]

Luther's realization—that God's free gift of forgiveness is available to each person on earth—emphasized the value God gives to each individual created in His image. What a contrast to the beliefs of communism!

Luther's teaching on the life of faith, as opposed to earning salvation by good works, was the beginning of the great Protestant Reformation that reshaped Europe during the next two centuries. Today, the principle of forgiveness by faith is followed by hundreds of millions of people worldwide. In America, we owe much of our historical and religious roots to what Luther began in Germany.

These two examples show that a false view of God leads to sin and corruption—and many times cruelty and great human tragedy. On the other hand, a proper understanding of God leads to a life of blessing for oneself and many generations to follow.

You may dismiss this by thinking, *I am no Karl Marx or Martin Luther. I am not a world leader or a person with great influence.* None of us are. Yet how

14 | GOD WHO ARE YOU ANYWAY?

we view God will change the way we live and relate with others. Consider the couple who takes in a foster child because they know God loves that little one; they may live next door to parents who neglect or abuse their child. One person cheats his customers because he thinks "no one will ever know"; another repays a loan despite severe financial hardships, because he has a reverential respect for a God who notes men's actions and expects honesty.

> We can trace all our human problems to our view of God.

All of our actions, like Marx's and Luther's, are driven by our view of God and how He interacts with us. Nothing in life could be more important than knowing God accurately.

Does God Want to Relate to Us?

Understanding God is not a simple task. I readily admit that, like all human beings, I am incapable of completely explaining the attributes of our awesome God who reigns in overwhelming majesty. Who am I, a mere man, trying to describe the God of the universe who is all-powerful, holy, and righteous? In fact, while I was writing this book, I was overcome with a sense of my unworthiness. I fell to my knees in tears and confessed, "Oh, Lord, I am not worthy to write about Your character. Forgive me for being so presumptuous." At that moment, the Lord seemed to put His arms around me, assuring me that He had called me to do this.

That's why I am so anxious to share with you, through this book, the truths about God: because I know without a doubt that God wants us to *really know* Him. God did not just content Himself with speaking to us through our limited language. Instead, He assumed our limited form—that of a human—setting aside His riches and splendor and honor to become like us! That, of course, was the miraculous day when God was born as a baby in a manger in the small village of Bethlehem. That baby's name is Jesus Christ, the Son of God and Savior of the world. This demonstration of God's love is beyond my comprehension and shows His great desire for us to know Him. God's willingness to become a man changed forever the way I can relate with Him.

How Can Knowing God Change My Life?

I can tell you from personal experience that an intimate walk with God never fails to produce an abundance of joy and adventure in people's lives. Let me share an example from one man's life, John Newton. His story demonstrates what a right view of God can do for each of us.

John Newton's mother was a devoted Christian, but she died when he was a child. As a young man, he decided to follow in the footsteps of his father, an English sea captain. He joined the British Royal Navy but was discharged because of unruly behavior. To escape further problems, he moved to the western coast of Africa and worked for a slave trader. He eventually became captain of a slave ship, and he treated the slaves despicably. What a loathsome man he had become!

On one voyage, his ship was severely battered by a fierce storm. Fearing for his life, he surrendered himself to God, setting his life on a new course. Over the next few years as he became convinced that slavery was abhorrent, he gave up his slave trading and later even crusaded against slavery. His life changed so much that he studied to become a minister. When he preached, he was known as the "old converted sea captain." All because he had personally met and come to know God. He wrote one of the most famous hymns in English, "Amazing Grace." In it, he describes his own transformation:

Amazing grace, how sweet the sound,
That saved a wretch like me.
I once was lost, but now am found,
Was blind, but now I see.

Who else but almighty God could change a calloused man engaged in the slave trade into a compassionate minister and anti-slavery crusader?

Have you experienced this change? Has God been intimately involved in your life? For more than fifty years, I have walked and talked with our loving heavenly Father. It has been the greatest adventure of my lifetime. The more I get to know Him, the more peace, joy, love, and excitement I experience. He has proven to be my best friend, someone I can trust in every situation.

> How we view God will change the way we live and relate to others.

My desire is not just to share information about God with you—although that is important. But I trust that the Holy Spirit will help me communicate my heart about God. Hopefully, you will be encouraged to embrace the right view of God and know Him well enough to love, trust, and obey Him as never before.

As we explore the truths of these pages together, discovering who God is and His love and plan for us, I am confident that your life will never be the same. Let us continue by looking more closely at how we can know God intimately.

Talk About It: I AM Personal

"I have called you friends, for everything that I learned from My Father I have made known to you."
(John 15:15, NIV)

1. Look at your timetable of your life events (created in Chapter 1). Would you say your experiences have shaped how you see God, or has your view of God shaped how you see your experiences?

2. How do you view God today? Take the "View of God" quiz at the end of this chapter to help give you insight into how you see God. Think of it as a mirror.

3. Why do you think you view God this way?

4. Do you see God as personal or distant? Most people believe God is knowable to some degree, but experiencing a deep and personal relationship with Him eludes them. Why do you think this is?

5. How does your view of God influence your relationship with Him?

6. How does your view of God affect your relationship with others?

7. What is your biggest obstacle to knowing God more deeply and authentically? Does your timeline give you any insight?

Focus on God

On an index card or your favorite electronic device, write the following statement and verse, or just take a picture of it:

**God, because You are personal,
I will seek a deep relationship with You.**

*"I have called you friends, for everything that
I learned from My Father I have made known to you."*
(John 15:15, NIV)

Carry it with you throughout the week. Look at it when you get up, when you go to bed, and at least once during the day as a way of intentionally shifting your focus from yourself to God.

Each day, take a few minutes to meditate on the fact that God is personal and wants a relationship with you. Talk with God about the things that hold you back in your relationship with Him. He knows the obstacles, the hurt, the fear. Nothing surprises Him or is too big for Him to handle. Put it all out there. Ask Him to help you overcome the obstacles. If you do, by the time you are done with this book your relationship with God will be deeper and more fulfilling than ever.

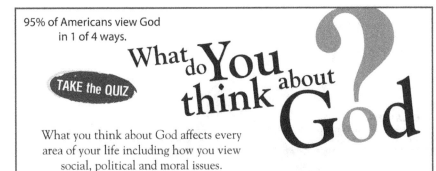

95% of Americans view God in 1 of 4 ways.

TAKE the QUIZ

What do You think about God?

What you think about God affects every area of your life including how you view social, political and moral issues.

Quickly discover YOUR view of God

Circle the number that best represents your answer to each question. Then write the number in the open box to the right. After you answer all ten questions, separately add the numbers in the "E" and then the "J" columns. Now, mark your E and J scores on the graph on the following page.

What do YOU think God is like?	Strongly Disagree	Disagree	Neither Agree nor Disagree	Agree	Strongly Agree	E score	J score
1. Concerned with the well-being of the world.	0	4	8	15	20		
2. Angered by my sin.	0	4	8	15	20		
3. Directly involved in affairs of the world.	0	4	8	15	20		
4. Concerned with my personal well-being.	0	4	8	15	20		
5. Angered by human sin.	0	4	8	15	20		
6. Directly involved in my affairs.	0	4	8	15	20		

How well do the following words describe YOUR view of God?	Not at All	Not Very Well	Not Sure	Fairly Well	Very Well	E score	J score
7. Punishing	0	4	8	15	20		
8. Severe	0	4	8	15	20		
9. Ever-present	0	4	8	15	20		
10. Wrathful	0	4	8	15	20		
					Total	E score	J score

What do You think about God?

Mark your "E" score on the lower left scale. Mark your "J" score on the lower-right scale. Then follow the grid lines until they cross to show which view of God you identify with most closely.

NOW FIND **YOUR SPOT** ON THE CHART

JUST:
Judging, not very Loving.
Sees God as: Stern and unapproachable.
Tends to view God as Judge, but primarily in the next life.

BALANCED:
Fully engaged with humanity.
Sees God as: Loving but firm.
Tends to view God as a Judge with a heart.

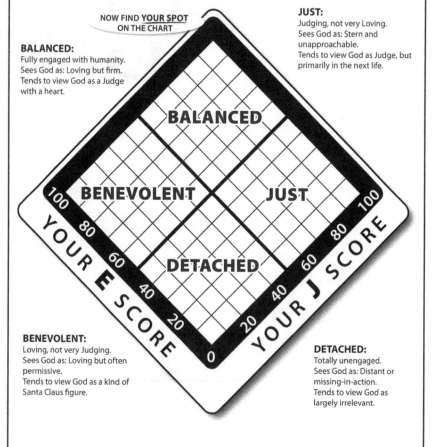

BALANCED

BENEVOLENT   JUST

DETACHED

YOUR E SCORE   100 80 60 40 20 0   YOUR J SCORE   100 80 60 40 20

BENEVOLENT:
Loving, not very Judging.
Sees God as: Loving but often permissive.
Tends to view God as a kind of Santa Claus figure.

DETACHED:
Totally unengaged.
Sees God as: Distant or missing-in-action.
Tends to view God as largely irrelevant.

To learn more about how each view tends to see God, or how each view tends to see societal issues, or if you would like to know more about how to develop a more balanced view of God please go to www.ViewOfGod.com.

Based on the study *American Piety in the 21st Century* released by Baylor University

CHAPTER 3

You Can Have a Relationship With Me

I n 1978 at the height of the Cold War between the Soviet Union and the United States, the Soviet government, at the request of the Russian church, invited me to visit that vast land. During my visit to eight cities, I sensed that millions of people were imprisoned by fear resulting from mental and physical abuse. The KGB, the secret police of the Soviet government, seemed to squeeze every individual to discover information about the activities and views of political dissidents, followers of Christ, and Jews. Under this kind of suspicion and tyranny, no one trusted anyone. Even family members turned against each other in this oppressive uncertainty.

While few of us in the West live under such conditions today, you may have often wondered, *Who can I really trust?* Perhaps you have a friend or two you consider trustworthy. But beyond that, who can you trust with the things that you consider most private and valuable?

I am sure you will agree that trustworthiness is in short supply today. At every level of government, there are officials who feel that dishonesty serves a purpose in politics. Within our financial institutions, businessmen have used

> The amount of trust you have in God depends on how you view Him.

the wealth of others to their personal advantage, often depriving those who are most vulnerable, senior citizens, of their retirement funds. People break contracts without remorse under the pretense of smart business practices. Husbands and wives, some who have been married for decades, betray their spouses for their own selfish, lustful desires. Families, especially innocent children, are shattered by broken promises. Good friends become enemies over lapses in honesty.

If a close friend or relative has betrayed your trust, how did that betrayal affect your relationship? Did it influence how much you trust other people today?

In many cases our past experiences, backgrounds, and personalities shape how we view other people and how we form relationships with them. If someone we trusted hurt us, we hesitate to trust anyone else again. If a parent or sibling treated us shamefully, we respond by protecting ourselves from other close relationships. Although trust is an important part of any healthy friendship, for many of us, building trust is one of the most difficult elements of our relationships.

But what about God? Can He be trusted? How far are you willing to go in trusting Him? The amount of trust you have in God depends on how you view Him. Some people think of Him as a big bully, a cosmic policeman, or a divine Santa Claus. Others believe He is like their insensitive, selfish parents who do whatever they want because they have the size or power.

Some consider God to be hard to get along with, someone to fear. Others think of Him as a heartless dictator waiting to punish them for doing wrong. Perhaps you see Him as a kindly grandfather who just shakes His head over the terrible plight of humankind but does not get involved. Do you see Him as loving, gracious, tender, and compassionate? Or as critical, jealous, vindictive, and haughty?

I hear from many Christians who are discouraged in their quest to know God more fully. They claim to have tried to learn what God is like but have come up short. Maybe they failed on a commitment they made to God and feel the communication lines are down between themselves and heaven. Others believe that God has abandoned them or treated them unfairly. Some simply do not know what God is like and have decided that they probably will never know more than they do now. Millions of people cry out, *"Who are you, God?"*

We Can Have an Intimate Relationship With the God of Creation

In Chapter 2, we learned how important it is to know God and to have the right view of Him. But how can we develop a relationship with a Being who is beyond our comprehension? The process toward intimacy is similar to getting to know a new neighbor.

Imagine that a new couple moves in next door to you. What impression do you get of what they are like? You probably notice the furniture and belongings carried into their house, and the type of car in their driveway. The first time you meet them, you most likely find out what they do for a living. Are they lawyers or construction workers, computer specialists or businessmen, teachers or factory workers? You probably ask questions about their hobbies and interests. Do they enjoy gardening or do they pride themselves in how well they play golf? These facts give you a little insight into what kind of people they are.

As you get to know your neighbors better, you also discover more about their character. Are they kind, generous, amiable, and compassionate? Or do they speak harshly, criticize, and act rudely toward others? Do they have good character?

With time, you may get to know your neighbors more intimately. Are they ambitious or lazy? Do they shade the truth or are they honest? Do they keep their word? Do they practice values similar to yours or do they live by a different set of rules? How do they react under stressful situations? This closer relationship uncovers the deeper qualities of their inner lives.

Of course, God is not like a next-door neighbor. He is so much more than that. His characteristics are far above what we as humans can accomplish or even understand. But because He is loving and gracious toward us, He reveals His character to us so we can relate more intimately with Him. As in any relationship, developing intimacy is a process. Someone has aptly said, "If we take one step toward God, He will take two steps toward us."

> Knowing God intimately can transform your life.

Would you not agree that the most astounding news we can ever hear is that God, the almighty Creator of heaven and earth, invites us to have an intimate relationship with Him? He makes it simple for us to do so. Knowing God intimately can transform your life into one of passion, joy, adventure, and peace.

God Is a Personal Spirit

Someone asked Buddha, the founder of Buddhism, if God existed. He replied, "The question is not relevant. If there were a God, man could not comprehend him anyway. So what good would it be to have such a God?"

Some "religious" people consider God a force, an evil spirit, or something encased in wood or stone. As a result, their concept of God is hazy or impersonal. If God were merely an energy force or a composite of the universe as New Age philosophies teach, knowing Him personally would be impossible. And if God were merely an idol, made by man's hand from wood or some precious metal, our efforts to know Him would be futile. How could a human have a relationship with an inanimate object?

But God's Word reveals God as a personal Spirit; therefore, we can know Him personally. This may seem like such a simple concept, but it is the underlying truth on which we base our understanding of God.

The Bible shows that God has a distinct personality. The book of John in the New Testament says that God is Spirit (John 4:24). Although He does not have a physical body as we do, God possesses all the characteristics of a personality: He thinks, feels, and wills. The Bible gives us several proofs that we can know God personally.

Many Old and New Testament believers knew God and were considered His friends. Let me give you a few examples.

God called Abraham, the "father" of the Hebrew nation, "My friend" (Isaiah 41:8). Moses met with God "face to face" when he talked to God in the tabernacle. Can you imagine how this personal experience must have changed his life? The Book of Exodus describes this encounter, which occurred just before Moses received the Ten Commandments:

> Whenever Moses went to the Tabernacle, all the people…would rise and stand in their tent doors. As he entered, the pillar of cloud would come down and stand at the door while the LORD spoke with Moses. Then all the people worshiped from their tent doors, bowing low to the pillar of cloud. Inside the tent the LORD spoke to Moses face to face, as a man speaks to his friend. (Exodus 33:8–11)

Both Enoch and Noah were said to have enjoyed "close fellowship with God" (Genesis 5:24; 6:9); Job talked of a time "when God's intimate friendship blessed my house" (Job 29:4, NIV). And in the New Testament, Jesus, the Son of God, told His disciples, "You are My friends" (John 15:14).

God has names. Many couples use great care in giving their newborn baby a name that has significance to their family. In the same way, each of God's many names reveals something important about His character. In the Bible, He is called Almighty, Eternal God, Heavenly Father, Lord of Hosts, Living God, Most High, and Jehovah, along with many other names. In Chapter 1, we learned the incredible truth behind God's most important name, "I AM," or Jehovah.

God is described throughout the Bible by a personal pronoun. He is not described as an "it," but as "He," a word that denotes a definite gender and personality. An impersonal force cannot be described this way.

God acts as a distinct personality. The Bible consistently demonstrates that God is a conscious, self-aware Being, someone who thinks and makes decisions. For example, He is the Creator. How could an inanimate object of gold or silver or some impersonal force design the intricacies of the universe? That takes planning, unlimited intelligence, and supernatural power. Also, the Bible tells us that God "sees," "speaks," and "hears" (Genesis 16:13; Number 23:19; 1 Kings 8:30). God exhibits a range of emotions from righteous anger to holy jealousy to love and grief.

God Is Three Persons in One

As we learn more about God's personality, we will find many areas that are hard to understand. This is because God is so far above our limited understanding that we cannot grasp the fullness of His nature. The fact that God is three-in-one is one of these difficult concepts. Yet this truth is one of the most important aspects of God's relationship with us.

What does God say about Himself?

Theologians have called God's triune nature the Trinity. The members of the Trinity are involved with everything together, yet they also have distinct roles. This is hinted at in the first chapter in the Bible. Genesis 1:26 reads, "Let *us* make people in *our* image" (emphasis added). The plural pronouns "us" and "our" mean that more than one Person was involved. Who else but God was present during creation? No one. Therefore, the Trinity in its simplest terms means one God manifested in three Persons with three distinctive roles.

God the Father is first in the Trinity. In general, He orchestrates action. For example, He sent to earth God the Son, Jesus, and bestowed His authority upon Him (John 17).

God the Son is the second Person of the Trinity. Jesus Christ is fully God and fully human (John 10:30; Colossians 2:9). He is the cornerstone and head of the worldwide Church (Colossians 1:18). Jesus now sits at the right hand of God the Father interceding for His Church (Romans 8:34).

God the Holy Spirit, the third Person of the Trinity, is our Comforter. As the "active arm" of God on earth, He lives within believers and guides us into all truth (Romans 8:11; John 16:13). He convicts us of sin and helps us know God and His will (John 16:8; 1 Corinthians 2:10).

Yet God is still one. It is difficult for us, with our limited comprehension, to understand how God the Father, God the Son, and God the Holy Spirit are distinct personalities, co-equal, yet one at the same time. Our best efforts to understand this relationship fall far short.

One popular analogy is to compare the Trinity to water. It can be three distinct forms: liquid, ice, or steam. The same chemical formula, H_2O, can assume each form under different temperatures. In a similar way, God assumes three different "forms" to accomplish His purposes.

Here is another analogy. We all play different roles in our lives. I am a husband, father, and grandfather, and the head of an international organization. I perform different duties in each role, yet I am the same person. God also performs different roles—heavenly Father, loving Son, and comforting Spirit.

Of course, the Trinity is far more complex and profound than any awkward illustration I can give. One of my seminary professors once said, "If you try to understand the Trinity, you will lose your mind... If you deny the Trinity, you will lose your soul."

The reason I take the time to explain the mysterious relationship between the three members of the Trinity is that this truth underlies all the work of God. These are a few examples:

- God the Father orchestrated creation (Genesis 1:1). God the Son performed the work of creation (Colossian 1:16). God the Holy Spirit was also involved (Psalm 104:30).
- All three members agreed upon Christ's birth in human form (Luke 1:35). Christ's baptism, which marked the beginning of His earthly ministry, was attended and approved by all three members (Matthew 3:16,17).
- Christ's resurrection was the work of the Trinity: God the Father raised Christ from the dead (Acts 2:32). Jesus laid down His life and took it up on His own accord (John 10:18). The Holy Spirit was the power in the resurrection (Romans 1:4).
- All three members of the Trinity participate in the miracle of the new birth when a person becomes a child of God (1 Peter 1:2).
- All three members of the Trinity participate in the atonement—when we receive forgiveness of our sins (Hebrews 9:14). And then all three Persons of the Trinity come to live in the new believer's life (John 14:15–23).

Each member of the Trinity has His own role to play, but each is fully God. God is not three separate Gods like some might envision, but has complete unity.

No Person in the Trinity is less important, less powerful, or less of anything than any other Person. As we discover more about God, we will see how the Trinity works in our behalf.

With God, Life Is Never Boring

Today, after more than fifty years of getting to know God, I have more joy in the Lord's presence than I have ever had. My communication with Him grows sweeter and sweeter. There is no one in the universe with whom I would rather spend time than my heavenly Father. I do not have adequate words to describe to you the many things He has done for me and the marvelous ways He has guided my life to make it an exciting adventure. My number one priority in life is to maintain my love for Him and to demonstrate my love by my obedience.

To this end, Vonette and I begin every day on our knees reading His holy, inspired Word and surrendering the activities of our day to His guidance. I want to be a suit of clothes for the Lord Jesus. I invite Him to walk around in my body as His temple. My heart's passion is to let Him think with my mind, love with my heart, speak with my lips, and continue to seek and save sinners through me. This is what He came to earth to do 2,000 years ago.

As we explore the amazing attributes of our glorious Lord, I encourage you to walk with Him, talk with Him, worship and praise Him, and give Him your cares and worries. He yearns to be your loving Savior and wrap His strong arms around you. You need never feel lonely or abandoned again.

God Helps Us Get to Know Him

Through their own ability, human beings cannot advance in their knowledge of God beyond a few biographical facts. But God in His love and mercy has taken steps to make Himself known to us in many ways. Because God is so far above us in every aspect, the process begins with Him as He reveals Himself to those who hunger and thirst to know Him.

The most important place we can turn to find the truth about what God is like is in His holy Word, the Bible. It gives us the most accurate picture of almighty God. I strongly urge you to ask the question, as you read this or any other book, "What does God say about Himself?"

Furthermore, it is crucial to view each of God's attributes in light of the rest of His character. I hope you will take the time to explore how each attribute shapes the next. For instance, have you ever thought about the fact that if God were not holy, you could not trust His love to be pure and without flaw? Or if God were not absolute truth, you could not trust Him to always be faithful and keep His promises to you?

Only by understanding God's attributes within the broader context of His other attributes can we begin to fully develop the depth of trust that will allow us to experience His peace each day.

Talk About It: You Can Have a Relationship With Me

"I will be your Father, and you will be
My sons and daughters, says the LORD Almighty."
(2 Corinthians 6:18)

1. What do you think of the statement, "You can't trust someone you don't know?" How does this impact our relationship with God?
2. On a scale of 1–10, how would you rate your trust in God? What are the top two reasons why?
3. On a scale of 1–10, how would you rate God's desire to have a close relationship with you? How does that make you feel?
4. Read Jeremiah 31:3. What does this verse reveal about God's desire for a deep and personal relationship with you?
5. Describe what you would do to get to know someone better. How does this apply to getting to know God better?
6. How does it make you feel when someone assumes they know what you think or feel but are totally off base? Do you think there are areas where you could be off base in how you see God?
7. How can you begin to remedy any misconceptions about God that you may unwittingly have?

Focus on God

God longs to be in a relationship with you that grows with each new day. He won't force you to know Him, but if you ask Him to help you know Him He will jump at the chance! No matter where you are in your spiritual journey, you can always know Him better. You can start by praying something like the following in your own words. If you really mean it, He *will* answer.

> Dear God, I want to know You as You really are, the Creator God of the universe, our heavenly Father. You hold everything in Your hand, and You know my past, present, and future. Help me to love, trust, and obey You with all my heart, soul, mind, and will. Thank You for giving me an opportunity to know You intimately as my heavenly Father and to tell others about You and Your marvelous love. Amen.

Continue to review the statement and verse you wrote down last week, at least three times each day, to remind yourself that God is personal and wants a deeper relationship with you.

**God, because You are personal,
I will seek a deep relationship with You.**

*"I have called you friends, for everything that
I learned from My Father I have made known to you."*
(John 15:15, NIV)

CHAPTER 4

I AM All-Powerful

When you think of the word power, what comes to mind? One of the major accomplishments of the National Aeronautics and Space Administration (NASA) is the International Space Station that our country has built in cooperation with Russia, Japan, Brazil, and several other European countries. If you visit the Space Center in Houston, you can view a documentary film about the space station. On a huge screen several stories high, space ships carrying materials for the space station are shown blasting into the sky. The power of the rockets can be seen as the huge screen fills with boiling clouds of fire and smoke from the booster engines. The roar thunders throughout the room. What power in those engines!

Sometimes we as humans become so caught up in our own power that we forget how very limited we are. We are like ants trying to scale Mt. Everest. After crawling over blades of grass and fallen twigs, ants think they have traveled a great distance. But when their journey is compared to the distant mountaintop ahead, they have hardly begun. When was the last time you tried to accomplish something completely beyond your ability? Perhaps you have valiantly concentrated all your energy on the challenge at hand, only to find that it was not enough to do what needed to be done. Afterward, you felt exhausted and defeated.

However, God is capable of doing anything—as long as it does not violate His other attributes. (For example, He cannot lie, change, or deny Himself.) Otherwise, no task is too large or too difficult for Him. He never fails or gets tired. Because He is all-powerful, He has the ability and the strength to do whatever He pleases. His power is not restrained or inhibited in any way by His created beings. God generates power within Himself and does what He chooses to do whenever He chooses to do it. His power is not an abstract idea but a force to be reckoned with. Theologians use the term *omnipotence* to describe the awesome, unlimited power of God.

God's Power in Creation

When I tour a historic mansion and scrutinize the building's details—the quality, design, and décor—I can draw some conclusions about its builder. Is the foundation strong? Are the walls and floors plumb and square? How well are the most intricate details constructed? Does the design flow from one room to another?

We live on a grand estate called Earth. As we look at the beauty and intricacies of our residence, we marvel at the genius of the design. When we gaze up into the heavens, we are overcome with awe at the vastness of what our Creator has brought into being. In one of the most beautiful passages in the Bible, King David describes how nature testifies to the power of God:

> The heavens proclaim the glory of God. The skies display His craftsmanship.
> Day after day they continue to speak; night after night they make Him known.
> They speak without a sound or word; their voice is never heard.
> Yet their message has gone throughout the earth,
> and their words to all the world. (Psalm 19:1–4)

To get just a small idea of God's creative power, let us consider our universe. We live on one of nine planets that revolve around the sun. As the dominant light of our solar system, our sun gives off far more energy in one second than all mankind has produced since creation. With a diameter of approximately 860,000 miles, the sun could hold one million planets the size of the Earth. Yet our sun is only an average-size star.

Our sun is just one among 100 billion stars in our galaxy, the Milky Way. The Pistol Star gives off 10 million times the power generated by our sun, and a million stars the size of our sun can fit easily within its sphere. It takes 100,000 light-years to travel from one side of the Milky Way to the other. (One light-year is 5.88 trillion miles or the distance light travels in one year.) Our galaxy is moving through space at a phenomenal speed of one million miles per hour! If the Milky Way were compared to the size of the North American continent, our solar system would be about the size of a coffee cup!

Yet our Milky Way is not a huge galaxy. One of our neighbors, the Andromeda Spiral galaxy, is 2 million light-years away and contains about 400 billion stars. No one knows how many galaxies there are in the universe, but scientists estimate that there are billions of them.[7]

Isaiah writes, "Look up into the heavens. Who created all the stars? He brings them out one after another, calling each by its name. And He counts them to see that none are lost or have strayed away" (Isaiah 40:26). Scientists estimate that there are ten billion trillion stars in the universe, or about as many stars as there are grains of sand on all of our planet's seashores. If all the stars were divided equally among the people of the world, each person would receive almost two trillion stars.

Yet, with the unfathomable vastness of our universe, God spoke and the heavens and earth came into being; He laid the foundations of the world (Psalm 33:6,9; Job 38:4). His invisible qualities—His eternal power and divine nature—can be clearly seen and understood from His creation. Even people who have never received a verbal witness about God have no excuse for not knowing Him because of His power displayed in creation (Romans 1:20). He alone is the Almighty Sovereign of the universe.

Truly, God is omnipotent. Allow me to give you three truths about His infinite power.

> God is capable of doing anything—as long as it does not violate His other attributes.

God Is the Ultimate Source of All Power

Our homes depend on a central source for electrical power and can be plunged into darkness due to a storm or other disturbance. This power is transmitted into our homes on slender cables, which can break or wear out. But God's power is inherent in His nature. He does not derive His power from any other source; all power has always been His and will continue to be His for eternity. Remember, He is:

Eternal—He has no beginning and no end
Self-existent—no other power created Him
Self-sufficient—He needs no other power source outside Himself
Infinite—His power has no limits

Any power that we have comes ultimately from God. King David acknowledged in one of his prayers, "In Your hands are strength and power to exalt and give strength to all" (1 Chronicles 29:12, NIV). Paul prayed for the Ephesians that they would "begin to understand the incredible greatness of His power for us who believe Him" (Ephesians 1:19).

God Is More Powerful than Anything

God has more power than all the forces of nature. The combined energy of earth's storms, winds, ocean waves, and other natural forces do not equal a fraction of God's omnipotence. He expresses His power through the laws of nature, which He has instituted—although God is not bound by these laws.

I have flown millions of miles, but I remember the most violent storm I ever encountered. Vonette and I were on our way from New York City to Washington, DC, when suddenly the airplane began to buck like a wild mustang throwing its first rider. It felt as though the plane was out of control, like a leaf blown about in the wind. The sky seemed to explode with brilliant flashes of lightning.

As we rode through the storm, Vonette and I were reminded of when Jesus calmed the wind and waves. The disciples shouted to the Lord, "Save us, we're sinking!" Vonette and I began to pray, "Oh, Lord, You have not lost Your power over nature. We ask You to still the storm and to save us, though we're ready to meet You now if it is Your will. But if You have something yet for us to do in this life, we ask You not to allow the enemy to destroy us and all these other passengers."

Almost immediately, the turbulence stopped. The plane was stabilized and we continued on our course. Our petitions to God turned into praise and thanksgiving. Later we discovered that the plane had been severely damaged—lightning had punched two holes in the fuselage and knocked out the radar. Our lives were truly in danger. Yes, our God is more powerful than the greatest storm.

> We need not fear that anyone has the power to hinder God's will.

God is also more powerful than all the rulers on earth. Do the nuclear capabilities, chemical weapons, and military strength of other countries frighten you? We do not need to fear. The prophet Isaiah writes, "All the nations of the world are nothing in comparison with Him. They are but a drop in the bucket, dust on the scales" (Isaiah 40:15). After learning firsthand of God's power, King Nebuchadnezzar acknowledges, "He does as He pleases with the powers of heaven and the peoples of the earth. No one can hold back His hand or say to Him: 'What have You done?'" (Daniel 4:35, NIV).

We need not fear that any person or nation has the power to hinder God's will. He is so far above our earthly governments that they can do nothing outside His power. No ruler or army can change any plan that God has made.

God is also infinitely more powerful than Satan and his evil legions. God is not intimidated by the devil's rebellious hatred. God is the Creator; Satan is a created being who can operate only within the prescribed limits God places on him. Satan is nothing compared to God.

Jesus told His disciples that "the prince of this world [Satan] now stands condemned" (John 16:11, NIV). Demons screamed in fear when they saw Jesus. The Book of Matthew records Jesus' encounter with two men who were demon-possessed. The demons immediately recognized the Son of God's power over them by saying, "Have you come here to torture us before the appointed time?" They requested that He let them go into a nearby herd of pigs. He said one powerful word—"Go." And they did. In response, the pigs ran over a cliff to their deaths (Matthew 8:28–32, NIV).

As Christians, sometimes we feel that Satan has the upper hand. But our almighty God fights for us. Romans 16:20 gives this promise: "The God of peace will soon crush Satan under your feet." How encouraging that promise is when we are battling the evil forces that confront us every day!

God Has the Power to Do Anything

Whatever God chooses will come to pass because He has the omnipotent ability to make it happen. God told Isaiah, "Everything I plan will come to pass, for I will do whatever I wish" (Isaiah 46:10). Speaking to God, Job acknowledged, "I know that You can do all things; no plan of Yours can be thwarted" (Job 42:2, NIV). Consider some of the things our almighty God can do without any effort.

God has the power to create anything from nothing.

The psalmist writes, "The LORD merely spoke, and the heavens were created. He breathed the word, and all the stars were born… Let everyone stand in awe of Him. For when He spoke, the world began! It appeared at His command" (Psalm 33:6–9). When God spoke, the sky was filled with stars. Pastor Tony Evans writes, "It takes no more effort for God to create a universe than it does for Him to create an ant."[8] God's power is so unlimited that He could speak a few trillion more universes into existence, then the next day a few trillion more, then the same every day for a trillion years. It would not lessen His power one bit!

God has the power to sustain everything He has created.

Deists believe that God created the world then withdrew, letting His creation run automatically like a watch with a battery. It is up to us to maintain what is in the world, they say. Yet that is not how God is depicted in the Bible. The ongoing existence of all creation depends on our all-powerful God every second of every day. The writer of Hebrews affirms: "The Son…sustains the universe by the mighty power of His command" (Hebrews 1:3).

God has the power to judge sin and rebellion.

One of the great mysteries of life is why God allows evil on the earth. We will probably never find a complete answer to this puzzle during our short lives on this planet. At the same time, we can know for sure that God will use His mighty power for the destruction of evil. He has given us examples in His Word: the great flood in Noah's time and God's judgment of Sodom and Gomorrah. Every injustice will be righted; every act of sin and rebellion will be accounted for. The sincere follower of Jesus should also keep in mind what the Bible says in Romans 8:28: "God causes everything to work together for the good of those who love God and are called according to His purpose for them."

Our Response

Because God is a personal Spirit and we can have a relationship with Him, His power is more than just a fact to file away. As we discover more about who God *really* is, it should motivate us to seek His presence and fellowship.

> As believers, we have access to the greatest force in the universe.

Worship is our natural response to God as we begin to better understand who He really is. His limitless power inspires an overwhelming sense of awe. But what does it mean to worship God? Picture a huge, ornate room with an immense throne at one end. The room is filled with people and angels praising God. The throng opens up to reveal a carpeted aisle that leads right to the throne.

Suddenly, you realize that you must walk up that aisle and stand before the elevated throne. Your eyes look up to catch sight of the Person who sits in the honored seat. That Being is so full of light and power and righteousness that your eyes cannot bear to look at Him.

What can you say that will mean anything to this glorious King? Your mouth is dry and you cannot speak. There are no words adequate for the moment.

All you can do is bow down before Him in humble adoration, servitude, and worship.

Throughout this book, we will learn the importance and the simple truths about worshiping our great Creator. The most basic element of worship is attitude. Our worship should begin with an attitude of awe for who God is and what He can do. We must realize how weak we are compared to the infinite power of God.

Once we have a right view of God, we will begin to praise Him. King David expressed this attitude when he was gathering materials to build a glorious temple to almighty God:

> "O LORD, the God of our ancestor Israel, may You be praised forever and ever! Yours, O LORD, is the greatness, the power, the glory, the victory, and the majesty. Everything in the heavens and on earth is Yours, O LORD, and this is Your kingdom. We adore You as the one who is over all things…our God, we thank You and praise Your glorious name!" (1 Chronicles 29:10,11,13)

Do his words reflect your awe of God's power? Take a few moments right now to praise God. As believers, we have access to the greatest force in the universe—the awesome power of God. In our next chapter, we will examine how God uses His unlimited power in our behalf.

Talk About It: I AM All-Powerful
"O Sovereign LORD! You made the heavens and earth by Your strong hand and powerful arm. Nothing is too hard for You!"
(Jeremiah 32:17)

1. When you think of the fact that God is all-powerful, does it help or hinder your relationship with Him? Why?
2. Does the fact that God's power will never be used to violate His other attributes make Him more or less trustworthy in your sight? Why?

3. What is the difference between God being all-powerful and simply having super-human strength? Consider how the following attributes apply to His power when answering:

    Eternal—He has no beginning and no end

    Self-existent—no other power created Him

    Self-sufficient—He needs no other power source outside Himself

    Infinite— His power has no limits

4. Do you think most people picture God as truly all-powerful, or as simply having super-human strength? Explain your answer.

5. Do you have a sliver of doubt about the fact that there has never been and will never be anyone or anything more powerful than God? How does your life reflect your answer?

6. How would your life change if you completely trusted God's power (e.g., your worship, life choices, sense of peace, view of others)?

7. Think of one thing you could do this week that would help you live in, or reflect, His power.

FOCUS ON GOD

On an index card or your favorite electronic device, write the following statement and verse, or just take a picture of it:

**God, because You are all-powerful,
I know You can help me with anything.**

"O Sovereign Lord!… Nothing is too hard for You."
(Jeremiah 32:17)

Carry it with you throughout the week. Look at it when you get up, when you go to bed, and at least once during the day as a way of intentionally shifting your focus from yourself to God's unlimited power. Ask God to help you see His power at work in your life.

In the book of Psalms we get a glimpse of God's power:

The LORD merely spoke, and the heavens were created. He breathed the word, and all the stars were born. He gave the sea its boundaries and locked the oceans in vast reservoirs. Let everyone in the world fear the LORD, and let everyone stand in awe of Him. For when He spoke, the world began! It appeared at His command. The LORD shatters the plans of the nations and thwarts all their schemes. But the LORD's plans stand firm forever; His intentions can never be shaken. (Psalm 33:6–11)

CHAPTER 5

My Power Gives You Strength

Have you ever felt so weak you weren't sure how you would make it another day? Have you ever been asked to do something you knew was beyond your ability? Our strength is limited, but God promises to give power to those who trust Him.

Some time ago, I had to fly from Los Angeles to New York for a mere three-hour stop, then fly to Portland, Oregon, to speak to several hundred pastors at a conference. When I reached Portland, I was bone tired. Every fiber of my being ached with fatigue. As I stood in the terminal, I felt impressed to pray, "Lord, do You have something that You would like to share with me?"

Immediately, I felt another impression to turn to the 40th chapter of Isaiah. I began to read a familiar passage, which took on new meaning for me. "Don't you know by now that the everlasting God, the Creator of the farthest parts of the earth, never grows faint or weary? ... He gives power to the tired and worn out, and strength to the weak" (Isaiah 40:28,29, TLB). I could identify with the writer, for I was absolutely worn out.

I continued to read: "Even the youths shall be exhausted, and the young men will all give up. But they that wait upon the Lord shall renew their strength. They

41

shall mount up with wings like eagles; they shall run and not be weary; they shall walk and not faint" (Isaiah 40:30,31, TLB).

At that moment, it was as though a great infusion of power flooded my very being. I was so excited as I thought about who God is and what He had said to me. I felt I could have thrown my luggage over the airport terminal and run to the meeting some miles away. Suddenly, I could hardly wait to stand before those pastors and proclaim to them the glory and power of our great and faithful God and Savior. Within thirty minutes or so, I did have that privilege, and God empowered and anointed me for the occasion in a marvelous way.

In all my years as a believer, I have found God faithful to use His power in the behalf of those who seek Him. A right understanding of who God is will revolutionize the life of every believer. It will launch them into the exciting adventure of supernatural living in the power of this mighty God. As we grow in our understanding of who God is, we naturally develop a deeper trust as well.

But perhaps you have asked yourself: How much can I expect God to do through me? How involved is He in what I see going on around me? What is He willing to accomplish in my life?

God Uses His Power Purposefully

When we look at the cosmic universe, we see order and design. Everything is in its place; everything has its purpose. If creation has so much purpose and design, then human history must also have purpose and design.

Many people are skeptical about God's willingness to get intimately involved in their affairs. They may agree that God has a general purpose for everything, but they wonder: *Do we live by luck or the breaks produced by our own hard work and cleverness?* They question if God even knows or cares about the details in their lives.

In His Word, however, God shows that He has a plan for this world and every person in it: "I have a plan for the whole earth, for My mighty power reaches throughout the world" (Isaiah 14:26).

God has unlimited power within Himself and does what He wants with it. This would be terrifying if God were a tyrant who meted out His power indiscriminately. Fortunately, the Bible says God acts out of love and righteousness (attributes that we will examine later). Some of us may question why God does not answer our prayers when and how we ask. But God is not a "genie" or Santa Claus who gives us everything we ask for just the way we want it, just as loving parents do not give their children everything they want. God knows what we need far better than we do. He uses His power to fulfill His purposes, plans, and will for us and everyone involved in our situations. Can you think of at least one prayer request for which you are now thankful God did not answer the way you wanted? Often we pray selfishly or from our fleshly natures. But as we align our ways and desires with His perfect will, and pray in faith, we will see His power demonstrated more frequently in answered prayer.

> God's power is dedicated to the accomplishment of His purposes, not ours.

When we study God's Word from Genesis to Revelation, we get a glimpse into how He directs history and nations. The psalmist writes: "Come and see what our God has done, what awesome miracles He does for His people! ... By His great power He rules forever. He watches every movement of the nations" (Psalm 66:5,7). Although events at times make no sense to us, God knows the end from the beginning, and has us in the palm of His hand.

Man is at best a microbe on the "grain of sand" we call earth, yet God created us for a purpose and uses His power in our lives to accomplish that purpose.

God's Power Is Shown Through His Son

From a human perspective the crucifixion appeared to be an epic failure—God's Son dying at the hands of mere men. But from God's perspective it was the ultimate display of His power. First Corinthians 1:24 tells us that God demonstrates His power through His Son. We can see evidence of this in His virgin birth. God planned before the foundation of the world to send His Son to die for us.

God's ultimate display of power was raising Jesus Christ from the dead. After Jesus' death by crucifixion, His enemies put a Roman seal on the tomb and set guards to make sure no one disturbed His body. Yet their efforts meant nothing to God. When He was ready to display His power, He simply rolled the stone away from the tomb and Jesus walked out alive and well.

Paul writes that the power available to us as believers is "the same mighty power that raised Christ from the dead and seated Him in the place of honor at God's right hand in the heavenly realms" (Ephesians 1:19,20). Does that not thrill you? The amount of power available to us through God's Spirit is equal to the power God used to raise Christ from the dead! Like Paul, we can honestly say, "I can do everything through Him who gives me strength" (Philippians 4:13, NIV).

Reflecting God's Power

In the midst of the barren desert between Los Angeles and Las Vegas stands a 300-foot tower. On top of this tower rests a black receiver that is 45 feet high and 23 feet wide, surrounded by 70 heat-conducting tubes. Tens of thousands of people who drive across the desert during the daylight hours see what looks like a brilliant ball of fire glowing from the top of the tower. This is the world's largest solar-powered electricity-generating station: Solar One.

How can a receiver turn into a glowing ball with a temperature exceeding 1,175° F? The secret is on the ground. On the desert floor surrounding the tower are 1,818 computer-controlled frames, each holding 12 giant mirrors that track the sun daily from the time it rises until it sets.

When sunlight strikes these mirrors, it is reflected onto the receiver at the top of the tower. The heat generated at the receiver is then transformed into electrical energy through a system of thermal storage and a turbine generator. When the network of mirrors is working in harmony, tremendous power is generated from the sun.

Note that the tower itself does not have the ability to generate power. This process is possible only because light from the sun—the real source of the power—is reflected onto a helpless receiver.

Have you considered that God wants us to reflect His power on earth? As we begin to understand our God's vast and magnificent power, our lives cannot help but be transformed. Everything about us will change—our attitudes, actions, motives, desires, our lifestyle, and even our view of God. As we are transformed, we light up the world around us. Our society which was once darkened by fear, ignorance, and hopelessness will become lightened with our witness of God's power, care, and intervention in our lives.

God Wants Us to Be Vessels for His Power

Just because God has the power to do anything should not cause us to assume that we can use that power for selfish purposes. His power is dedicated to the accomplishment of His purposes, not ours. He will bring about the future that He desires. As our all-powerful God and loving Father, His ways are infinitely better than ours.

God is seeking faithful servants through whom He can display His incredible power. Paul was one of countless servants of Christ who was available for God's mighty power. Acts 19:11 records that "God did extraordinary miracles through Paul" (NIV). Through Paul's prayers, other Christians also understood what it means to be "strengthened with all power according to His glorious might" (Colossians 1:11, NIV). The ways God desires to use us are beyond counting, but let me mention five that will help us reflect God's glory.

God gives us power to conquer evil.

We have already seen that God's power is infinitely greater than the forces of evil. We can apply that truth to our own battle with Satan and his helpers—no matter what they throw at us.

When God instructed Moses to lead the Israelite people out of Egypt, conflict developed between God's servants (Moses and his brother, Aaron) and Pharaoh's magicians. These accomplished sorcerers could have intimidated Moses and Aaron. Their demonic power was clearly evident when they threw their rods to the floor and the rods became serpents. But God demonstrated His superior power when Aaron's rod devoured the other serpents. This was a graphic illustration of how much greater God's power is than any other.

Satan's power is most clearly demonstrated through false religious systems. Millions have followed him to disastrous endings. From the 900 followers of Jim Jones who tragically died in Jonestown, Guyana, to Heaven's Gate cult members who committed suicide at the command of their leader, many have been deluded by Satan's wiles. But when we walk with God, we need not be afraid. The devil and his forces are no match for God. God's Word promises that we can have victory in our spiritual battles. James 4:7,8 says, "Resist the devil, and he will flee from you. Draw close to God, and God will draw close to you."

Although we are weak at times, we can stand firm and say "no"; we can quit any habit or addiction; and we can speak up to tell the truth at any time. How do we do these difficult feats? In the power of the name of Jesus Christ and faith in our almighty and powerful God allowing His Spirit to empower us.

God gives us power to live a holy life.

I like to compare the Christian battle against sin to an individual swimming upstream against a surging current. His progress is slow and tortuous; he is constantly swept backward by powerful undercurrents. Hovering near the swimmer is a speedboat with a powerful motor. He can continue to try to swim upstream or he can choose to climb aboard the speedboat, which can easily whisk him up the river. Staying in the water means he must trust in his own efforts. Accepting a ride in the speedboat allows him to take advantage of a power far greater than his own.

We have a similar choice. When battling evil spiritual forces, worldly influences, and our own fleshly temptations, we can either fail miserably by fighting temptation in our own efforts or defeat that sin-current that drags us down by living in the unlimited power of the Holy Spirit (Galatians 5:16).

Peter explains, "As we know Jesus better, His divine power gives us everything we need for living a godly life. He has called us to receive His own glory and goodness!" (2 Peter 1:3). We do not have to make our own lives holy or clean up our messy lives before we invite God in; we can appropriate God's holiness through His Holy Spirit living His life within us (Romans 6:1–8; Ephesians 5:18).

The Scriptures assure us "that if we ask anything according to His will, He hears us. And if we know that He hears us—whatever we ask—we know that we have what we asked of Him" (1 John 5:14,15, NIV). We can become holy vessels of the all-powerful God by committing to live holy lives and being filled with the power of the Holy Spirit.

God gives us power in our weakness.

Since nothing is too hard for God, we do not have a need too great for Him to meet nor a problem too complicated for Him to solve. We can never face a foe too strong for Him to conquer. We can never pray a prayer too difficult for Him to answer.

His ways are always above our ways, and when we submit to His will, we experience peace and He builds patience into our lives. Our frailties in His hands become strengths. When Paul repeatedly asked God to remove a physical ailment that was tormenting him, God responded, "My gracious favor is all you need. My power works best in your weakness" (2 Corinthians 12:9). God uses our weakness to highlight His magnificent power. Just as He helped me speak to those hundreds of pastors in Portland, He will enable you to do more than you could ever imagine.

> God uses our weakness to highlight His magnificent power.

God gives us power to proclaim the gospel.

One important aspect of living a holy life is talking about the good news of God's love and forgiveness with everyone we meet. Paul writes, "Everywhere we go, we tell everyone about Christ… I work very hard at this, as I depend on Christ's mighty power that works within me" (Colossians 1:28,29).

Because of my love for Jesus and gratitude for what He's done for me, I actively look for situations to share my story with others. Each time I am with someone for five minutes or more, I consider it a God-given opportunity to talk about the incredible things God has done in my life. It doesn't matter whether I am in an airport, a taxi, a restaurant, or the grocery store. How can I do this? Because God through His Holy Spirit gives me the power to represent Him (Acts 1:8).

You may be thinking: *Bill Bright is the president of a worldwide organization dedicated to introducing people to Christ. Surely, proclaiming the gospel is easier for him than for me. I could never witness like that.*

I am naturally a shy and reserved person, so sharing my faith is sometimes difficult for me. I must continually rely on the power of the Holy Spirit to be a fruitful witness. When I obey God's command to tell others of Jesus, God makes the experience joyful and meaningful. He reminds me that I am not responsible for convicting the sinner or drawing others to Him. He is. I am just to follow His command in love, by the power of His Holy Spirit.

At Campus Crusade for Christ we have trained millions of believers around the world to share their faith in Jesus. We have learned that successful witnessing is simply taking the initiative to share Christ with everyone who will listen, in the power of the Holy Spirit, and leaving the results to God.

God gives us power to fulfill His plan for our lives.

God wants to strengthen us so we can serve Him in the fulfillment of His purposes. That plan includes allowing us the privilege of making an eternal difference in the lives of others. But that is possible only as we come to know God as He really is. He is our God who can do anything through us that He chooses to do: "By His mighty power at work within us, He is able to accomplish infinitely more than we would ever dare to ask or hope" (Ephesians 3:20).

> Are you called to *great* faith, or faith in a *great* God?

If we really believe that God is all-powerful, we will no longer walk in fear and unbelief. We will place our faith in God—not necessarily *great faith* in God, but rather faith in a *great God* who is omnipotent. In turn, He will lead us into a life full of adventure and purpose. I have found no better way to live!

Pastor David Jeremiah explains that the unlimited power that raised Jesus Christ from the grave is available to us today:

Most believers give lip service to God but live their lives in their own strength. They operate in their own energy about 80% of the time. Then they have a power outage. You know what a power outage is? It's going to the doctor and finding out there is something wrong with you that they can't fix. And realizing that you don't have control. It's going into an office where you have been going for 25 years where you feel secure, and getting a pink slip saying that you have been laid off from your job. Now you don't know what to do. Most of us as believers don't really touch the power of God until we have our own power outage. Then we discover that when we are weak, God is strong. I tell you that the power of God that was in Jesus Christ is the power that is available to you today. So we, too, can say with the Apostle Paul, "I can do all things through Christ who strengthens me" (Philippians 4:13).[9]

God's power is something we can trust. Yet God's character involves much more than power. His strength is used in conjunction with His many other qualities. For instance, unlimited power without perfect love is a frightening thing. Fortunately for us, God is both. Unfortunately, most Christians are miserable or living in spiritual defeat because they really don't fully grasp God's love for them. If this describes you, or someone you know, I assure you there is hope, as we will discover in the next two chapters!

Talk About It: My Power Gives You Strength

"O Sovereign LORD! You made the heavens and earth by Your strong hand and powerful arm. Nothing is too hard for You!"
(Jeremiah 32:17)

1. What can we expect from God's power? What should we *not* expect?
2. God doesn't always use His power the way we want. Read the story of Mary, Martha, and Lazarus in John 11:1–44.

    What was Jesus' relationship with the three siblings?

    Why didn't Jesus go to them immediately when they asked?

    What did they believe Jesus was powerful enough to do?

    How did their actions reflect their belief?

    How might you have responded if you had been Mary or Martha?
3. Reflect on your timeline. Have you ever had God say "no" to something you asked for and later been grateful He didn't use His power to do what you wanted Him to do? Why?
4. Why can we trust God's use of His limitless power?
5. Explain some of the ways you have experienced God's power at work in your life.

6. What is the key to experiencing God's power?

7. On a scale of 1–10, how much of your life do you operate in your own strength and how much in God's?

8. In the following list, which are easier for you to trust God has the power to help you overcome and which (if any) seem impossible?

addictions	broken relationships	jealousy
poor self-image	critical attitude	sexual temptations
fear	worry	suffering
abuse	rejection	financial crisis
illness	other people's choices	questioning God

9. If Jeremiah 32:17 is really true, how can you draw on His power in the areas of your life that feel impossible to change?

FOCUS ON GOD

Continue to review the statement and verse you wrote down last week, at least three times each day, to remind yourself that God can help you with anything.

**God, because You are all-powerful,
I know You can help me with anything.**

"O Sovereign LORD!... Nothing is too hard for You."
(Jeremiah 32:17)

To learn more about how to experience God's power in your daily life, review Appendix B, "How to Be Filled With the Holy Spirit." I suggest that you review it with a friend so you can talk about it.

CHAPTER 6

I AM Love

Love. It's a word filled with conflicting expectations and emotions. What does it mean to you? Have your dreams of love been fulfilled? Has love let you down, left you brokenhearted, jaded, and wary? Are you confused by the widely diverse understanding of what love looks like? You are not alone. Consider what happened in the summer of 1969.

The plan seemed so wonderful at the time. More than 100,000 people would camp out in a pristine glade in upstate New York where everyone would get along and love each other. This meeting was part of a movement—one that its followers believed would change the world. The movement really began in 1967, which some called the "Summer of Love." Its members were called hippies. The slogan expressed noble ideals: love, not hate; peace, not war. One of its cornerstones was unrestrained sex for self-gratification, termed "free love."

The Woodstock Festival in the summer of 1969 culminated this national "Love-In." It became the defining event of an entire generation of Americans. Instead of the expected 100,000 hippies descending on a quiet countryside, 1.5 million young people wearing beads and feathers flooded the area for three days of music.

Was Woodstock really a place of peace and love? Peter Townsend, a member of the megaband "The Who" which played during Woodstock, said, "What was going on off the stage was just beyond comprehension—stretchers and dead bodies, and people throwing up, and people having [drug] trips...I thought the whole of America had gone mad."[10]

Tempers flared; people were assaulted; a concession stand was almost ripped apart; roads were clogged for a twenty-mile radius. Nudity, sex, and drug dealing were going on everywhere. One young man was crushed in his sleeping bag by a backhoe. And when the uncontrollable crowd went on their way, they left behind acres of trash.

What was supposed to be a monument to free love and brotherhood was actually a hedonistic mess resulting in total chaos. Selfishness and a disregard for others and even the environment reigned. The "Summer of Love" had turned into a time of disaster and disappointment.

> God loves us, not because of who we are, but because of who He is.

Love is a universal need of all humanity. Everyone wants to be loved. But what is love? Tragically, our world understands very little about authentic love. We must turn to our loving Creator to understand what love is all about.

Recognizing God's power does not comfort us if we do not understand His love, mercy, and faithfulness. God's love is not just words on a page, but was demonstrated in the deepest kind of sacrifice—Christ's death on the cross.

God Is the Source of All Love

Love is the supreme expression of God's personhood and flows out of His goodness. It affects all His other attributes. The Bible does not say, "God is holiness" or "God is power," but "God is love" (1 John 4:8). God's heart overflows with His supernatural and unconditional love for us. The psalmist proclaims, "The LORD is good. His unfailing love continues forever" (Psalm 100:5).

People are sometimes willing to violate standards of honesty, righteousness, and morality to please others, but God never compromises His standards. His love is pure and holy; it does not suppress or negate any of His other attributes.

In New Testament times, there were three primary words for love: *eros* (sensual love), *phileo* (brotherly love), and *agape* (unconditional, supernatural love). Our world speaks mainly of *eros* or *phileo* love, but God's love is *agape*, the purest, deepest kind of love.

Many years ago I spoke on God's unconditional love at a mission's conference for the famous Park Street Church in Boston. A missionary with whom I had attended seminary twenty years earlier approached me afterward. "I would never preach a sermon like that," he scolded. "I leave talking about God's love to the theological liberals. My message emphasizes faith."

This man had lost sight of one of God's greatest qualities. Paul writes, "We know how dearly God loves us, because He has given us the Holy Spirit to fill our hearts with His love" (Romans 5:5).

God's love is the only reason we exist. It is the *why* of creation, whereas His power is the *how*. Love demands an object; therefore we are created as the object of God's love. Love flows from Him as a pure river of grace and mercy without detracting in any way from His holiness and righteousness. Everywhere we look we see evidence of God's loving concern for our well-being. Love is our doorway to knowing God intimately.

God's love is expressed to all people, not just those who love Him. He loved us first before we loved Him—even when we were unlovable. That is hard for us to accept at times. Yet all people benefit from His loving care: "He has shown kindness by giving you rain from heaven and crops in their seasons; He provides you with

> Embracing God's unconditional love will transform your life.

plenty of food and fills your hearts with joy" (Acts 14:17, NIV). When the sun rises, its warm rays are an expression of God's love; when the rains come, they demonstrate God's love to all.

God's Love Is Beyond Explanation

Dwight L. Moody, a famous pastor at the turn of the 20th century, tells of an experience shortly after building Moody Church. The congregation wanted to emphasize the love of God so they put "God is love" over the pulpit in lights. Every night they lit the sign so passersby could see them through the windows. Moody reports:

> A man walking past there one night glanced in through the door and saw the text. He was a poor prodigal, and he kept going. And as he walked away, he said to himself, "God is love? No. God is not love. God does not love me. He does not love me, for I am a poor, miserable sinner. If God were love, He would love me. God is not love." Yet there the text was, burning down into his soul. He went on a little further, turned around and came back, and went into the meeting. He didn't hear what the sermon was, but the text got into his heart…

He stayed after the meeting was over, and I found him there weeping like a child. But as I unfolded the Scripture and told him how God had loved him from his earliest childhood all along, the light of the gospel broke into his mind, and he went away rejoicing.[11]

Why would God stoop to love such unworthy people as us? Our limited mortal minds can barely begin to comprehend the vastness and constancy of God's perfect love. However, as with the man in the story, when we allow God's love to penetrate our hearts we can't help but love, appreciate, worship, and praise Him all the more in return.

God's Love Is Free

One night, I was speaking to several hundred men gathered in a homeless shelter. To illustrate to these men the love and grace of God, I pulled a $10 bill from my pocket and said, "The first person who comes to take this from my hand may have it as a free gift." Out of the hundreds of people seated before me, not a single person moved.

Finally, a middle-aged man, shabbily dressed like the rest, stood timidly to his feet and asked, "Do you really mean it?"

I said, "Sure, come and get it; it is yours."

He almost ran to grasp it, then he thanked me. The rest of the crowd began mumbling, as if to say, "Why didn't I go and accept the gift?"

This gave me a marvelous opportunity to emphasize that we do not earn God's love. God's love is a gift to all who will receive it by faith; He offers it to us freely. Nothing we do will make God love us any more; nothing we do will make Him love us any less. God loves us, not because of who we are, but because of who He is. God is love.

Usually, in our world, the rich, beautiful, talented, and intelligent receive the most attention and "love." But our social situation has no bearing on God's love for us. When Jesus entered Jericho, He had to pass by that greedy tax collector, Zacchaeus, who was shunned by everyone in town. Zacchaeus's spiritual hunger was so great that he climbed into a tree to see Jesus. When Jesus passed under the tree, He looked up and said, "Zacchaeus, come down immediately. I must stay at your house today" (Luke 19:5, NIV).

Zacchaeus did not need a second invitation. Scrambling out of the tree, he quickly welcomed Jesus into his home.

God's love reaches out to everyone, inviting them to enter the circle of His love. As in the case of Zacchaeus and the prodigal described by D. L. Moody, God's love sets a person free—no matter who that person is. God's unchanging love is reaching out to you right now.

God's Love Never Changes

"I don't love you anymore!" Just reading those words is heartbreaking. Some of the most devastating words a child can hear from his parents are, "I won't love you if you do that." The hurt of conditional love is also contained in the words of the teenage boy who says to a girl, "If you won't have sex with me, you don't love me." She yields to his embraces in a desperate attempt to hold someone who loves her, but when he gets what he wants, he leaves her. That same hurt reverberates like the echo in a canyon when after many years of marriage one partner says, "I don't love you anymore."

The one love we can count on, *no matter what,* is the love of our Creator. You and I can be completely confident that God's love for us is the same yesterday, today, and forever. Because of His great love, God's sacrificial plan for our salvation was set in motion in eternity past: "He chose us in Him before the creation of the world to be holy and blameless in His sight. In love He predestined us to be adopted as His sons through Jesus Christ" (Ephesians 1:4,5, NIV). There was never a moment when God did not purpose in His love to make the ultimate sacrifice for us. He planned to leave heaven's glory, beauty, and peace and take on the body of a man. You and I, who are not even worthy to call His name, are so loved that we were always on His mind!

Just before His betrayal, Jesus enjoyed the Passover meal with His disciples. They were about to experience incredible trauma when they saw their Master led away by soldiers, put on trial, and crucified. The Book of John explains Jesus' intentions during that Last Supper: "Jesus knew that the time had come for Him to leave this world and go to the Father. Having loved His own who were in the world, He now showed them the full extent of His love" (John 13:1, NIV).

First Jesus had a meal of fellowship, then He washed the disciples' feet. As the Lord washed Peter's feet, Peter proclaimed, "I will lay down my life for you."

Jesus responded, "Will you really lay down your life for Me? I tell you the truth, before the rooster crows, you will disown Me three times!" (John 13:37,38, NIV).

That is exactly what Peter did. During Christ's darkest hours, Peter turned his back on his Lord (Luke 22:32). Did Jesus reject Peter because of his betrayal? No! In fact, after His resurrection Jesus said to Peter in Matthew 16:18, "Now I say to you that you are Peter [which means 'rock'], and upon this rock I will build My church." Not only did Jesus forgive Peter's cowardice, but He also fully restored him because of His love for him.

> Once we grasp God's great love for us, we worship Him as a sincere response.

When we receive Jesus as our Savior and Lord, God envelops and infuses us with His everlasting love (Jeremiah 31:3). We enter into a special eternal relationship with Him. John recognized this and exclaimed: "How great is the love the Father has lavished on us, that we should be called children of God!" (1 John 3:1, NIV). This love will be with us for eternity.

God's Love for Us Is Pure

In Milwaukee, Wisconsin, a homeowner was approached by a man who wanted to borrow his barbecue grill. Being goodhearted, he let the man take it. When the borrower returned it several days later, he offered the grill owner four tickets to a Milwaukee Brewers baseball game. The owner was delighted, and even though the Brewers lost the game that day, he and his family had a good time. When they returned home, they discovered that thieves had cleaned out their house of all furniture and appliances while they were gone. What had appeared like a magnanimous gift of tickets turned out to be a trick to get the family to leave so their house could be burglarized.

Sometimes, we find ourselves wondering when God's goodness to us will end and we will find the "bottom line." But we do not need to be suspicious about the good things God offers us. He will never misuse our love for Him.

Nothing we do will take away His love for us. Paul writes, "I am convinced that nothing can ever separate us from His love. Death can't, and life can't. The angels can't, and the demons can't. Our fears for today, our worries about tomorrow, and even the powers of hell can't keep God's love away. Whether we are high above the sky or in the deepest ocean, nothing in all creation will ever be able to separate us from the love of God that is revealed in Christ Jesus our Lord" (Romans 8:38,39). We need never fear that His blessings are a disguise for other intentions. All God's actions toward us flow out of His pure love for us.

God's Love Works for Our Good

When iron ore is dug out of a mountain, it is worth only a few dollars per ton. But when that same ore is placed in a Bessemer furnace and put under tremendous heat and pressure, it is changed into a high grade of surgical steel.

God uses adversity in our lives, not to destroy us, but to build our faith and to refine us into the kind of people He created us to be. He does not want us to live as self-centered weaklings. During those difficult times, God assures us that He will work for our good (Romans 8:28). Only He knows the future and how things will turn out. Most of the time we selfishly ask for things that we want, but they are not necessarily the things that are good for us. I am so glad that God has not always answered my prayers and given me what I wanted. I am sure I would have made situations worse. I am going to trust God, His wisdom, and His plan for my life through my adversity.

Because He loves us, God has prepared an incredible future for us. First He gives us a full and meaningful life on earth. This is not a temporary provision, nor is it available only when we feel holy enough to accept it (Romans 5:1,2). In addition, God gives us a heavenly future with Christ (John 14:2,3). That is the hope of the one loved by God!

The words of this grand old hymn express God's love so clearly:

O the deep, deep love of Jesus,
Vast, unmeasured, boundless, free!
Rolling as a mighty ocean
In its fullness over me;
Underneath me, all around me,
Is the current of Thy love;
Leading onward, leading homeward,
To my glorious rest above.[12]

Once we grasp God's great love for us, we worship Him, not as a religious exercise or ritual, but as a sincere response to the love He has already shown for us! Where else will we find the unconditional love and acceptance we so desperately need? Certainly not in some hedonistic "Love-In" or an immoral sexual relationship. Such authentic and unselfish love can come only from the tender heart of a perfect God.

Every day, thank Him and praise Him for His unconditional, perfect love. Praise Him when you wake up in the morning, thank Him as you work, and tell Him how much you love Him before you go to sleep. Respond to His limitless, ever-present love to you by expressing your heart of love to Him.

Experiencing and wholeheartedly embracing God's unconditional love will transform your life and the lives of those around you. The more His love fills your heart, the more it will overflow into *every* relationship!

Talk About It: I AM Love

"And may you have the power to understand, as all God's people should, how wide, how long, how high, and how deep His love is."
(Ephesians 3:18)

1. How have your relationships with others (parents, spouse, friends, etc.) influenced how you view God's love?

2. How do you define real love? How do you know if someone's love is authentic?

3. Read 1 Corinthians 13:4–7, inserting "God" into each verse ("God's love is patient and kind. His love is not jealous..."). How does God's love differ from our love?

4. In this chapter you read, "Love is the supreme expression of God's personhood and flows out of His goodness. It affects all His other attributes." Consider one or two of God's other attributes listed in the I AM statements at the beginning of the book. How do you think His love affects those attributes?

5. Which of the following facts about God's love do you think is the most challenging for people to fully believe, and why?
   • God's love is free.
   • God's love never changes.
   • God's love for us is perfectly pure.
   • God's love works for our good.

6. When you think about God's love for you, which of the above facts is the hardest for you to truly believe? Why?

7. Read Ephesians 3:19. What hinders you the most from experiencing God's love for you?

FOCUS ON GOD

On an index card or your favorite electronic device, write the following statement and verse, or just take a picture of it:

**God, because You are love,
I know You are unconditionally committed to my well-being.**

*"We know how much God loves us, and we have
put our trust in His love. God is love…"*
(1 John 4:16)

Carry it with you throughout the week. Look at it when you get up, when you go to bed, and at least once during the day as a way of intentionally shifting your focus to God's unconditional love for you.

Ask God to help you experience *His* love this week.

CHAPTER 7

My Love Flows Through You

Our heavenly Father loves us, His children, in innumerable ways. As we follow Him, He gives us the incredible privilege of conveying His love to a broken and hurting world.

My dear friends Vek Huong and Samouen Taing direct the *JESUS* film project in Cambodia, which seeks to give every Cambodian an opportunity to know Jesus Christ through film. Their country went through one of the most devastating and horrific times in history when the Communist dictator, Pol Pot, held the small country in a grip of terror and torture. Today, a visitor can see the evidence in the Killing Fields Memorial just outside of Phnom Penh, the capital city. On display are 90,000 skulls piled seventy feet high. Shelf after shelf holds the bleached bones of men, women, and children. Out of a population of 8 million, 1.5 million or more were slaughtered, many in tortuous ways that are difficult to describe.

A few days before the collapse of Cambodia this young couple was asked if they would like to be evacuated. Huong replied, "We have decided to serve our Lord Jesus Christ by reaching Cambodia for Him until the last days of our lives."[13]

No one heard from the couple for four years. In that time, they wandered throughout the country, faced starvation and deprivation, but kept their faith in their Lord. To celebrate their anniversary, the only food they had were some rat heads and skin. They asked God to spare their lives, but were also willing to die if that was His plan for their lives.

After a long ordeal, they made their way to a refugee camp in Thailand where a reporter met them and published their names. Someone recognized their names and informed our leadership that they had been found. They were reunited with their Campus Crusade family with great joy.

Their experiences did not deter them. After their rescue from the refugee camp Samouen said, "Cambodia is our home. We will continue to serve here. We both have sad memories here. My parents and Huong's mother were killed by the Khmer Rouge. God gave us back our lives so we could serve Him, so that we could reach Cambodia for Christ. This is our second life."[14]

Because of Christ's love, Vek and Samouen returned to their homeland to direct the ministry in Cambodia. We who have experienced God's unconditional love are commanded to share that love with others. John writes, "We know how much God loves us, and we have put our trust in Him. God is love, and all who live in love live in God, and God lives in them" (1 John 4:16). The secret is letting God use us as His instruments to love others. We begin that process by loving God. As Jesus said, "Come, follow Me, and I will make you fishers of men" (Matthew 4:19, NIV). First we must "follow." Only then will God turn us into effective "fishers of men."

God Wants Us to Love Him Wholeheartedly

Jesus declared, "'You must love the LORD your God with all your heart, all your soul, and all your mind.' This is the first and greatest commandment" (Matthew 22:37,38). God, in His sovereignty, has created us so we find our greatest joy and fulfillment in loving Him.

One day when I was preparing a talk, my young son Zac suddenly appeared with his stack of books and sat silently beside me. I was deeply moved to think that there were dozens of places in our home where he could have gone to read. I broke the silence: "Zac, I want you to know how much it means to me that you have come to sit with me."

My heart melted to hear my son say, "Dad, that's the reason I've come. I just want to be with you."

In the same way, the great heart of God longs for fellowship with us. With incredible blessings in hand, He waits for us to open our eyes and ears and reach out in faith to receive them. Oh, how He desires to walk and talk with us as He did with Adam and Eve in the Garden of Eden.

> The great heart of God longs for relationship with us.

One of the great preachers and Bible teachers of our time, Charles Stanley, delivered a message at one of our staff training sessions in which he revealed that he had grown up not knowing the love of a father. He had come to faith in Christ, gone to seminary, and built a large church. One day when he was feeling burned out and at the end of his rope, he invited some trusted men to join him for a time of reflection on his life. For several hours he told them his story, how unloved he had felt as a child, how even as an adult he was not experiencing the love of God.

Finally, one of the men asked him to rest his head on his folded arms on the table. "Imagine God putting His arms around you while you focus on the statement, 'God loves me.'"

As Stanley did so, tears began to flow. He felt overwhelmed by the love of his heavenly Father. What had been an intellectual exercise of faith in the love of God had become very personal. For the first time in his life he experienced the love Jesus spoke of in John 15:9: "I have loved you even as the Father has loved Me."

I encourage you to pour out your heart to Him; tell Him of your hurts, fears, and hopes. Read His letters of love found in the Bible. Then come into His presence through stillness or praise and worship. As you linger in His presence, His Spirit will commune with your spirit to refresh your body, soul, mind, and emotions.

God Wants Us to Love Our Neighbors

As our intimate relationship with God deepens, we become more like His Son, Jesus Christ. As a result, we are better able to love others as God loves us. John writes, "Dear friends, since God loved us that much, we surely ought to love each other" (1 John 4:11). God wants us to express His supernatural, *agape* love to others. We become examples of God's love to the world as we love our neighbors through the enabling of His Holy Spirit.

I am reminded of the story of the Navajo Indian woman who had been cured of a serious ailment by a missionary doctor. She was greatly impressed by the love he manifested. "If Jesus is anything like the doctor," she said, "I can trust Him forever."

That woman did not need anyone to explain God's love to her. She saw it in action through the doctor. God wants His people to be living examples of His love to others.

God Wants Us to Love Our Enemies

Jesus taught His disciples, "Love your enemies and pray for those who persecute you" (Matthew 5:44, NIV). That is difficult, if not impossible, without yielding control of our lives to the Holy Spirit who lives in every believer.

When Christians begin to love God, they will love their enemies.

One man who demonstrated God's love for his enemies is Richard Wurmbrand, a Romanian pastor who was imprisoned and tortured for his faith. During the Nazi Holocaust, his family lost parents, several sisters, and a brother, as well as orphaned children they had taken in. During those terrible days, he was introduced to a German soldier who boasted how he had killed Jews—even those who held little children in their arms.

This man did not realize that Wurmbrand was a Jew. Since Wurmbrand is a good German name and he was a Christian pastor, the soldier assumed that Richard was not Jewish. During the soldier's boasts of cruelty against Jews, Wurmbrand did not say a word. Instead, he invited the man to his home.

The soldier accepted the invitation. When they arrived, Wurmbrand explained that his wife was sick in bed. After conversing until late at night, the Romanian pastor said, "Sir, I have to tell you something. But promise me that you will listen to me ten minutes quietly. After ten minutes, you can say whatever you like." The soldier readily agreed.

Richard Wurmbrand then said, "In the other room, my wife is sleeping. She is Jewish, and I am Jewish too. Her family, which is also my family, perished in one of the big Nazi concentration camps. You boasted that you have killed in the same concentration camp where our family was sent. So you presumably are the very murderer of my family.

"Now I propose to you an experiment. We will pass into the other room and will tell my wife who you are. I can assure you my wife will not say one word of reproach, will not look angrily at you, will smile at you as at every guest. She will consider you as an honored guest. She will go and prepare for you coffee and some cookies. You will be received just like everybody else. If my wife, who is only human, can do this, if she can love you like this, knowing what you have done and can forgive you, then how much more will Jesus, who is love."[15]

The tall soldier tore at his jacket, crying, "What have I done, what have I done? I am guilty of so much blood." This man who had never before heard a prayer knelt with the pastor and asked God for forgiveness.

Then the two men came into the room where Mrs. Wurmbrand lay. She had heard nothing about what had happened in the next room, but when her husband woke her, she did exactly as he described she would. When she heard that the soldier had repented of his sins, she fell around his neck. They both wept. Pastor Wurmbrand writes of the scene, "It was a scene of love like in heaven. That is what Jesus can do. He is love."[16]

When Christians begin to love God, they will love their enemies. The world today, as in the first century, will marvel when they see our loving attitudes and actions (John 13:35).

Loving by Faith

My prayer for you is the same as Paul prayed for the believers in Ephesus: "May your roots go down deep into the soil of God's marvelous love. And may you have the power to understand, as all God's people should, how wide, how long, how high, and how deep His love really is" (Ephesians 3:17,18).

We have the potential to love anyone God puts in our path. One of the greatest lessons I have learned in my Christian life is "how to love by faith."[17] We may think we have lost our love for our spouse, for example. Yet when we *by faith* invite God's unconditional love for an "unlovable" spouse to flow through us, we will discover a rekindled love that is alive and well. That is true as well for an "unlovable" boss, associate, or employee. Nothing breaks up the hardened ground of unforgiveness and bitterness like sincere acts and words of love.

There is no power on earth stronger than supernatural love.

Sometimes you and I must take the first step of restoration, by faith, to love. A positive response from others may not always be immediate, but keep on choosing by faith to love and reach out. There is no power on earth stronger than supernatural love.

An attorney came to my office at Arrowhead Springs, California, one day to complain that he just could not get along with one of his partners. They hated each other, he reported. So I suggested he tell his partner that he loved him and ask him for forgiveness for not loving him.

"I could *never* do that," he protested. But after I explained the concept of how to love by faith, he agreed to approach his partner. He went into the office early the next morning and said to his partner: "Some time ago I became a Christian and my critical attitude toward you has changed. I've come to ask you to forgive me and to tell you that I love you."

His partner practically fell out of his chair because he was so amazed at the dramatically changed attitude of the man before him. He asked, "How can I have what you have?" The attorney led his partner to faith in Christ, and they became good friends. A few days later they came to tell me of the miracle of their reconciliation and of God's supernatural love.

Begin right now to love by faith. Make a list of everyone you do not like or have a hard time loving or those who have hurt you. Perhaps your list will include your boss, a coworker, your spouse, your children, a parent, a fellow believer, or a neighbor. Now ask the Holy Spirit to fill you with love for that person and claim by faith Christ's great love for them. Then the next time you meet them, by faith draw upon God's limitless, inexhaustible, overwhelming love for them. Through the enabling of the Holy Spirit, demonstrate your love by your actions.

A Love We Want to Share

A newly engaged couple cannot help but share their happy news with anyone who will listen. A woman who has been cured of cancer cries tears of joy and calls all of her friends to share the good news. It can be similar for one who has just begun a relationship with Jesus. Have you ever been around a new Christian who is so in love with Jesus that he cannot stop talking about our Savior? Whether we are an introvert or an extrovert, it is hard to be quiet about the things that excite us and change our lives.

Unfortunately, like the church of Ephesus, as recorded in the Book of Revelation, many believers lose their first love and stop talking about the God who loved them so much that He gave His Son to die in their place on the cross.

The contrast between a new Christian and a "veteran" Christian is illustrated by the story of the young man who rushed back to his apartment one night after a Billy Graham meeting. He and his roommate had lived and worked together for several years. "I must tell you something," he said to his friend. "Tonight I invited Christ to be my Savior, and He has changed my life!"

His friend smiled and said, "Wonderful! I have been a Christian for several years, all the time hoping that you would receive Christ as your Savior."

Surprised, the new Christian said, "Ever since I've known you, I have been trying to live up to your standards, but have failed miserably. Why didn't you tell me how I could know Christ?"

Paul writes, "Christ's love compels us, because we are convinced that one died for all, and therefore all died. And He died for all, that those who live should no longer live for themselves but for Him who died for them and was raised again" (2 Corinthians 5:14,15, NIV). When we genuinely realize how much God has sacrificed for us, our love for Him will stay warm and fruitful. We will not be able to keep the Good News to ourselves. God's love *is* the Good News we share with those who have no idea what it means to be loved by Christ.

Let us continually, day to day and moment to moment, drink deeply from the wellsprings of God's love. And after you are refreshed with that living water, pour some out onto dry, thirsty people around you. I assure you that seeing others respond to God's love and forgiveness will be one of the most joyful experiences you will ever have.

However, one question still remains: Is God's love dependable? How can I know that His love will always be perfectly pure? How can I trust that He will always love me no matter what I have done? If you don't understand God's holiness you will never be confident of His love. Let's explore in the next two chapters what it means for God to be holy.

Talk About It: My Love Flows Through You

"This is My commandment: Love each other in the same way I have loved you. There is no greater love than to lay down one's life for one's friends."
(John 15:12,13)

1. On a scale of 1–10, how would you say you are doing at loving God?
2. In Matthew 22:37,38, Jesus said, "'You must love the LORD your God with all your heart, all your soul, and all your mind.' This is the first and greatest commandment." How can you live this out in your daily life? Why do you think God wants us to love Him so completely?
3. In his book *The Five Love Languages,* Gary Chapman outlines five primary ways we can give and receive love. How do you think we can apply the love languages shown below as we seek to love God in ways that bring Him joy?
   - Quality time
   - Acts of Service
   - Gifts
   - Words of encouragement (praise)
4. God says He wants you to:
   - Love Him with your whole heart (Matthew 22:37)
   - Love your neighbor as yourself (Matthew 22:39)
   - Love your enemies (Matthew 5:44)

Which of the above is the most challenging for you? Why?

5. What is your response to the concept of "loving by faith"? Is there someone in your life you need to begin to love by faith? What is your first step?

6. Jesus' love changes lives. Who was the first person who ever told you about Jesus' love for you?

Have you ever told anyone how much Jesus loves them? Is there someone in your life who needs to hear about the love of Jesus expressed on the cross? Pray and ask God daily to give you an opportunity to talk with them about His love for them, and then start looking for the opportunity God will provide.

(See Appendix A, "Would You Like to Know God Personally?" to help you communicate God's love. Or go to BrightMedia.org for helpful tools and suggestions.)

FOCUS ON GOD

Continue to review the statement and verse you wrote down last week, at least three times each day, to remind yourself that God loves you unconditionally.

**God, because You are love,
I know You are unconditionally committed to my well-being.**

*"We know how much God loves us, and we have
put our trust in His love. God is love..."*
(1 John 4:16)

This week, live in this confidence:

"And I am convinced that nothing can ever separate us from God's love. Neither death nor life, neither angels nor demons, neither our fears for today nor our worries about tomorrow—not even the powers of hell can separate us from God's love. No power in the sky above or in the earth below—indeed,

nothing in all creation will ever be able to separate us from the love of God that is revealed in Christ Jesus our Lord." (Romans 8:38,39)

...and then extend His love to others.

CHAPTER 8

I AM Holy

God's holiness has been largely ignored by modern Christianity. Of all God's attributes, nothing compares to the splendor and beauty of His holiness. It is chief among His attributes. That means His character is perfect in every way. His moral excellence is the standard of absolute integrity. God's pristine purity and perfection infinitely set Him apart from His creation. Everything God does bears the imprint of His unblemished holiness. His holiness never diminishes.

Holiness is a wonderful, awe-inspiring attribute, but it is also a fearful reality for those who fall short of perfection. Our flaws are exposed in the consuming fire of His holiness. But in the midst of the fire God also extends great hope.

The Power of Fire

They were called the Great Fires of 1988. That year, wildfires swept through 1.4 million acres of Yellowstone National Park. The park was like a huge lumberyard filled with millions of wooden poles stuck at intervals far enough apart to allow good air circulation but close enough for each old lodgepole pine to torch its neighbor. Pine needles and dead twigs littered the ground, providing tinder-dry fodder for the unquenchable appetite of the fires.

On September 6, spot fires were seen around the historic Old Faithful Inn, the world's largest log structure. Twenty-five miles north, a fire storm raged across 50 acres of forest.

The next day wind gusts propelled the flames south. By afternoon, a large wall of intensifying black and brown smoke hovered close to the Inn, but firefighters felt confident that they could contain any outbreaks. Suddenly, fingers of fires around the Inn curled together to make a powerful fist that pounded the area. Then 50-mile-an-hour, fire-generated winds thundered in, sounding like the continuous roar of a jet taking off. Spot fires jumped up in numerous places close to the vulnerable buildings. A wall of flame higher than the tops of the trees advanced with terrifying speed.

Firefighters worked furiously, soaking the Inn with water to protect it from the flames. Then as quickly as the fire had come, it turned to the northeast. The danger was past. Twenty-four buildings had burned, but Old Faithful Inn had been saved.[18]

Months later, the forest grew with new vigor. The heat from the fires split open the hulls of the pine cones, releasing their seeds and yielding a forest of little saplings sprouting everywhere. The dead underbrush had been burned away. New spears of grass turned the hillsides to spring green, and a bumper crop of wildflowers carpeted the meadows.

The Power of God's Holiness

Anyone who has been near a fire of that magnitude understands its tremendous power. When it roars through an area, everything is changed. Ancient trees turn into cinders. Buildings are reduced to ashes. Nothing can withstand its fury. But in their wake, wildfires also bring new growth and regeneration.

In the Bible, God's holiness is sometimes pictured as a fire. A. W. Tozer writes:

Only fire can give even a remote conception of it. In fire He appeared at the burning bush; in the pillar of fire He dwelt through all the long wilderness journey. The fire that glowed between the wings of the cherubim in the holy place was called the Shekinah, the Presence, through the years of Israel's glory, and when the Old had given place to the New, He came at Pentecost as a fiery flame and rested upon each disciple.[19]

What does a fire do? It destroys the dead, purifies, and transforms the landscape. It is powerful, beautiful, and awesome. No one can stand up to the heat and fury of a firestorm. Nothing can bring regeneration like a forest fire.

God's holiness has even greater power. Moses, who saw God's holiness in the burning bush, asked, "Who else among the gods is like you, O LORD? Who is glorious in holiness like you—so awesome in splendor, performing such wonders?" (Exodus 15:11).

> God's holiness is chief among His attributes.

Our God Is Exalted in Holy Majesty

Our unwillingness to acknowledge God's holiness reflects our failure to recognize who God really is. The Hebrew root word for "to be holy" means to cut or to separate. The Old Testament reveals that God is above and separate from all that He created. He is exalted above everything in holy majesty.

We may also define *holy* as completely set apart from sin.[20] Holiness reflects a flawless, unblemished moral purity. God does not just match a standard of purity—He is the standard.

I feel totally inadequate to describe this attribute of God. How can I, or any sinful human being, find the right words to explain how pure and high God is in His holiness? How can I describe something that is so far removed from my experience and nature? However, if we desire to know God intimately and see our lives transformed, we must begin to grasp God's holiness, His supreme attribute.

When I think of God's holiness, I am convicted by the sinful nature of my own being. We are all like a man wearing a beautiful white suit who was invited to go down into the depths of a coal mine. In the darkness of the mine, he was not aware that his suit was becoming soiled. But when he resurfaced into the dazzling light of the noonday sun, he was fully aware that his suit had become sooty and dirty. The light of God's holiness reveals the darkness of our sin.

Isaiah was a prominent citizen of Judah during the eighth century BC, a prophet who followed God's commands and served his Lord. Today, we would consider him one of the "spiritual elite," a man of integrity and honor. At one point, Isaiah had a vision of heaven and the holiness of the Creator:

> I saw the Lord. He was sitting on a lofty throne, and the train of His robe filled the Temple. Hovering around Him were mighty seraphim, each with six wings. With two wings they covered their faces, with two they covered their feet, and with the remaining two they flew. In a great chorus they sang, "Holy, holy, holy is the LORD Almighty! The whole earth is filled with His glory!" The glorious singing shook the Temple to its foundations, and the entire sanctuary was filled with smoke. (Isaiah 6:1–4)

Prior to his vision, Isaiah was focused on the sins of others, calling them to repentance. Now that he found himself in the very presence of our holy God, he became dramatically aware of his own sin and unrighteousness. Terrified, he exclaimed, "My destruction is sealed, for I am a sinful man and a member of a sinful race. Yet I have seen the King, the LORD Almighty!" (Isaiah 6:5).

When the angels surround the glorious throne of God, they sing, "Holy, holy, holy is the LORD Almighty." Stephen Charnock comments, "Do you hear, in any angelical song, any other perfection of the Divine Nature thrice repeated? Where do we read of them crying out, 'eternal, eternal, eternal' or 'faithful, faithful, faithful' Lord God of hosts?"[21]

This repetition, "holy, holy, holy," tells us that God's holiness is the supreme attribute of His being, the foundation of His eternal existence. All His other attributes are marked by His holiness. His sovereignty and His role as judge are rooted in and flow out of His holiness. In fact, theologians speak of God's holiness as His "central and supreme perfection."[22] It sets Him apart from everything and everyone.

God's Holiness Requires Separation

God's holiness requires separation from anything that is not perfect and pure. Permit me to take you back to the Old Testament times when the Israelites worshiped God in a large tent or pavilion, called a tabernacle, which they carried through the wilderness and into the Promised Land. The tabernacle provided a daily reminder of God's holiness and His distinct separation from sinful mankind.

> God does not just match a standard of purity— He is the standard.

The tabernacle had three sections: the large outer courtyard surrounding the tabernacle, the Holy Place, and the Holy of Holies within the tabernacle. Each area was hidden from the other two by curtains.

Any priest who entered God's tabernacle first had to sacrifice an animal on the Brazen Altar to atone for sin. These burnt sacrifices were offered twice a day, once in the morning and once in the evening. Next was the Laver in which the priest washed his hands and feet before he appeared before the Lord—once again a symbol of our need for cleansing from sin. Then he was ready to enter the Holy Place.

Inside the Holy Place were three articles: the gold-plated Table of Showbread, the solid gold Lampstand, and the Altar of Incense. The Table of Showbread held the special Bread of the Presence; the Lampstand continually burned pure oil; and the Altar of Incense held fragrant incense which was offered every morning.

But the Holy of Holies was the place where God's presence resided. It was hidden from view by a curtain so heavy that it took four men to move it. Only the High Priest was allowed to enter this place—and only once a year. If anyone else tried, God would strike him dead. Inside the Holy of Holies was the gold-plated Ark of the Covenant, the dwelling place of God Himself, where once a year the High Priest offered sacrifices for his own sins and the sins of the people.

Why was the place of God's presence in the tabernacle hidden from view? Because God is so holy that no one can look upon His glory and live without prior atonement for the forgiveness of sin.

The Israelites offered a lamb as a sacrifice for sin. It was a picture of Jesus Christ, the Lamb of God, and His sacrifice on the cross to provide a covering against the wrath of God on all sin. The only thing that can satisfy the judgment of sin demanded by God's holiness is the shedding of pure, innocent blood. Only Jesus' blood met this high standard. Apart from that, we would remain separated from God for all eternity because of His purity and perfection.

The idea that God would allow His own Son to be brutally murdered on a cross bothers many people. However, it clearly reveals the depth of God's revulsion to our sin because He is holy. That, in fact, is one of the primary lessons we learn from the Old Testament repeatedly—God cannot tolerate sin. However, Jesus' willing sacrifice for us on the cross also demonstrates how passionately God loves us. Until we recognize how much our holy God hates our sin, we will never understand how deeply He loves us.

God's Wrath Is Part of His Holiness

The Bible admonishes us to have a healthy fear of God. He is the absolutely pure and righteous being who abhors evil. He cannot tolerate any unrighteousness. Habakkuk 1:13 tells us, "Your eyes are too pure to look on evil; You cannot tolerate wrong" (NIV). God cannot secretly inspire any evil in us, for in His very nature He cannot accept any evil in any form.

God's holiness requires consequences for sin. We have broken His standard of holiness, and His holiness demands that He judge sin, not ignore or excuse it.

God's holy wrath is evidenced throughout the Bible. Apart from Noah and his family, God destroyed all of humanity with a flood because of sin. The Lord rained down fire and burning sulfur upon Sodom and Gomorrah. God handed over His people, Israel, into captivity in Babylon because of their faithlessness. In the New Testament, God struck down Ananias and Sapphira because they lied. Yet God's wrath is not uncontrolled anger, like we may sometimes think. Instead, it is a planned and just act that has its roots in God's holiness.

> When you recognize how much God hates sin, you understand how deeply He loves you.

Many people believe that actions do not necessarily have consequences—at least not for them. Because they believe God is either irrelevant or just wants them to be happy, they justify all kinds of self-gratification. If you are not happy in your marriage, get a divorce. If you want to have sex outside of marriage, just use a condom. If you have an unwanted pregnancy, just get an abortion. If you commit a crime, hire a good lawyer. Stealing items from your employer is okay because everyone else is doing it. The lack of teaching in the Church on who God really is has weakened all of society and lowered standards for holy and righteous living both in the Church and in secular society.

"Our sins are not so wrong," we say. "What others do is much worse." The person who believes this has not confronted the holiness, justice, and righteousness of God. One small sin, one white lie, one hurtful word is enough to separate us from God's perfect holiness forever.

God's Holiness Is Demonstrated in His Lawgiving

In recent years, numerous laws passed by state and federal legislatures have been struck down by the Supreme Court. In some cases, the judges ruled that a law could not be fairly applied. Other laws the Supreme Court decided had a fatal flaw that would prevent justice from being evenly distributed.

As the supreme, absolutely holy lawgiver, God has never announced a law that was not perfect in all respects. He has no need of a Supreme Court to determine whether His laws are fair or can be evenly applied. All His laws are an expression of the purity of His holiness (Romans 7:12).

Jude's epistle provides numerous examples of people who rejected God's laws—and suffered the judgment of a holy God. Jude mentions "godless men, who change the grace of our God into a license for immorality" (Jude 4, NIV). They thought they could get away with their sin. Not so, Jude writes, for we are dealing with a holy God who, after delivering the people of Israel out of Egypt, "later destroyed those who did not believe" (Jude 5, NIV). Even the angels who rebelled against God "He has kept in darkness, bound with everlasting chains for judgment on the great Day" (Jude 6, NIV).

Over and over again, we set up our own standards of what ought to please God: "I deal fairly with people." "I do not abuse my wife or my children." "I give to the needs of others in the homeless shelter I support." "I'm a good neighbor."

We slight the holiness of God when we think we can manage on our own. We fool ourselves when we assume that keeping the Golden Rule will cover our sins. How ridiculous our standards are when compared to His perfect standards of righteousness. When Joshua gave his farewell address to the people of Israel after they had settled into the Promised Land, he knew that the people still worshiped foreign gods. He told them, "You are not able to serve the LORD, for He is a holy and jealous God. He will not forgive your rebellion and sins" (Joshua 24:19).

None of our manmade standards of behavior meet the requirements of a holy God. God's holiness mandates that we keep all His laws perfectly at all times. If we don't then the only way we can come into His presence is by having our sins paid for by the blood of the "Lamb of God," Jesus Christ. Only through Christ's payment can our holy God extend His mercy to us.

If you have never accepted Jesus' payment for your sin, why wait another minute? Turn to Appendix A right now and find out how you can begin a relationship with our holy, loving God!

Responding to God's Holiness

If we could just grasp even a part of the magnificent holiness of God and the miracle of His mercy to His sinful creatures, then our homes, offices, schools, and in fact, the whole earth would shake with people kneeling and falling prostrate on the ground in worship and adoration of Him. Such a view would precipitate a healthy fear of God, which is a necessary starting point for seeing our lives transformed (Proverbs 9:10).

True knowledge of God's holiness always elicits a worshipful response from us. Moses fell to his face before the burning bush. Isaiah said, "Woe is me!" We cannot stand in the presence of God without acknowledging His holiness and seeing our own sin. Author Beth Moore writes in *A Woman's Heart: God's Dwelling Place*:

The light of God's glory shines two ways: it sheds light on the knowledge of God so we can see Him more clearly, but it also sheds light on us so that we can see our own sin more clearly. Remember, the closer you approach the light, the brighter it shines on you. This is the marvelous two-edged sword of intimacy. We see Him more clearly and we see ourselves more clearly. It is the perfect safeguard against pride. You can mark His word on this: true intimacy breeds true humility![23]

When we concentrate on God's holiness—His moral perfections and absolute purity—the only appropriate response is humble adoration. Adoration is the basis for all worship.

Whenever I meditate on the holiness of God, I am impressed with how worthy He is of our worship. I think of the verse, "Worship the LORD in the splendor of His holiness; tremble before Him, all the earth" (Psalm 96:9, NIV). I want to become absorbed with His holiness, rather than with His might, His wisdom, or His other magnificent attributes.

As we meditate on God's supreme holiness, we cannot help but be overcome with a sense of awe. Music can help us express our awe for our Lord. Many Christian hymns capture the spirit of worship. I encourage you to select one of them, such as "Holy, Holy, Holy," and begin to worship God in song and praise daily.

Talk About It: I AM Holy

"Holy, holy, holy is the LORD ALMIGHTY;
THE WHOLE EARTH IS FULL OF HIS GLORY!"
(Isaiah 6:3, NIV)

1. In your words, describe what you think the Bible means by "holy." Think of specific words that describe what it means for God to be holy.
2. Holy = Perfectly pure; set apart (in His own category). What do you think people might perceive as some of the pros and cons of God being perfectly holy?

3. How does God's perfect holiness impact His integrity? If He were not perfectly holy, how would that impact your ability to trust all His other attributes?

4. Why do you think God's holiness can elicit security and comfort as well as fear?

5. Read Isaiah 6:1–5. What was it that overwhelmed Isaiah? Describe how Isaiah may have seen himself in relationship to his fellow Israelites before and after the vision. What caused the shift in Isaiah's perspective and focus?

6. If you encountered God the way Isaiah did, imagine how you might respond. How do you think standing in God's presence would affect your attitudes, behavior, and desire to live a holy life? How do you think that might affect how you worship Him?

7. How does God's holiness give you greater insight into how God feels about your sin and why Jesus had to pay the penalty for your sin?

FOCUS ON GOD

On an index card or your favorite electronic device, write the following statement and verse, or just take a picture of it:

**God, because You are holy,
I will devote myself to You in purity, worship, and service.**

*"Holy, holy, holy is the LORD Almighty;
the whole earth is full of His glory!"*
(Isaiah 6:3, NIV)

Look at it when you get up, when you go to bed, and at least once during the day as a way of intentionally shifting your focus from yourself to God. During one of those times each day take a few minutes to meditate on God's holiness: His absolute perfection.

Also, take some time this week to worship God for His holiness. Pray. Sing along with praise music that focuses on God's holiness. Verbalize words or phrases of adoration. A good way to learn to do this is by reading aloud verses like Isaiah 6:3, Exodus 15:11, or many of the Psalms, such as Psalm 96 and 99.

CHAPTER 9

I Can Make Your Heart Pure

Have you been trying to live the Christian life but feel like a failure? Do you feel stuck? Many people who sit in church every Sunday are discouraged because no matter how hard they try to please God, they are not experiencing the abundant life Jesus promised.

There are really only two reasons why most Christians live in defeat. The first is that they have never fully surrendered their lives. The second is that they don't really understand who God is and therefore they are trying to live the Christian life in their own strength. Either of these will prevent you from experiencing victory over sin and the abundant joy that comes when our hearts are filled with His pure and perfect love.

Some time ago a man who held an influential position in a Christian ministry confided in me that he had never surrendered his life to Christ, although for years he pretended that he had done so. He said and did all the right things so that his friends and all who met him would think he was a committed follower of Christ. But he admitted to deliberately saying "no" to the Holy Spirit's leading and choosing to live a lie.

I was shocked that anyone who was exposed to the inspired Word of God, Christian fellowship, and ministry would dare to deliberately disobey God. But as we talked, I learned that he was simply afraid to live a holy life. The thought of complete surrender to the Lord was unappealing to him, and as a result, he had run from God for many years.

Holy Living: You Can't Do It on Your Own

Like with this man, a false view of holiness causes many Christians to stop short of complete surrender to God. They have a distorted view of holiness because they define it from a secular viewpoint. They imagine a holy person as some kind of religious fanatic, a "kook," or an isolated monk devoted to prayer and fasting. Others think that holiness has only to do with the way a person dresses or socializes. These misinformed believers decide they do not want to give up their lifestyle, pleasures, and pride and allow God to renew their minds. They do not let Him mold them into people with tastes and desires that bring true happiness and joy in fellowship with Him.

Tragically, some believers allow their childhood experiences with strict, legalistic parents or churches to distort their view of God, His holiness, and His expectations. I have heard some confess, "I tried to live up to the high expectations of my parents or pastor, but I have failed many times. I just can't live the Christian life!" I agree.

> It is impossible to live a holy life on your own.

It is impossible to live a holy life on your own. Even with determination and our best efforts, we will always fail. We can never become holy in our own strength and abilities.

But the story does not end with our feeble efforts. Paul proclaims:

There is no condemnation [guilt] for those who belong to Christ Jesus. For the power of the life-giving Spirit has freed you through Christ Jesus from the power of sin that leads to death. The law of Moses could not save us, because of our sinful nature. But God put into effect a different plan to save us. He sent His own Son in a human body like ours, except that ours are sinful. God destroyed sin's control over us by giving His Son as a sacrifice for our sins. He did this so that the requirement of the law would be fully accomplished for us who no longer follow our sinful nature but instead follow the Spirit. (Romans 8:1–4)

This is the secret: We can live a holy life if we yield to the Holy Spirit who came to glorify Jesus Christ. Jesus is the only person to ever live a holy life, and now He resides within every believer through His Holy Spirit. His presence and power give us the strength to live a holy life moment by moment.

Holy, righteous living, by surrendering to God's Spirit, is the secret to a life of joy, power, victory, and fruitfulness. When we are holy, we are set apart and separated from sin for God's special use. God gives us the power to experience a whole new life based on His holiness and purity. But we must obey His direction and laws by submitting control of our lives to His Holy Spirit. If you would like to learn more about how to allow the Spirit of God to empower you to live a holy life, turn to Appendix B, "How to Be Filled With the Holy Spirit." The Holy Spirit is the secret to living a victorious Christian life.

In this chapter, we will learn about several ways God wants us to respond to His holiness.

Because God is holy, we must give Him reverent respect.

In 1996, I was privileged to receive the prestigious international Templeton Prize for Progress in Religion. As part of the honor, Vonette and I went to Buckingham Palace to meet with Prince Philip and Sir John Templeton. Because we were meeting royalty, we were very conscious of our appearance and our behavior.

Do we have less concern when we come before our Sovereign God, the ruler of the universe? He deserves much more reverence and respect than any human being who ever lived! He is not the "man upstairs." He is the great, holy, righteous, all-powerful, loving, creator God.

> Living a pure life is possible only through the enabling of the Holy Spirit.

Many Scripture passages tell us to fear God. King David writes, "Serve the LORD with reverent fear, and rejoice with trembling" (Psalm 2:11). Solomon explains, "The fear of the LORD is the beginning of wisdom, and knowledge of the Holy One is understanding" (Proverbs 9:10, NIV).

Fearing God does not mean to be afraid of God, but rather to express reverential awe and deep respect before Him.

Vonette and I get on our knees every morning to praise and worship God out of reverential awe for Him. I encourage you to examine:

- How you come before God: Do you bow your head or kneel out of respect?
- How you honor His name: Do your words and actions make it clear to others that you really believe His name is sacred? Do you ever misuse the name of Jesus? Do you ever financially support movies that misuse His holy name?
- How you respect His Word: Do you read it daily? Do you study it? Do you memorize it? Is it your standard for daily conduct? Is it your source for discerning truth?

In your daily quiet time with Him, give Him the honor He deserves. Seek to spend more time worshiping Him than asking for your own needs.

Because God is holy, we must turn away from evil.

God created the universe to function according to His standard of holiness. God's holiness is so complete that He cannot permit even one sin. Not one.

Picture God's holiness in this way. Envision a beautiful bride on her wedding day, dressed in white and looking radiant. The white dress symbolizes purity. It does not have a spot or wrinkle anywhere. If one ink spot stained the dress, people would focus on the ugliness of the stain rather than the loveliness of the bride. That is a picture of God's purity. God, who has never sinned in any way, is so pure and holy that He "cannot tolerate the slightest sin" (Psalm 5:4). His heaven is pure and holy, absolutely free of all sin and evil.

No matter how religious, self-disciplined, or good we may try to be, we cannot expect God to allow us into His heaven when we have sin-stains in our lives. If God allowed one sin to mar His pure dwelling place, it would cease to be a holy city. Since God cannot tolerate sin, our sinful, human situation is hopeless.

This is where a miraculous paradox comes in. Jesus Christ came to take away the sins of the world. He became sin for us. The perfect, holy Son of God took on the stain of our sin. He endured and satisfied the judgment of a pure God for our misdeeds—not just one or two sins, but every sin you and I have ever committed or will commit in our lifetimes!

Remember how the Holy of Holies in the tabernacle illustrated God's holiness and His separation from humans? The heavy curtain separated sinful people from God's presence. The sacrifices of lambs and goats symbolized a holy God who would take upon Himself the sins of the world. This ultimate sacrifice also included death—Christ's death on the cross.

The physical agony of the cross was nothing compared to the spiritual agony of God becoming sin for us! All the sins and evil ever committed, or that ever will be committed, were laid on Jesus Christ just before He died. Although Jesus abhorred sin and evil, He willingly took on the sins of all people. The Book of Hebrews explains this so much better than I ever could:

> What God wants is for us to be made holy by the sacrifice of the body of Jesus Christ once for all time… For by that one offering He perfected forever all those whom He is making holy… Now when sins have been forgiven, there is no need to offer any more sacrifices. And so, dear brothers and sisters, we can boldly enter heaven's Most Holy Place because of the blood of Jesus. This is the new, life-giving way that Christ has opened up for us through the sacred curtain, by means of His death for us. (Hebrews 10:10,14,18–20)

That is why during Christ's crucifixion God miraculously tore in two the heavy curtain that kept men and women from the Holy of Holies. Christ had paid the ultimate price. Those who accept God's forgiveness become spotless and pure so they now have access to God. In fact, all believers become God's holy temple as the Holy Spirit comes to live within them at the moment of their spiritual birth.

As His temples—His Most Holy Place—our lives are no longer temples of evil, immorality, stealing, or lying. Because God lives within us, we should abhor evil the way He does. When we understand how holy God is and what His Son endured to make us the temple of the living God, our motivation should be to live pure and sin-free lives.

Of course, living a pure life is possible only through the enabling of the Holy Spirit. We are given power over sin and temptation as we are indwelt, filled, and empowered by Him.

According to God's Word, we do not have to sin. But if we do sin, there is Someone to plead for us before the Father. This is explained in 1 John 2:1,2: "My dear children, I am writing this to you so that you will not sin. But if you do sin, there is someone to plead for you before the Father. He is Jesus Christ, the one who pleases God completely. He is the sacrifice for our sins. He takes away not only our sins but the sins of all the world."

Holy living involves a daily decision to follow Jesus.

Becoming holy is more than obedience; it is a liberating, cleansing freedom from all unwholesomeness. Sin in our lives creates a barrier to fellowship with God. It blocks the communication lines between us and God so He does not heed our prayers (Isaiah 59:1,2). Restored fellowship with God comes by confessing our sin and turning from it. As the holiness of God is absorbed into every fiber of our being, we become even more sensitive to sin and learn to abhor it all the more as we walk in an intimate, joyful relationship with Him.

Because God is holy, we must walk in His light.

"They plan to stone you!" I heard the words and knew that just like many of the early Christians, I had a decision to make. In the 1960s, I went to Rangoon, Burma, to speak to a gathering of students. When I arrived, I was told that a group of radical Communist students planned to kill me by stoning me at the meeting. Empowered by the Holy Spirit I went anyway.

When I began my speech, there was so much heckling that I could not be heard. Since I knew that God inhabits the praises of His people, I asked the few

Christians in the audience to join me in singing the praise chorus, *Hallelujah*. Satan cannot stand it when believers praise God. As we exalted God, the hecklers leaped from their chairs, dropped their stones, and ran out of the meeting. We continued with the meeting and several students asked Christ to become their Savior and Lord.

Sin and evil always seek refuge in darkness. But God's holy radiance exposes and destroys the darkness of sin and evil. Paul writes, "God lives in light so brilliant that no human can approach Him" (1 Timothy 6:16). The more we meditate on the holiness of God, the more we become aware of our sinfulness. In comparison to His purity, everything else appears dull and dirty.

First John 1 says that "God is light and there is no darkness in Him at all… If we are living in the light of God's presence, … then we have fellowship with each other, and the blood of Jesus, His Son, cleanses us from every sin" (1 John 1:5,7). Jesus said, "I am the light of the world. If you follow Me, you won't be stumbling through the darkness, because you will have the light that leads to life" (John 8:12). As we follow Jesus, His light illumines our way and unbelievers see the holiness of God through our attitudes and actions.

Because God is holy, we must completely surrender to Him.
Scripture gives us God's directive: "Now you must be holy in everything you do, just as God—who chose you to be His children—is holy" (1 Peter 1:15). Christians have been set apart by God for this divine purpose. If you want to see the holiness of God, examine the life and teachings of Jesus Christ. He is the visible expression of God's holiness. God wants us to place our lives under His lordship and conform to the moral character of His Son and reflect the beauty of His holiness and character.

Out of respect for God, I want to be holy as He is holy and never disappoint Him in any way. I would rather die than bring dishonor to His holy name. I have often prayed that if there is any possibility that I might be unfaithful to my beloved wife or in any other way bring dishonor to our Lord, that He would take my life before it happened.

George Müller, well-known for his great faith and ministry to orphans, was asked the secret of his fruitful service for the Lord. He said, "There was a day when I died...utterly died." As he spoke, he bent lower and lower until he almost touched the floor. "I died to George Müller—his opinions, his preferences, tastes, and will—died to the world, its approval or censure—died to the approval or blame even of my brethren and friends—and since then I have studied only to show myself approved unto God."

Everyone I know who has been greatly used by God for the cause of Christ has gone through an experience of "dying to self" as described in Galatians 2:20. It is not until we know the reality of "death to self" that we can live for Christ and God can truly use and bless us. My Galatians 2:20 experience happened in the spring of 1951 when Vonette and I signed a contract to become slaves of Christ. I daily reaffirm this contract.

Holy living involves a daily decision to surrender to the lordship of Christ. It involves yielding our will to God and adopting His perspective for life (Romans 12:1,2). God wants our minds and hearts to be filled with His holy qualities. As our lives are transformed, we will project the light of His holiness into the darkness of our evil world. Real life—abundant life—begins with dying to self.

Because God is Holy, we must worship Him alone.

God is very possessive of our affections. He warned the Israelites, "Do not worship any other gods besides Me. Do not make idols of any kind... You must never worship or bow down to them, for I, the LORD your God, am a jealous God who will not share your affection with any other god!" (Exodus 20:3–5). He alone has the right to occupy the throne of our heart. He is to be exalted to the highest place in our lives. Everything else must be of lower importance.

Yet we are all guilty at one time or another of modern versions of idolatry. The false gods and idols of our society may not be as obvious as those of ancient Israel or other cultures, but their presence is just as real. They clamor for our attention. They bargain for our allegiance. Here are some of the most common:

- *The idol of affluence.* Many are convinced that wealth is the key to happiness. They place their trust in bank accounts and hoarded assets. The spirit of greed has gradually transformed their values so that money is now their master.

- *The idol of pleasure.* Multitudes are convinced that pleasure is the chief goal in life. Couch potatoes vegetate in front of the TV screen. Sports fanatics cannot watch enough games. Others seek happiness in food, alcohol, or drugs. They seek entertainment, thrills, adventure, and escape in their futile search for happiness.
- *The idol of achievement.* The ambitious sacrifice themselves to this god. Pride is their relentless taskmaster. For these workaholics, accomplishments are the building blocks of self-esteem. No challenge is too great in their quest for significance.
- *The idol of infatuation.* Some people idolize a celebrity, a hero, a friend, or even a relative. Their entire world revolves around that individual. The spirit of obsession amplifies healthy feelings of love and admiration into unholy worship.
- *The idol of self-worship.* Many are convinced by the spirit of vanity that appearance is everything. Their life is preoccupied with beauty, fashion, and body-building.
- *The idol of sensuality.* The spirit of lust has ensnared many with immorality. For them God's gift of sex has been distorted into perversion and tragically often ends in addiction, abortion, disease, and death.

Substitute gods usurp the worship and devotion that rightfully belong to our holy God. In reality, these idols can never fill the God-shaped vacuum within our hearts. God's Word calls us to a higher focus: "You must be holy because I am holy" (1 Peter 1:16).

As believers who belong to the universal Church, we are the bride of Christ. God promises that the Church will one day shine faultless before Him. At the end of this age, Christ will present us to God clothed in Christ's purity and holiness (Ephesians 5:25–27).

I can hardly wait for that day. That will be the moment when all of us, the Church of Christ universal with millions upon millions of believers, will give glory to God as the spotless bride of Christ. It will be one of the most moving moments in all eternity. We can prepare ourselves for that momentous occasion today by living our lives in the light of God's holiness and purity by faith through the enabling power of the Holy Spirit.

Talk About It: I Can Make Your Heart Pure

"For by that one offering He forever made
perfect those who are being made holy."
(Hebrews 10:14)

1. On a scale of 1–10, how would you say you're doing at living the Christian life? (1=complete failure; 5=working hard but not good enough; 10=pure joy)
2. First Peter 1:16 says, "You must be holy because I am holy." What do you think prevents most Christians from living lives that reflect God's holiness?
3. Based on your personal observations of modern culture, which of the idols mentioned in the chapter do we most tend to elevate (knowingly or unknowingly) above our holy God? Why?

idol of affluence	idol of pleasure
idol of achievement	idol of infatuation
idol of self-worship	idol of sensuality

4. According to Hebrews 10:14, when you accept Christ's payment for your sin, two things change. You are _____ perfect and you are _____ _____ holy. What do you think that means?
5. Read Romans 8:1–4. To what degree are you experiencing the reality of these words in your daily life?
6. Read Hebrews 10:14 again. Do you think God is okay with the fact that you are in process? Why?
7. Because of who God is, He never requires something of us without giving us what we need to accomplish what He asks. According to this chapter, what has He given us to enable us to live a holy life?

FOCUS ON GOD

Continue to review the statement and verse regarding God's holiness you wrote down last week, meditating daily on God's perfect holiness.

God, because You are holy,
I will devote myself to You in purity, worship, and service.

*"Holy, holy, holy is the L*ORD *Almighty;*
the whole earth is full of His glory!"
(Isaiah 6:3, NIV)

As temptations arise this week, thank God for His Holy Spirit and ask Him to help you turn away from sin.

CHAPTER 10

I AM Everywhere All the Time

In 1985 during the week between Christmas and New Year's Day, my fellow staff members and I were involved in a conference televised simultaneously on every continent via 97 down-link locations. Using the newest satellite technology, I spoke from Seoul, South Korea, in the early morning hours while audiences around the world watched in their corresponding time zones. The following day, I traveled to Manila to speak at the televised conference. The third day I was in Berlin, and the fourth night in Mexico City. I traveled more than 40,000 miles in five days and spoke more than twenty times.

Although physically present in only one city at a time, I was present on television sets around the world. In every part of the globe, people saw my face in full color. Those who had met me personally could say, "Yes, that's Bill Bright, because that's a perfect picture of him." Viewers also heard my voice, and those who had previously heard me in person could say, "It's Bill Bright, all right! I recognize the inflections in his voice and the way he pronounces words."

In a narrow sense, I was "present" through my face on the screen and the voice that came out of the speakers, but I was not really present. Viewers could not touch me. I could not see the people in the worldwide audience. I did not know if they were standing or sitting, and I was not aware of what they were thinking, planning, or doing.

But God is present everywhere at the same time. It's not that He is physically present in one city and present by voice and picture in another city, as I was by the technology of electronics; He is present in the fullest sense everywhere at once. How does He do it? This is how God explains His presence when speaking to Jeremiah: "'Am I only a God nearby,' declares the LORD, 'and not a God far away? … Do not I fill heaven and earth?'" (Jeremiah 23:23,24, NIV).

God's ability to be present everywhere is called *omnipresence*. It means that there is not a sliver of space anywhere in the universe where He is not dynamically and powerfully present with all of His wonderful personal attributes. Everywhere throughout the world, to the utmost reaches of the universe and in heaven, God is always and immediately present with all of who He is!

God's Spirit-Presence

Can you imagine being completely free of all the limitations of time and space? We cannot, of course. But God can, and is! He is not limited by a body, but is a Spirit who moves wherever He wishes.

How can we explain His Spirit-presence? Many writers have compared it to the wind. No one can see the wind; it comes and goes as it pleases. No one can box it in or stop it from blowing. Yet we can see the results of wind. We see its massive strength in roiling tornadoes, hurricanes, and typhoons. The wind can also be gentle, like the whisper of a breeze off the ocean. It can bring the smell of soft rain on the leaves or the freshness of spring through an open window. Is this not like the wonderful contrast of our God who can both topple rulers and calm the fears of a little child?

> God is present in the mountains and the stars, but He is not these things.

Meteorologists try to predict the wind, yet with only partial success. In Central Florida, the meeting of hot and cold air masses spawned deadly tornadoes which took weather forecasters by surprise. The devastation caused the loss of more than forty lives and millions of dollars in property. In a similar way, God's presence and work cannot be predicted for He does what He wills (of course, He will not contradict His nature). Jesus also used the wind analogy to describe the work of the Holy Spirit: "Just as you can hear the wind but can't tell where it comes from or where it is going, so you can't explain how people are born of the Spirit" (John 3:8).

Yet a wind analogy is inadequate to completely describe the awesome presence of our infinite Creator who lives outside the time-space dimension in which we find ourselves bound. Unlike the wind, He is literally in every place in the entire universe at the same time! Not a single atom in any galaxy is hidden from His sight.

Solomon, the famous biblical king who was given unparalleled wisdom from God, built a temple for our majestic God. Awed by the holy task, Solomon asks, "Will God really live on earth? Why, even the highest heavens cannot contain you. How much less this Temple I have built!" (1 Kings 8:27). Truly, a temple of gold could never contain God, since even the heavens cannot hold him.

God's Spirit Is Different Than His Creation

Many religions believe that God's existence is somehow bound up with His creation. A. W. Tozer writes of one such scene:

> Canon W. G. H. Holmes of India told of seeing Hindu worshipers tapping on trees and stones and whispering, "Are you there? Are you there?" to the god they hoped might reside within.[24]

The belief that God is everything and everything is God is called *pantheism*. Like these Hindus, if you touch a tree, you touch God. To carry it further, this belief leads to the conclusion that since everything is god, we are gods. These fallacies take away God's majesty and make Him common and ordinary. But pantheism is not what the Bible means when it describes God's omnipresence. A well-known author explains the difference this way::

The Bible says that God is Spirit, so technically, He doesn't dwell in three-dimensional space as we do (John 15:15). His *presence* is everywhere, but not His *essence* (that would be the heresy known as pantheism). God is no less present in one portion of the universe than any other. And He is no more present anywhere than where you are right now. In other words, anyone, anywhere in the universe might say, "The Lord is in this place." Wherever you are, God is right there, right now.[25]

Think of the difference this way. The Bible illustrates God's creative power as a potter who forms a pot out of clay. We would never confuse the pot and the potter. They are distinct in nature and substance. So it is with God. He is distinct from His creation, so far above it in every way that we cannot equate His essence with His creation. Yet because He has no limitations, God is also present in every corner of His universe. This means that He is present in the mountains and the stars, but He is not these things.

In this chapter, we will consider three truths that provide the basis for an understanding of the omnipresence of God. These truths are promises on which we can base our lives.

God's Presence Sustains the Universe

There is no place within all of creation that is not supported by the divine presence of God. Acts 17:28 records, "In Him we live and move and exist." Let me use an example that is very personal to each of us. God was present when you and I were fashioned in the womb. Psalm 139:13–16 says:

> You created my inmost being; You knit me together in my mother's womb. I praise You because I am fearfully and wonderfully made; Your works are wonderful, I know that full well. My frame was not hidden from You when I was made in the secret place. When I was woven together in the depths of the earth, Your eyes saw my unformed body. All the days ordained for me were written in Your book before one of them came to be. (NIV)

We are the result of God's marvelous workmanship. He designed us. He made our bodies wonderfully complex. He was present from the moment of conception, is present every moment we live, and will be present when we die.

Let us think for a moment about what God sustains for each of us. It is estimated that as adults our bodies contain sixty trillion cells that have all been carefully organized to perform life's various functions in harmony. Consider these other facts about the human body:

- Our nose can recognize up to 10,000 different aromas.
- Our tongue has about 6,000 taste buds.
- Our brain contains ten billion nerve cells. Each brain nerve cell is connected to as many as 10,000 other nerve cells throughout the body.
- Our body has so many blood vessels that their combined length could circle the planet two and a half times.

God also customized each of us with our own special DNA blueprint, which is contained within every single cell. It has been estimated that if our individual blueprint were written out in a book, it would require 200,000 pages.[26] And God knows every word on every page!

Can you imagine if factories all over our country were manufacturing intricate human bodies? With our human record, what a mess it would turn out to be! The assembly line would grind to a halt because of back-orders on hands and feet. Hearts would malfunction due to system design defects; recalls would bring back hundreds of thousands of misassembled brains.

Now think of the millions of living organisms, from viruses to elephants, and the trillions of systems, from galaxies to earth's numerous ecosystems. It all runs without tune-ups or teardowns and rebuilds. We hire experts to build and keep sophisticated computers functioning at maximum capacity, yet many people believe that our amazing universe has no Designer and no Sustainer! But it does—our loving, creative, ever-present God.

God Reveals His Presence in Different Ways

God reveals His presence to us, which allows us to have an intimate relationship with Him. Let us consider several ways in which God manifests His presence to us.

God's "illuminating presence" affects every person.

Like turning on a light in a dark room, the light of God's presence opens our eyes to truth. Paul explains that God "made His light shine in our hearts to give us the light of the knowledge of the glory of God in the face of Christ" (2 Corinthians 4:6, NIV).

We begin to know God when the light of His presence exposes our sin. Paul writes, "It is shameful even to talk about the things that ungodly people do in secret. But when the light shines on them, it becomes clear how evil these things are" (Ephesians 5:12,13). Once we recognize our sinfulness and turn from it, God in His grace can reconcile us to Him through the death of His Son, Jesus, on the cross.

> God wants us to consciously live in His presence every day.

King David was well aware that God is present everywhere at once, and what that meant for him. At times, he may not have wanted God's presence—for example, during his adulterous affair with Bathsheba. In Psalm 139:7, he asks, "Where can I go from Your Spirit? Where can I flee from Your presence?" (NIV). But after he was forgiven and for the rest of his life, he reflected on God's companionship. He realized that at any given moment, God was present in Israel, in all of the nations around it, even in the distant regions. David also counted on God's presence during troubling times (Psalm 34:18). This affirmation of God's help came from the heart of a man who had walked in God's illuminating presence and found Him faithful—even during his disobedience.

We can have this same assurance. Hebrews 13:5 says, "Never will I leave you; never will I forsake you" (NIV). This promise gives us hope for the future and confidence in our gracious God.

God's "inspirational presence" is revealed in special places
and at special times.

God has revealed Himself to men in unique ways. God spoke to Moses on Mount Horeb through a burning bush. Later on Mount Sinai, God came down in a pillar of cloud and passed in front of Moses. God's glorious presence so filled Solomon's temple that the people fell face down on the ground and worshiped the magnificent God of Israel. Paul saw the Lord in a blinding light on the road to Damascus.

On countless other occasions, God makes His presence especially known to ordinary believers. The setting may be a devotional time, church service, or during a revival. God chooses the time and place to reveal Himself to us in special ways, and when He does, we never forget the joy of being in His inspirational presence.

I have experienced God's special presence many times since surrendering my life to Him in 1945, although I have never seen Him or heard His audible voice. One dramatic experience happened early in my ministry when He gave me a vision for Campus Crusade for Christ. One evening at about midnight during my final year in seminary, I was studying for a Greek exam. Vonette was asleep in a nearby room. Without warning, I sensed the presence of God in a way I had never known before. Within moments, I had the overwhelming impression that the Lord had flashed His instructions for my life on the screen of my mind.

This was the greatest moment of my Christian life. In a very definite way, God commanded me to invest my life in helping to fulfill the Great Commission in my generation.[27] I was to begin by helping to win and disciple students of the world for Christ. How I would do this was not spelled out in detail. That came later to my fellow staff and me as the Lord has given additional insights for the implementation of the original vision.

I awakened Vonette, and together we praised God for His direction and promised that through His grace and strength we would obey Him. Today I can tell you it has been the greatest adventure of my life to follow His lead and watch Him fulfill His plan before my eyes.

God's "incarnate presence" is manifested in Jesus Christ.

Perhaps you have heard the story of the little girl who was afraid of the dark and whose mother kept insisting, "God is watching over you. He will take care of you." But the little girl insisted, "Mommy, I want a God with skin on." And that, of course, is the reason God visited this planet in physical form. God became a man, the God-man Jesus. The God with skin on.

> Wherever you go, God is already there.

John tells us, "The Word [Jesus] became human and lived here on earth among us…No one has ever seen God. But His only Son, who is Himself God, is near to the Father's heart; He has told us about Him" (John 1:14,18). Our awesome God was willing to restrict Himself to a physical body so He could live among us and teach us about Himself. This is the most tangible way God has revealed His presence to us. "Christ is the visible image of the invisible God" (Colossians 1:15).

God's "indwelling presence" resides within every believer.

How would Jesus' followers continue to have fellowship with Him once He left this earth to return to His Father's side? Just before Jesus returned to heaven, He told His disciples, "I will ask the Father, and He will give you another Counselor [the Holy Spirit] to be with you forever—the Spirit of truth… He lives with you and will be in you" (John 14:16,17, NIV). Paul wrote, "Don't you know that you yourselves are God's temple and that God's Spirit lives in you?" (1 Corinthians 3:16,17, NIV).

Unbelievers cannot begin to comprehend why we are so confident that God is filling us with His presence. Though God is omnipresent in their universe just like He is in ours, they cannot sense His presence, so they deny He is there. Jesus explained this to His disciples: "The world cannot accept Him [the Holy Spirit], because it neither sees Him nor knows Him. But you know Him" (John 14:17, NIV).

Do we deny that the wind exists because we cannot see it? Of course not, for we can feel it. The God who is present everywhere is felt by those sensitive to the Spirit of God.

God Wants Us to Consciously Live in His Presence

Indeed, our confidence is in the ever-present nature of God. We can be sure that He sees us, walks with us, and loves us no matter where we are. That fact leads us to our third truth: God wants us to consciously live in His presence every day.

A classic little book, *The Practice of the Presence of God*, gives the essence of living moment by moment in God's presence. Its author was a humble monk named Brother Lawrence, who served his Lord by washing pots and pans in a French monastery during the 16th century. Joseph de Beaufort, his close friend, says of Brother Lawrence, "The worst trial he could imagine was losing his sense of God's presence, which had been with him for so long a time."[28]

Brother Lawrence spoke openly about his practice of living in the presence of God:

All we have to do is to recognize God as being intimately present within us. Then we may speak directly to Him every time we need to ask for help, to know His will in moments of uncertainty, and to do whatever He wants us to do in a way that pleases Him. We should offer our work to Him before we begin, and thank Him afterwards for the privilege of having done them for His sake. This continuous conversation would also include praising and loving God incessantly for His infinite goodness and perfection.[29]

Every morning, I make it a practice to fall to my knees in prayer beside my bed. I ask my Lord to live His life in and through me throughout the day. My request is that He will walk around in my body, speak with my lips, use my hands and feet for His glory, and control my thoughts so they honor Him.

I encourage you to begin a daily practice of praising God during all your activities. But praise is just the beginning of a lifestyle of practicing the presence of God. Along with Brother Lawrence, learn to carry on a "continuous conversation" with your heavenly Father as you go through your day. Remember, wherever you go, He is already there. In our next chapter, we will see how God's omnipresence means that He will always help us.

Talk About It: I AM Everywhere All the Time

"Am I only a God nearby," declares the LORD, "and not a God far away?
Can anyone hide in secret places so that I cannot see him?" declares the
LORD. "Do not I fill heaven and earth?"
(Jeremiah 23:23,24, NIV)

1. What does the Bible mean when it says God is everywhere? How is that different from the Hindu or pantheistic view of God's presence? What real difference does it make?

2. Read Psalm 139:7. The reality that God is everywhere at all times can evoke different emotional responses. What do you think some responses might be? Why is that?

3. Think of an attribute of God that is particularly meaningful to you right now. If God were not everywhere, all the time, how would it affect that attribute and your willingness to trust God?

4. Acts 17:28 records, "In Him we live and move and exist." He is with you from the moment you were created. Look at the timeline you wrote out in Chapter 1. Looking at the timeline, when have you seen evidence of His presence in your life?

5. Like turning on a light in a dark room, the light of God's presence opens our eyes to truth. According to Ephesians 1:18 and 5:13,14, what does God's illuminating presence reveal?

6. What is His illuminating presence revealing in your life? Do you need to confess and repent of something He is showing you? Has God shed light on any lies you have believed about Him or yourself that are robbing you of the joy of His presence in your life today?

7. What did Brother Lawrence's "continuous conversation" with God look like? What impact do you think that had on his attitude, behavior, or sense of isolation? If you wanted to have a "continuous conversation" with God as did Brother Lawrence, what do you think the next step would be for you?

FOCUS ON GOD

On an index card or your favorite electronic device, write the following statement and verse, or just take a picture of it:

**God, because You are everywhere all the time,
I know You are always with me.**

"Never will I leave you; never will I forsake you."
(Hebrews 13:5, NIV)

Look at it when you get up, when you go to bed, and at least once during the day as a way of intentionally shifting your focus from yourself to God. During one of those times each day, take a few minutes to think about the positive benefits in your life of God's omnipresence.

This week, seek to live in God's presence moment by moment, as Brother Lawrence did, through seeking to carry on a "continual conversation" with our ever-present God. You may find it helpful to often ask yourself, "Have I prayed about this?" as you go through your day.

CHAPTER 11

I Will Always Be With You

Have you ever felt completely alone? The feeling of isolation can destroy even the strongest among us. The enemy of our souls does not want us to experience the presence of God, because he knows we are easily discouraged and defeated when we feel alone.

When I awaken in the morning, God is with me. When I kneel to worship Him, He is with me. When I arrive at the office or at the airport for one of my many trips, He is still with me. When I turn out the lights at night anywhere in the world, He is already there.

Likewise, God is with you at the grocery store, in the hospital, at school, at the office, and in your home. He is with you when everything is going well, and still with you when you feel your world is crashing down around you.

As followers of Jesus we can be confident that Christ is present with us as well as all of our fellow believers in the United States, Canada, Mexico, Germany, Russia, Indonesia, Egypt, Brazil, Nigeria, and every other country—all at the same time.

God is not limited by time or space or height or depth—or even our level of faith. He is always with us whether we are taking giant steps of faith or we are taking the first baby steps of faith. He lives inside of every person who trusts in God through faith in Jesus Christ.

> God is not limited by our level of faith.

God Is Present With Us in All Places

Let us apply this attribute to the events of our lives. First, God's omnipresence means that we cannot go anywhere that God is not beside us. The psalmist writes, "If I go up to the heavens, You are there; if I make my bed in the depths, You are there. If I rise on the wings of the dawn, if I settle on the far side of the sea, even there Your hand will guide me, Your right hand will hold me fast" (Psalm 139:8–10, NIV). God sees us, walks with us, and cares for us no matter where we are.

During NASA's Apollo 13 flight, Jim Lovell, Jack Swigert, and Fred Haise were scheduled to walk on the moon. Just after they blasted off, an explosion on their ship endangered their lives. Not only did they have to abort their plans to land on the moon, but it also looked as if they would not have enough engine power and cabin oxygen to return to Earth alive. One of the tensest times during the flight was when the space ship orbited behind the moon. For agonizing hours, the astronauts sailed through the darkness on the far side of the moon, out of reach of radio contact with Mission Control in Houston. All over our country, Americans prayed for the safety of the astronauts. The country breathed a sigh of relief when radio contact was reestablished and when Apollo 13 was successfully brought back home.

How could God hear all the prayers for the astronauts? Because God is no less present behind the shadow of the moon than right beside you right now. In fact, without God's omnipresence, prayer would be ineffective. God promises His people, "Before they call I will answer; while they are still speaking, I will hear" (Isaiah 65:24). When I am in Orlando and pray for a colleague in Thailand, God is with both of us. He is fully present in Orlando to hear my prayer, and at the same time fully present in Thailand to act in behalf of the one for whom I am praying! The basis for all prayer rests on the fact that God is omnipresent.

God Is Present in All Our Circumstances

Have you had an experience that left you wondering where God is? Sometimes we do not feel God's presence, but emotions can be misleading. No matter what we feel, God is still there.

David often felt abandoned by God. In Psalm 22, he implores, "My God, my God! Why have You forsaken me? Why do You remain so distant? Why do You ignore my cries for help? Every day I call to You, my God, but You do not answer" (Psalm 22:1,2). Yet later in the same psalm he states his trust in God's presence:

> Yet you brought me safely from my mother's womb and led me to trust You when I was a nursing infant. I was thrust upon You at my birth. You have been my God from the moment I was born... Praise the LORD, all you who fear Him! ... For He has not ignored the suffering of the needy. He has not turned and walked away. He has listened to their cries for help. (Psalm 22:9,23,24)

Two Dutch women during World War II experienced God's omnipresence. Corrie and Betsie ten Boom became involved in hiding Jewish people during the Nazi occupation of their country. As a consequence, the Nazis sent the two middle-aged women to Ravensbrück, one of the most dreaded concentration camps. There they endured incredible depravation and suffering. Yet they ministered to hundreds of other prisoners who needed to hear about their Lord and Savior. Their barracks were transformed into a Bible study and prayer center, and the cruel, harsh attitudes of many prisoners were turned to compassion and love.

Eventually, Betsie became deathly ill. As she was taken to the prison hospital, Corrie tried to shield Betsie from the sleet that stung their bodies. After the orderlies set Betsie's stretcher on the hospital floor, Corrie leaned down to hear the words on her sister's weak lips, "...must tell people what we have learned here. We must tell them that there is no pit so deep that He is not deeper still. They will listen to us, Corrie, because we have been there."[30]

Betsie died the following day. Soon after, Corrie was miraculously discharged from the camp—only days before all women her age were put to death. For the rest of her life, Corrie traveled the globe telling her story of God's presence and faithfulness even in the worst of places.

Our confidence is that there is no pit so deep that God is not there. We cannot face a situation in which He does not walk beside us.

God Is With Us During Every Crisis

What crisis are you facing right now? Unemployment, serious health problems, the break-up of your marriage, rebellious teenage children, rejection by those who once loved you? God walks with us, gives us strength, understands our pain, and knows how to handle our problems. He will help us if we only ask Him and are willing to do things His way and in His time.

Isaiah 43:1–3 records God's precious promise to be with us in times of crisis:

The LORD who created you says: "Do not be afraid, for I have ransomed you. I have called you by name; you are Mine. When you go through deep waters and great trouble, I will be with you. When you go through rivers of difficulty, you will not drown! When you walk through the fire of oppression, you will not be burned up; the flames will not consume you. For I am the LORD, your God, the Holy One of Israel, your Savior."

One of the most basic crises each of us faces is our own death. For many people, even Christians, the terror of leaving this world is very real. One of my colleagues faced such a crisis just after her thirtieth birthday. Days after her doctor admitted her to the hospital, she began having problems breathing. Although she pressed the call button for the nurse, no one responded.

Panicked, she realized that she was dying in a hospital bed—and no one knew. As her breathing became more labored, she began to lose consciousness. She was helpless, yet she desperately wanted to live to see her young daughter and husband again.

Within seconds of her panic, a supernatural peace flooded over her. God impressed this promise clearly on her heart: "If you awake and are in heaven, I am with you. If you awake and are in this hospital bed, I am with you. Either way, I am just as close to you."

With that promise ringing in her ears, she put her future in God's hands. Then through eyelids barely cracked, she saw the elevator doors slide open in the hall outside her room. Out walked her pastor! By the time he reached her bedside, she drifted into unconsciousness. But because of his quick response, her life was saved.

> No matter what we feel, God is still there.

The comforting words of Psalm 23:4 ring beautifully. "Even when I walk through the dark valley of death, I will not be afraid, for You are close beside me. Your rod and Your staff protect and comfort me." I encourage you to memorize and meditate upon this beloved psalm.

God Is With Us When We Tell Others about Him

Jesus promises, "Be sure of this: I am with you always, even to the end of the age" (Matthew 28:20). He said this as part of the Great Commission in Matthew 28:18–20—the challenge to go into the entire world and preach the gospel and disciple those who place their trust in Christ. It is when we are fulfilling the Great Commission that Jesus' promise to be with us becomes most precious. He has given us the challenge to reach every person on earth with God's message of love and forgiveness. Yet He did not leave us alone to accomplish this impossible task. He sent us His Holy Spirit to empower us to do what is humanly impossible—but possible with God.

I take great comfort in the fact that Jesus is with every one of our ministry's 20,500 full-time staff and over 660,000 trained volunteers in 181 countries of the world.[31] His Holy Spirit is the one who works within the hearts of all believers so that His work will be accomplished.

You can take comfort in knowing that God is present and working during any ministry opportunity He gives you. As you speak about your faith in Jesus Christ with your neighbor, God is with you. When you teach your children about God's love, God is with you. When you talk about Jesus with that coworker who is an atheist, God is with you. God will bring forth the fruit and help us be faithful to Him in introducing others to Christ.

Nothing We Do Is Hidden from God

Jesus promised that our heavenly Father, "who sees what is done in secret, will reward you" (Matthew 6:4, NIV). Just think about that. When we privately do something good that no one else knows about, God still sees it and rewards us accordingly.

When a Sunday school teacher labors to teach preschoolers about God's love, she may not receive many affirmations from others, yet the Lord sees every smile and hug she gives them. When a godly pastor spends hours in his office in heartfelt prayer for people who dislike him, try to thwart his ministry, or are apathetic about the church, God sees his deep concern. For the bedridden elderly person who adopts a prayer ministry in behalf of loved ones, neighbors, and friends, God hears. For the godly parent who prays hours into the night for a prodigal child, God sees. God knows about the businessman, betrayed by his business partner, who does not take revenge but responds in forgiveness and love. To these faithful servants, our ever-present God says, "Love your enemies, do good to them, and lend to them without expecting to get anything back. Then your reward will be great" (Luke 6:35, NIV).

On the other hand, God also sees the wrong things we commit in secret. We only fool ourselves by thinking that no one will ever know. Scripture says, "Nothing in all creation can hide from Him. Everything is naked and exposed before His eyes. This is the God to whom we must explain all that we have done" (Hebrews 4:13).

There is no place we can hide when we do wrong. God sees and is beside us. As believers, we may break our fellowship with God when we sin, but He does not leave us. He is still dwelling within us, convicting us, helping us to do what is right through His loving discipline, and waiting for us to repent of our wrongdoing.

Some people see God as a "great traffic cop" in the sky watching their every move. However, I like to think that He loves me so much that He cannot take

His eyes off me. I am the "apple of His eye." Thank You, Father, for watching over us.

Consciously Living in His Presence

God's omnipresence enables us to be in constant communion with Him and to depend on Him in every situation. But at times we ignore His presence because we are so preoccupied with our lives and focused on material concerns (food, clothing, shelter, finances, and jobs). Sometimes we even forget that He is with us while we are busy serving Him.

Brother Lawrence discovered the peace and joy Jesus promised when he began to practice the presence of God through his "continuous conversation" with his heavenly Father. For fifteen years, his responsibility was to wash greasy pots and pans in the monastery—a job he disliked. Practicing the presence of God transformed what he considered a chore into an exciting privilege. He writes, "My day-to-day life consists of giving God my simple, loving attention. If I'm distracted, He calls me back in tones that are supernaturally beautiful."[32] This is what he considered important in walking with God:

> The most holy and necessary practice in our spiritual life is the presence of God. That means finding constant pleasure in His divine company, speaking humbly and lovingly with Him in all seasons, at every moment, without limiting the conversation in any way.[33]

Living in God's presence means realizing that God is with you and is vitally concerned about every part of your life. Carrying on a "continuous conversation" with your heavenly Father is the key to experiencing joy and peace in your life. As I practice this, I find that throughout the day the Lord Jesus communicates with me through impressions in my mind that spring from meditating on His Word and talking to Him. This makes both prayer and the study of God's Word an exciting adventure for me. Let me give you some promises that you can rely on as you consciously practice the presence of God in your daily activities.

God promises when we are confused, He will guide us.

Confusion is rampant in our society—even among believers. People ask: Why are these things happening to me? Where should I go, and what should I do with my life?

We can have confidence that God will reveal Himself to us when we do not know where to turn. He promises, "I will instruct you and teach you in the way you should go; I will counsel you and watch over you" (Psalm 32:8, NIV). Through His Word, prayer, the leading of the Holy Spirit, and our open hearts, He will guide us along the pathway He has planned for us.

God promises when we are afraid, He will be with us.

When we are afraid, no matter where we are—at home alone, driving on the freeway during rush hour traffic, facing a hostile meeting, or walking alone at night—God is right beside us. He promises, "Do not fear, for I am with you; do not be dismayed, for I am your God. I will strengthen you and help you; I will uphold you with My righteous right hand" (Isaiah 41:10, NIV). What a comfort this is for us in our daily lives!

Claim this promise and consciously remember that God is with you during your times of fear and uncertainty. He will comfort you and give you courage to confront your fears as you carry on a "continuous conversation" with Him. He will also protect you so that you will never experience anything outside His will for your life.

God promises when we are tempted, He will help us resist.

My oldest son Zac once observed, "The greatest tragedy in life is when we stop talking to God." How true. Satan's main strategy with God's people has always been to whisper, "Don't call, don't ask, don't depend on God to do great things. You'll get along fine if you rely on your own cleverness and energy." The devil is not terribly frightened of our human efforts, but he knows his kingdom will be damaged when we lift our hearts to God.[34]

Although we can be tempted by our own flesh and by worldly influences, Satan is a major player in our desire to disobey God. Pastor David Jeremiah puts temptation in a new light:

Suppose you and one of your friends are on the border of doing something wrong. Both of you know it is wrong. But you are about to do it anyway. But if you should say to your friend, "Go right ahead and do it, but I think you should know that I just heard from heaven and God will be here in a few moments." Maybe your friend will respond, "Wow, if God is going to be here soon, maybe I will do this tomorrow or next week, but I don't want to do this if God is going to show up in a few minutes."[35]

Surprise! God has already shown up. He is here...now! When facing temptation, we should say to ourselves, "This is being carried out in the presence of Almighty God." Meditating on this truth will give you conviction to face temptation in your life.

I encourage you to practice the presence of God by asking our Lord to help you resist temptation. The Bible promises, "God is faithful. He will not allow any temptation to be more than you can stand" (1 Corinthians 10:13). The key is to stay engaged in a "continuous conversation" with God by the power of His Spirit.

God promises when we are hurting, He will comfort us.
How could Paul and Silas sing praises to God in the depths of a stinking, cold Roman prison? Their backs were raw because they had been beaten with whips and rods. Their feet were in stocks and the jailer had threatened to execute them if they tried to escape. Paul and Silas could sing because God was with them in the inner dungeon while they were hurting.

The psalmist writes, "The LORD is close to the brokenhearted; He rescues those who are crushed in spirit" (Psalm 34:18). Whether we experience physical, emotional, or mental pain, the Holy Spirit will comfort us and give us strength and courage to triumph over our hurts.

God is with you during your times of fear and uncertainty.

Several of our Campus Crusade for Christ staff members have lost small children to accidental death or disease. Vonette and I are thankful that this is a trial we have never had to endure, but we feel their pain. They tell me that it is one of the most agonizing crises that a person can ever go through. Tears flow for months; muscles are sore from sobbing. Many unbelieving couples break up afterwards due to guilt and blame. But many followers of Christ testify, "That was the most difficult thing I have ever experienced, but I have to tell you that God was so very near to me that I felt His presence like I have never felt Him before." Although Scripture is clear that God is present everywhere at once, believing parents who have lost children give evidence that God manifests His presence in special ways at particular times of need. In 2 Corinthians 1:3,4, Paul assures us, "God is our merciful Father and the source of all comfort. He comforts us in all our troubles so that we can comfort others."

God promises when we are discouraged, He will encourage us.

Do you struggle with insurmountable bills? Have friends betrayed you? Do you feel inadequate at your job or as a parent? Scripture instructs us, "Cast all your anxiety on Him because He cares for you" (1 Peter 5:7, NIV). We are encouraged in Joshua 1:9, "Do not be afraid or discouraged. For the LORD your God is with you wherever you go." Not only will God help you conquer every discouragement, He will help you climb every mountain in your life! And when you come through the valleys of discouragement, you will find that God was there all the time. Sometimes He was waiting patiently for you to exhaust your means and energy and turn to Him for His help. Recognizing His presence in the midst of our discouragement gives us hope. What a tremendous encouragement! We can trust that kind of God for anything!

God promises when we are lonely, He will be our companion.

Some of our loneliest moments can occur when we are in a crowd, and yet no one notices us. Our hearts ache when we think no one cares. But Jesus is our ever-present friend and refuge (John 15:15). He promises, "Never will I leave you; never will I forsake you" (Hebrews 13:5, NIV).

He is also with us as we face lonely tasks. When David Livingstone sailed to Africa for the first time as a missionary, a group of his friends accompanied him to the pier to wish him bon voyage. They were concerned for his safety and reminded him of the dangers of that unexplored land. One of the men even tried to convince him to remain in England. But Livingstone opened his Bible and read Jesus' words from Matthew 28:20: "Lo, I am with you always." He turned to the man who was especially concerned about his safety and smiled. "That, my friend, is the word of a gentleman… So let us be going."

No person or circumstance can ever remove us from the presence of our loving God. Paul writes, "I am convinced that nothing can ever separate us from His love. Death can't, and life can't. The angels can't, and the demons can't. Our fears for today, our worries about tomorrow, and even the powers of hell can't keep God's love away. Whether we are high above the sky or in the deepest ocean, nothing in all creation will ever be able to separate us from the love of God that is revealed in Christ Jesus our Lord" (Romans 8:38,39).

He is here with us right now and forever—because He is our ever-present God. He is our guide for life and for eternity. What an incredible truth! What a powerful motivation for us to know, love, trust, obey, worship, and enjoy the constant presence of our wonderful God and Savior.

Talk About It: I Will Always Be With You
"Never will I leave you; never will I forsake you."
(Hebrews 13:5, NIV)

1. What are some reasons people give for abandoning a relationship?
2. God promises He will never, *ever* abandon those who have accepted Jesus as their Lord and Savior. Why do you think this promise is hard for many to believe?
3. If a person does not feel God's presence, does it mean He's not there? What does the Bible say we are to do if we aren't experiencing the joy of His presence in our lives?
4. What did you think of the statement, "The greatest tragedy in life is when we stop talking to God." Why is that such a great tragedy?
5. Did you attempt to carry on a "continual conversation" with God this past week? If so, how well did you do and did it make any difference?

What do you think you could do that would help you better "practice the presence of God" each day?

6. If you were more aware of God's presence every minute of every day, how do you think it would make a practical difference in the choices you make?

7. We read about six promises God makes. Which ones are you most thankful for today, and why?

   a. When we are confused, God will guide us. (Psalm 32:8)

   b. When we are afraid, God will be with us. (Isaiah 41:10)

   c. When we are tempted, God will help us resist. (1 Corinthians 10:13)

   d. When we are hurting, God will comfort us. (Psalm 34:18)

   e. When we are discouraged, God will encourage us. (1 Peter 5:7)

   f. When we are lonely, God will be our companion. (Romans 8:38,39)

8. If God were not everywhere all the time, could He keep any of these promises?

FOCUS ON GOD

Continue to review the statement and verse you wrote down last week, at least three times each day, to remind yourself that God is always with you.

**God, because You are everywhere all the time,
I know You are always with me.**

"Never will I leave you; never will I forsake you."
(Hebrews 13:5, NIV)

And as you go throughout each day this week, continue to practice the presence of God by seeking to carry on the "continual conversation" with our ever-present God who loves you.

CHAPTER 12

I AM Merciful

She had no hope. They caught her in the act. Her guilt was undeniable and the sentence was certain: death! Stones in hand, her accusers prepared to hurl them at her in righteous fury.

A voice rose above the chatter of the crowd. "Teacher," a man said, "this woman was caught in the act of adultery. The law of Moses says to stone her. What do You say?" The Teacher, Jesus, held her fate in His hands, but it gave her little hope.

She was as surprised as the rest when Jesus stooped down and began writing in the dirt. If her life had not been on the line she might have even smiled at His casual disregard of the religious leaders. But tension mounted. They hurled the question again and again, "What do you say?!" Finally the Teacher stood to speak. She could barely breathe.

"Let the one who has never sinned throw the first stone!"

Silence fell on her accusers as His words hit their mark. One by one, the stones fell to the earth. With each thud, hope grew in her heart. After what felt like an eternity only the Teacher remained. "Where are your accusers?" He asked. "Didn't even one of them condemn you?"

"No, Lord," she replied.

His next words not only gave her hope when all hope was lost, but they continue to give us hope today.

"Neither do I. Go and sin no more."

With a few simple words Jesus acknowledged her sin, extended God's mercy and set her on a new path.

The story of the woman caught in adultery, from John 8:4–11, is a dramatic example of God's mercy, but each of us experience God's mercy every day in numerous other ways.

Jesus stated in the Sermon on the Mount, "[God] gives His sunlight to both the evil and the good, and He sends rain on the just and on the unjust, too" (Matthew 5:45). God provides the necessities of life for every human born on this planet. Many times we take His mercy for granted—until we experience a devastating blizzard with the mercury plummeting, or when summer temperatures soar into the 100s for days on end. Then we complain about how bad things are.

Unfortunately, we rarely thank God for the thousands of days of beautiful sunshine. How often do we stop to be thankful that, year after year, the flowers bloom, the rain falls, the sun shines, and the earth yields its fruit? Our grocery store shelves are stocked with food grown in the farmers' fields. When was the last time you felt gratitude for your enjoyment of food, friendships, music, art, and so many other things?

> At the cross, God's justice and mercy found complete fulfillment.

When we think of these blessings, our thoughts eventually end up at the doorstep of mercy. God's mercy leads Him to extend compassion. Our merciful God always seeks the welfare, both temporal (life on earth) and eternal (life in heaven forever), of His children and those who have not yet accepted His love and forgiveness. Although many people show mercy to others, God is the grand master of mercy. His very nature desires to relieve us of the self-imposed misery and distress we experience because of our sin. Let me give you an allegory of a merciful judge that dramatically illustrates how amazing God's mercy is.

The Merciful Judge

The wretched, shackled prisoner trembled with fear as he stood before the imposing bench of the toughest, fairest judge in the district. "You have been found guilty," the judge solemnly announced. Courtroom observers held their breath, waiting for what they were sure was to come.

Without a doubt the man was guilty. The evidence was clear. The judge had no choice but to pronounce a death sentence. There were no appeals for the horrendous crime, no stays of execution allowed.

Suddenly to everyone's shock, the judge did something unprecedented in legal history. He said to the prisoner, "Justice must be served. You are guilty. You are totally unlovable. Nevertheless, I love you, in spite of yourself. And because of my love for you, I have decided to take your place. I will take your punishment for you. I will die in your place. You are a free man. You can go now." The judge's gavel pounded. The courtroom was silent.

After a stunned moment, courtroom guards unlocked the prisoner's handcuffs and legs irons, removed the judge's robe, and snapped the irons on his wrists and ankles. As the judge was led away to death row, the shocked prisoner numbly walked out of the courtroom door to freedom, tears of gratitude streaming down his cheeks.

This, of course, is an allegory about God's mercy. God is the judge. Since He is perfectly just, all His actions must uphold justice. We are like the prisoner. We all deserve the death sentence, because we are all guilty of numerous sins. Romans 3:23 says, "All have sinned and fall short of the glory of God" (NIV). In His fairness, God must judge our sin with the punishment it deserves. Romans 6:23 says, "The wages of sin is death" (NIV). He cannot allow us to inhabit His perfect heaven, that place without a spot of uncleanness, a thought of wrongdoing, or a charge of guilt.

In the supreme act of mercy, God displayed divine favor and forbearance to us guilty offenders. He took our punishment upon Himself. That is what Jesus Christ did for us at Calvary: "The gift of God is eternal life in Christ Jesus our Lord" (Romans 6:23, NIV). He did it for the woman caught in adultery and He did it for you and me. By His sacrifice, all who put their trust in Him are declared "not guilty" and freed! That was true mercy and grace.

Our Merciful Savior

Because God is holy He cannot tolerate sin. Perfect justice requires that sin must always be punished—no exceptions. All our claims that we were tricked into sin or that we did not know our action was sin gets us nowhere with God.

If that sounds cruel and unfair, here is the good news! Jesus provided a dramatic reprieve from our sentence and punishment. Jesus was beaten, tortured, and hung on a cross to die in our place to satisfy God's demand for untainted justice. The perfect Judge became our merciful Savior!

Peter explains, "[Jesus] personally carried our sins in His body on the cross so that we can be dead to sin and live for what is right. By His wounds you are healed" (1 Peter 2:24). When Jesus came, His blood was spilled so we could experience God's mercy. Jesus' sacrifice is the ultimate expression of God's mercy.

> God's mercy toward the unrepentant sinner does not last forever.

Jesus Christ's sacrifice on the cross also satisfied God's just nature. God, the divine Judge, showed mercy and clemency for us guilty sinners. It is the mercy of God that sees man weighed down by sin and therefore in a sorry and pitiful condition, needing divine help. At the cross, God's attributes of *both* justice and mercy found complete fulfillment—simultaneously and without compromising either one! Is that not amazing?

God's Mercy Extends Beyond Our New Birth

God's mercy does not end with the forgiveness of our sins. As His children, He provides us an abundant life that is much more than we deserve or could ever expect. In His mercy, He provides what we need to begin growing in His Spirit. His mercy also gives us peace. He shows us compassion as we walk with Him day by day. And His mercy also means that He will discipline us as a father disciplines his child. Let us look at each of these aspects of God's mercy.

First, God does not forgive our sins, then just send us our own way. He has a plan for our lives that will bring us to maturity in His grace.

At 14 years old, Scott killed another gang member in a street fight. He was convicted and sent to a juvenile prison. While there, he attended a Bible study led by a Christian. Based on the Scripture passages he was shown, Scott recognized that God's mercy extended even to him. Though feeling terribly unworthy, he decided to become a follower of Christ.

While in the juvenile prison, he met regularly to study the Bible in order to grow in his new faith. He was still in his teens when he was released, but he did not want to go back to his inner city environment. Acting with the mercy of God, the Bible study leader took Scott into the home he and his wife had established as a discipling center for young men who showed genuine commitment to Jesus Christ while in prison.

Scott spent two years in the halfway house. He made such progress—completing his high school degree and growing as a Christian young man—that he was accepted as a student at a well-known Christian college. As a student, he began sharing the love and mercy of God with other young men incarcerated in the state juvenile detention centers. Not only did Scott personally experience God's mercy, but he then passed it on to others who were without hope.

Ephesians 2:4 describes God as being rich in mercy. Have you experienced this in your relationship with God? He has an unlimited abundance of mercy, which originates in His being. He extends His abundance of mercy to us all the days of our lives—and for eternity.

God's Mercy Brings Us Peace

Some years ago, I was invited to speak to the inmates of one of the most infamous high-security prisons in America: the Federal Penitentiary in Atlanta, Georgia. When I arrived at the penitentiary's assembly room, several of the inmates rushed over to me, embraced me, and called me "brother." They told me they had heard my messages on tape, and had been introduced to Christ or discipled by my books. Before I spoke, several stood and told about how they had been forgiven by God through faith in Christ's death on the cross and His resurrection. One man spoke of how he had murdered five people. Another man confessed to killing three. Others had committed similar crimes. They told of how they came to the prison full of hate and fear—and then they met Jesus and were transformed.

Tears streamed down my face as I listened to these stories of God's forgiveness, mercy, and love. Again and again different prisoners said, "I'm glad I'm here. If I had not been sent to prison, I would not know Christ, and I would probably be dead because of my life of crime."

These prisoners—these men behind bars—had experienced the wonder of God's eternal pardon from their sins. They had received peace of heart and mind. They were experiencing purpose and meaning for their lives, even in their prison cells.

God's mercy enables us to break free from the habits of sin that have bound us. As a result, we can have peace, joy, fulfillment, and purpose. We will find the true meaning for living—serving God. We will find the true joy in life—serving others. We will find true peace and fulfillment—living in God's presence and will moment by moment.

God's Mercy Means He Has Compassion for Us

What astounds me as an imperfect human being is that God genuinely feels pity and compassion for us during our trials and difficulties. We have the assurance that "the LORD comforts His people and will have compassion on His afflicted ones" (Isaiah 49:13, NIV). Our loving Father does not just feel our pain, He wants to relieve our pain. He will if we will trust and obey Him.

> We should never lose the awe and appreciation of what God has done for us.

The Gospels are filled with examples of how Jesus was moved with compassion to help those who were sick, suffering, and in need. The woman who had been ill with bleeding for many years was healed when she touched His garment. Jesus reached out His hands and healed a blind man, Bartimaeus. He spoke and healed ten lepers. And, of course, to the woman caught in adultery He spoke compassionately and forgave her. We can be sure that our merciful God is beside us through every trial we face and every pain we endure, and will help us live for His glory in every situation.

God's Mercy Is Evident in His Discipline

If you are a parent, you know that your feelings of compassion and mercy toward your child will often be tested. At times you will have to exercise discipline. A child does not know he is loved unless his parents set up behavior boundaries and then enforce them in love and fairness.

When Vonette and I disciplined our sons, Zac and Brad, we did so in love. When one of our sons disobeyed us, we would first explain why we were punishing him, then we would follow through with the appropriate discipline. When it was all over, we would hug our son and emphasize that we disciplined him because we loved him.

One day Zac came home from kindergarten with a puzzled look on his face. With a serious tone of voice, he announced, "I don't think many of the children at school have parents who love them like you love me."

Mystified, Vonette asked, "Why do you say that, honey?"

"Because they are so disobedient," he said confidently. Zac had figured out that lovingkindness includes discipline.

The loved child understands when someone cares enough to take the time to correct wrong behavior. That is the way God is with us. When we become part of His family through our spiritual birth, He corrects and rebukes us for the things we do wrong (Hebrews 12:6,7).

Some people believe God's ultimate desire is for us to be happy and therefore it is okay for us to do whatever gives us pleasure. But God, in His wisdom and mercy, disciplines us in order to teach us to say "no" to things that give only temporary pleasure, so that we can experience His deep and unwavering peace and joy. As we listen to His Spirit and obey His Word, we become fulfilled and joyful as members of His family.

God Displays His Mercy Through Us

The most exciting aspect of God's mercy is that we can be His example of mercy here on earth. Let me tell you a story about a beloved friend, a godly man whom I highly respect and admire.

Many years ago in Korea, Dr. Joon Gon Kim and his family were enjoying an evening together. Suddenly, an angry band of Communist guerrillas invaded their village, killing everyone in their path. In their trail of blood, the guerrillas left behind the dead bodies of Dr. Kim's wife and father. Dr. Kim was beaten and left for dead. In the cool rain of the night, he revived and fled for safety with his young daughter to the mountains. They were the sole survivors.

Can you imagine how we would feel if this happened to us? Since Dr. Kim is a man of God, he knew from Scripture that he must love his enemies and pray for those who persecute him. The Spirit of God impressed upon him to return to the village, seek out the Communist chief who led the guerrilla attack, and tell him that he loved him. Then he was to tell that man about God's love in Christ. Dr. Kim obeyed the impression God had given him. When he met the Communist chief, the man was dumbfounded because he had believed that the guerrillas had killed Dr. Kim. He knelt in prayer with Dr. Kim and committed his life to Christ. Within a short time, more Communists came to Christ, and Dr. Kim helped build a church for these and other Communist converts.

In 1958, Dr. Kim accepted the position as director of Korean Campus Crusade for Christ, our first international ministry. He is a living demonstration of God's mercy (Micah 6:8).

As I walk in the Spirit and grow in appreciation for the mercy of God to me, I find that mercy overflows from my life into the lives of others. If I plant the seeds of God's mercy in the hearts and minds of others, they produce a harvest of love for God and repentance of sin.

God's Mercy Has an End

Although God's mercy toward His own people extends throughout eternity, His mercy toward the unrepentant sinner does not last forever.

Before Alexander the Great would lay siege to a city, he would set up a light giving notice to those who lived within the city that if they came to him while that light was still burning, he would spare their lives. But once the light was out—no one should expect mercy.

In very much the same way, God sets up light after light and waits year after year for sinners to come to Him so that they also may secure eternal life. He does not want anyone to perish, so He is giving more time for everyone to repent (2 Peter 3:9).

But be aware that a time is coming when there will be no more mercy. God does not want us to be destroyed by our sinfulness, so He offers us mercy, but we must be willing to accept it before we run out of time. Those who feel they can wait until later to receive God's offer of mercy can never be certain that they will have the time or opportunity to receive it.

The time is so urgent to call people to repentance. We do not know who has a tomorrow, or whose hearts are soft toward God. Right now is the time to present them with God's message of mercy, to show them the mercy that God has liberally given us. Our Lord Jesus may return at any moment. While we ourselves must be ready, we must warn those who have not heard of His gracious mercy or who have not heeded God's call.

In light of His mercy to us, our hearts should be filled with gratitude, praise, and worship. We should reach beyond our Christian circles of comfort and extend God's mercy to those who hate or ignore us. Author David Morris writes, "When Jesus came to earth, He changed seats with us and took on all our sin, rejection, and shame so we could see ourselves from His perspective."[36] We should never lose the awe and appreciation of what God has done for us. We once wore filthy garments stained by sin and corruption; now we are clothed in spotless robes of righteousness—all because of the mercy of God! That perspective will change the way we worship, reverence, and serve our God. We will also see differently the need of the people to whom He is sending us.

Talk About It: I AM Merciful

"God is so rich in mercy, and He loved us so very much,
that even while we were dead because of our sins, He
gave us life when He raised Christ from the dead."
(Ephesians 2:4)

1. How do you usually react when you catch someone doing something they shouldn't? Have you ever been caught doing something you knew was wrong? What was your first thought? How did you feel?
2. Consider the definition of mercy: "Compassionate treatment, especially of those under one's power; clemency" (American Heritage Dictionary).

Have you ever experienced mercy from others or from God? What impact did that have on your life?

3. God offers His mercy to everyone but He doesn't force us to accept it; it is a gift. Why do you think some people have a hard time believing God's mercy is a gift that cannot be earned? How is that a reflection of their view of God's love, faithfulness, and power?

4. Read Luke 23:34 to see what Jesus said as He was hanging on the cross looking at His executioners. If Jesus could extend mercy to the men who humiliated and tortured Him, can you think of any sin you have ever committed that Jesus' mercy cannot cover?

5. Saul of Tarsus, (before he became the apostle Paul) murdered and imprisoned many devout followers of Jesus. Look up Philippians 3:13,14 to see what his attitude was years later.

   What do you think Paul meant about "forgetting the past," and what does that have to do with embracing God's mercy? How do you think that related to his ability to do what God asked him to do?

6. In John 8:11, how do Jesus' words to the woman caught in adultery reflect both His mercy and His holiness? Which of Jesus' words do you think provided greater motivation to the woman to change her behavior, and why?

FOCUS ON GOD

On an index card or your favorite electronic device, write the following statement and verse, or just take a picture of it:

**God, because You are merciful,
I know that through Christ all my sins are forgiven.**

"The Lord is full of compassion and mercy."
(James 5:11, NIV)

Look at it when you get up, when you go to bed, and at least once during the day as a way of intentionally shifting your focus from yourself to God. During one of those times each day, take a few minutes to think about the positive benefits in your life of God's mercy.

CHAPTER 13

Offer My Mercy to Others

Think of God's offer of mercy as a banquet to which you are invited. The most luscious foods overflow the table from end to end: spicy appetizers, gourmet entrées steaming on heated plates, a vast array of juicy fruits, iced deserts, and cool, sweet drinks. The table is so large that it has enough room for more than the few who have come. But strangely enough, outside the door to the banquet hall stands a crowd who will not enter. They cry out, "I'm so hungry, so hungry!" You can almost hear their starved stomachs rumbling. Yet for some reason, they will not step through the door and help themselves to the free banquet. A. W. Tozer gives this analogy when he writes:

> We may plead for mercy for a lifetime in unbelief, and at the end of our days be still no more than sadly hopeful that we shall somewhere, sometime, receive it. This is to starve to death just outside the banquet hall in which we have been warmly invited. Or we may, if we will, lay hold on the mercy of God by faith, not allow skepticism and unbelief to keep us from the feast of delicious foods prepared for us.[37]

God extended His mercy to us even before we were born, and before we acknowledged our need for His forgiveness. Without our Lord's sacrifice on the cross, we could not have a relationship with God. Now, because of Christ's willingness to die in our place, we can have a deep intimacy with the God who loves us unconditionally.

The Merciful Extend Mercy

One day Peter asked Jesus how many times he had to forgive someone. Peter thought that forgiving seven times was pretty good. "No!" Jesus replied, "seventy times seven!" (Matthew 18:22). Then Jesus gave an illustration showing how God looks on our responsibility to forgive:

One day, a king was going over his accounts, settling old debts. He saw that one of his servants owed him millions of dollars. The king ordered the servant brought before him. When he arrived, the king demanded that the servant pay every penny. But the amount was far beyond the servant's ability to pay, so the king ordered the man and his family and all his possessions be sold to pay the debt. The servant fell before the king and pleaded for mercy. The king felt pity and forgave him this tremendous debt.

That is such a wonderful picture of God's mercy. We are like the servant who could not pay the debt. But God, in His mercy, took pity on us and erased our sin debt completely.

But what did this servant do? He found a fellow servant who owed him a few thousand dollars and demanded payment. Just imagine. He came from the throne room where he had been extended so much mercy and grabbed his friend by the throat and demanded payment! The friend begged for mercy. But the servant would not forgive him and had him thrown into prison.

> How can we refuse to extend mercy when we have received so much mercy?

When the other servants saw the injustice, they went to the king and reported what had happened. The king was angry! He called in the servant and demanded to know why the man had acted so harshly toward his friend when he himself had been forgiven so much. Then the king commanded the servant be thrown into prison until he had paid every penny.

God gave His only Son to die in our place. That is mercy beyond comprehension, beyond description. How, then, can we ever refuse to give mercy to others when we have received so much mercy ourselves? What others may have done to you does not compare with what God has forgiven you. That is why God expects us to have mercy on others. To the degree that we show mercy to the poor, the wretched, and the guilty, we are like God. The lesson is clear: the merciful shall obtain mercy. And who among us is not a candidate for more of God's mercy?

Our Need for Mercy Helps Us Serve Others

Just like the unforgiving servant, sometimes the hardest place to extend mercy is the area where God has given us the most mercy—our area of weakness.

Ed DeWeese came home one afternoon to find that thieves had gone through his home. The TV, stereo equipment, and jewelry were missing—about $3,000 worth. He called his wife, Beth, at work and she rushed home. The police arrived and took a report. Because the DeWeeses had just moved in, they had not taken out homeowner's insurance. After the policemen left, they prayed, "Lord, we have no insurance and cannot afford to replace these things. Please return them to us."

That is when Ed's situation really hit him. He was an ex-offender. He had gone to jail for embezzlement—sophisticated burglary. He said to Beth, "We must first forgive."

After the thief had been arrested and released on bond, Ed asked a police officer to take him to the offender's home. When Ed met the man who had robbed him, he said, "I'm the man you ripped off. But brother, I forgive you in the name of Jesus."

Ed continued to visit the thief and gave a Bible to his little brother who had assisted in the crime. Soon, the robber told the police where the stolen things were hidden, and the officers recovered the DeWeeses's belongings. When the young man pleaded guilty to burglary, Ed testified in his behalf. He then helped the young man find a job. And Ed says, "Best of all, he and his brother did receive Christ as Savior."[38]

Our past failures can make us more sensitive to those who need mercy in the very areas in which we once needed mercy. We can minister to others in a more meaningful way because we understand and have experienced the reality of God's mercy in our area of weakness.

Mercy Means Letting Go of Old Hurts

Corrie ten Boom encountered a situation in which her willingness to forgive was challenged.

During 1944, Corrie experienced the horror of life under Hitler's National Socialists in the Ravensbrück concentration camp. Grim guards in blue uniforms and caps bearing the Nazi swastika stood in a line with leather crops swinging from their belts. The emaciated women dressed in prison garb worked long hours every day under the watchful eye of these godless tormentors. Corrie's sister, Betsie, died in Ravensbrück, a victim of the tortuous conditions.

In 1947, after the war, Corrie spoke to a group of Germans in a sparsely furnished Munich church basement. Her mission was to help those who were ravaged by the war. During her talk, she said, "I have a home in Holland for victims of the war. Those who have been able to forgive their former enemies have been able to rebuild their lives, no matter what the physical scars. Those, however, who have nursed their bitterness remain invalids. We, as Christians, have every reason to forgive each other, for our God richly lavishes His mercy on us—if we only ask Him."

When she finished her talk, she was approached by a balding, heavyset man in a gray overcoat, a brown felt hat clutched between his nervous hands. Horror filled her as she realized he had been one of those guards who had abused Betsie in the camp. His name was Joseph.

Joseph thrust out his hand. "A fine message, Fräulein! How good it is to know that, as you say, all our sins are at the bottom of the sea!"

Dumbfounded, Corrie did not take his hand.

He went on, "You mentioned Ravensbrück in your talk. I was a guard there. But since that time, I have become a Christian. I know that God has forgiven me for the cruel things I did there, but I would like to hear it from your lips as well. Fraulein, will you forgive me?"

Corrie remembered how he had pushed Betsie with the butt of his gun. She looked down at his outstretched hand. She whispered to herself, "Jesus, help me." Her hand slowly moved toward his. Their hands touched and God flooded her heart with genuine forgiveness as she finally vigorously shook his hand. With tears in her eyes, she said, "I forgive you, brother…with all my heart." Corrie didn't have the ability to forgive on her own. The pain was too deep. Her part was to be willing to forgive and ask God to help her forgive. God's part was to fill her heart with forgiveness. Corrie experienced God's mercy in the moment she chose to extend His mercy.

> Sometimes the hardest place to extend mercy is where God has given us the most mercy.

God loves us no matter what we have done. He forgives us when we ask Him. No sin is too big for His ocean of forgiveness. Since God richly lavishes His mercy on us, we must show mercy to one another. And that means choosing by faith, like Corrie, to let go of all those old hurts caused by others, asking God to enable us to forgive by the power of His Spirit.

Extending Mercy Has a Cost

Often the most difficult place to show mercy is in close relationships—our family and friends. A middle-aged man sat in the pastor's office, nervously wiping perspiration from his brow with the back of his hand. "There is absolutely no way I can tell this to my wife," he said. "She would be devastated. She would never forgive me. I just cannot tell her. But I want forgiveness. I need relief from all this guilt."

In this family's case, the wife's career had soared with success, while the husband's work had plateaued. She traveled on extended business trips, gaining all kinds of recognition and earning a big salary. Meanwhile, the husband was at home keeping the family fed and attending to household chores. In a weak moment when loneliness drove his attention elsewhere, his wife's best friend began to meet his sexual and emotional needs. He was caught in an ugly trap of betrayal, with seemingly no way out.

After counseling with the pastor, the husband went home and confessed his sin to his wife. He told her exactly what had happened and why. He admitted he was very wrong and assured her that his adulterous relationship with her friend was over. Much to his surprise, she forgave him, and they started all over again. This act of mercy came at no small cost to this rejected wife, but it ultimately led to the restoration of the relationship they once had.

God will reward us when we show mercy. One of mercy's rewards is the intimacy we enjoy in our human relationships. Another reward is the intimacy we experience in our relationship with our Lord. Since mercy is of the highest priority to God, when we are merciful, we become instruments of blessing and enjoy communication with God (Luke 6:35,36).

God's Mercy Helps Us in Our Failures

If you ask Steve about God's mercy, he can tell you that it is bottomless. He worked hard in his local church, raising four children with a wife he loved dearly. Yet he was not walking in God's Spirit. He began to have a problem—greed. Little by little, he began taking money from his job. In time, his $100,000 embezzlement was discovered, and he was taken to court. Still, Steve was not truly repentant. He did not realize his great need for God's mercy and help.

Because this was his first offense, the judge was lenient. Steve received a work-program sentence in which he had to spend his weekends doing community service. He was assigned to the sheriff's department. At first he did simple jobs like washing police cruisers, but soon police officials began trusting him with greater responsibilities. Eventually, they put him in charge of handling sales of items such as pepper spray. Over the next year, Steve began embezzling money from the sheriff's department until he had taken more than $20,000!

As you might guess, he was caught once again. But this time, the court did not have mercy on him, and he was sentenced to several years in prison. Because of a paperwork mix-up, he was sent to the state penitentiary for violent criminals. Suddenly, Steve's world collapsed. His wife divorced him and he was not able to see his children. Sitting in that prison cell surrounded by men for whom violence was a way of life, he decided to commit suicide. His birthday was coming up, and he felt as if his life was over.

His three daughters sent him a birthday letter in which they said, "Dad, all we ever wanted was you. We didn't want the money." Their words pierced Steve to his very soul. At that moment, he threw himself upon God's mercy— including his greed and his pride.

When Steve was paroled, he began rebuilding his life. At first, he felt so unworthy that he did not think he could ever serve God again. But little by little, God began to restore him and heal his hurt. Three years after his release, Steve felt God nudging him to work in the singles' ministry in his church. He approached the singles' pastor, his conviction papers in hand. "I want to be honest with you, Pastor Ron. I am a convicted felon. But if you could find any place for me to serve God, that's what I want to do."

After learning about Steve's past failures, Ron smiled and said, "Of course, we have a place for you to serve. We just won't put you in charge of any finances."

Since then, Steve has humbly served God in evangelism and church leadership ministry. In His mercy, God restored Steve gently and lovingly. He will do the same for you when you come before Him in humility. God wants us to be bold in asking Him for mercy when we need it (Hebrews 4:16). If we are in distress, guilt-ridden, persecuted, lonely, facing disaster, experiencing the contempt of others, struggling with our weakness, or undergoing some other difficulty, God wants us to come humbly to Him in prayer seeking His help.

Remember, people all around you need to be pointed to the mercy of God. Their hearts ache for that unconditional love and complete forgiveness. As ambassadors of Christ, we know the comfort of God's mercy and can show others how to receive this unlimited gift.

God's Mercy Does Not Eliminate All Consequences

Isn't it wonderful to celebrate the mercy God has given us? At the same time, God will not remove all the consequences of our actions just because He is merciful. In Steve's case, his sin of embezzlement still cost him his marriage and time in prison. The pain for his children was real. If he could go back and do it all over again, he would have relied on God's strength to keep him from sin rather than on God's mercy to rescue him afterwards.

When David and Bathsheba committed adultery, God forgave David after he confessed his sin. Nathan the prophet says about David's forgiveness, "The LORD has forgiven you, and you won't die for this sin. But you have given the enemies of the LORD great opportunity to despise and blaspheme Him, so your child will die" (2 Samuel 12:13,14). David experienced the consequences of his sin but God also restored him. Later, God even allowed David and Bathsheba to have another child. That child became the wisest man who ever lived: King Solomon.

God does not forgive halfway. He cleared the sin-debt against David. But God, in His wisdom, knows that if we never suffer consequences for our actions, we will not learn our lesson completely.

Mercy and Tolerance Cannot Coexist

People today, even many Christians, are more concerned about a need for *tolerance* than a need for *mercy*. There is a great difference! Josh McDowell, a world renowned author and speaker, says that tolerance and Christian love cannot coexist.

Similarly, tolerance and mercy cannot coexist. Tolerance says, "Don't judge me!" Mercy says, "I forgive you," clearly implying a wrong was committed. That is what Jesus modeled with the woman caught in adultery. The Word of God exhorts Christians to speak the truth in love (Ephesians 4:15). Mercy rooted in love demands that a person be told if he is doing something self-destructive or harmful to others.

> Tolerance toward wrong behavior is not love; it is a cheap counterfeit.

The problem we encounter in separating mercy and tolerance is that we live in an age where the majority of our society does not accept the idea of absolute truth. The biblical concept of sin has been replaced by a demand for tolerance of any culturally sanctioned activity. Consequently, tolerance has replaced mercy, especially in government, schools, colleges, industry, and the media. Tolerance is demanded for almost every bizarre and perverted belief and behavior.

When tolerance reigns and absolutes are eliminated, when diversity becomes the catch-all phrase for accepting even gross sinful and self-centered behavior, then people feel no need for the mercy of God. Instead, many rationalize their behavior with excuses like these:

"Even if I am unfaithful to my wife, I'm sure God will understand. After all, He knows I have needs that are not being met."

"Remember, this is my first time getting caught with drugs. I am basically a good man who looks after my wife and kids, and I know God will recognize that."

What has happened? We have tried to reduce God to our size, to our standards, and to what we believe He ought to be like. This makes us feel comfortable. Too often we want *Him* to respond like *we* would respond to sin and injustice. We want *Him* to accept *us* on our standards of behavior. Since we are tolerant and non-judgmental with other's sins, we want everyone including God to be tolerant with ours. In this way, we do not have to change our ways or feel guilty about them. "Live and let live" is the world's philosophy, but it is not God's.

God set the example. He extends mercy and maintains His standards perfectly. He made the dearest sacrifice for our forgiveness; yet He judges and disciplines people for their sin. He loves unconditionally; yet He completely understands our weaknesses and failings. That is what mercy is all about. Unlike tolerance, it does not sweep bad things under the rug. Mercy sees the whole picture, maintains right from wrong, and loves with the whole heart.

Can you do that? None of us can without the help of the Holy Spirit. Through Him, we can extend mercy without compromising truth. Tolerance toward wrong behavior is not love; it is a cheap counterfeit—a lie. Mercy, which extends unconditional forgiveness, is the loving response. Let us then follow Christ's example as we receive mercy from God and in return extend mercy to all we meet.

God's omnipresence means that He is always with us. His mercy means that He will fully forgive us and set our relationship with Him on the right path. And as we will see in the next two chapters, His absolute truth means that we can always trust Him to be truthful with us and to show us what is right.

Talk About It: Offer My Mercy to Others

"O people, the LORD has already told you what is good,
and this is what He requires: to do what is right, to
love mercy, and to walk humbly with your God."
(Micah 6:8)

1. In Micah 6:8 we learn that God wants us to "love mercy." How could you demonstrate this in your daily life?

2. Tolerance and mercy are often confused. Explain the differences between them.

3. Do you agree or disagree with this statement: "Sometimes the hardest place to extend mercy is the area where God has given us the most mercy—our area of weakness." Why?

4. Read Matthew 18:23–35. How do you respond when you read about the ungrateful servant?

5. Peter thought he was being extremely generous with mercy when he asked if he should forgive someone seven times, and Jesus' response was a jaw-dropping "seventy times seven!" (Matthew 18:21,22). What makes it hard for you to extend mercy? What do you think would help you extend mercy more readily?

6. What do you think are the personal benefits to you when you extend mercy to those who have hurt you? Does extending mercy mean you are supposed to blindly trust them from then on? Why or why not?

FOCUS ON GOD

Continue to review the statement and verse you wrote down last week, at least three times each day, to remind yourself of God's incredible mercy.

God, because You are merciful,
I know that through Christ all my sins are forgiven.

"The Lord is full of compassion and mercy."
(James 5:11, NIV)

Have other people sinned against you? Are you holding onto the hurt and having a difficult time forgiving? This week, make a list of the people it's hard to forgive and ask God to give you a heart of mercy and forgiveness as you focus on Him.

Now tear up the list and refuse to let them take up any more of your thoughts or emotional energy. When they come to mind in the future, immediately change your focus by talking to God about them. Turn those moments into reminders of your need to carry on a "continuous conversation" with the God of mercy.

CHAPTER 14

I AM Absolute Truth

Many years ago a banquet speaker was introduced as a very smart businessman. The audience was told that his business, growing and selling potatoes in Maine, netted him $25,000 the previous year. After a long introduction, he stood to speak. "Before I begin," he said, "I must set the record straight. What was said about my business is only partially true. First, it was not Maine, but Texas. It was not potatoes, but oil. It was not $25,000, but $250,000. And it was not a profit, but a loss. And one more thing about this introduction—it was not me who lost the money, it was my brother."

As the story illustrates, truth matters. And in some situations, it *really* matters. Knowing what is true helps us make good decisions. In some instances it can save our life.

Josh McDowell speaks to college students all over the world, and one of his most frequent topics is "safe sex." Josh was invited to give the concluding talk during "Safe Sex Week" at the University of North Dakota to 3,000 students in a jammed auditorium. When he began by saying, "You've been brainwashed," a rumble spread through the crowd. Josh describes what happened next:

When the students settled down, I continued, "You've had an entire week of 'safer sex' indoctrination: speakers, experts, videos, films, classes, and symposiums. You've been challenged, motivated, encouraged, indoctrinated, and pressured about using condoms to ensure safe sex. To top it all off, you were given a 'safer sex packet.' But you've been lied to."

At this point, the crowd was becoming a little indignant with me. Then I lowered the boom with one more question: "After all the information on 'safer sex' you have received this week, how many of you know the statistical failure rate of the condom?" *Not one hand went up!* Suddenly, the auditorium was as quiet as a cemetery. They looked at each other with expressions of astonishment. They realized they hadn't been told the whole truth about safer sex.[39]

Josh finds a similar reaction in every university crowd he addresses. Invariably, the students have been thoroughly coached about how to have "safer sex," but are never told how unsafe "safer sex" really is. In essence, what they heard was a lie.

Statistics fly in the face of "safe sex." Research conducted by Planned Parenthood (a group advocating the practice of safer sex) states that within one year of using a condom to prevent pregnancy, the pregnancy rate is more than 10 percent for all ages, and the rate is almost double for teens.[40] Statistics also show that a girl who becomes sexually active at 14 years old and practices birth control has an 87 percent chance of becoming pregnant before she graduates from high school.[41] If she is your daughter, niece, or a friend's child, does she not deserve to know the *whole truth* before she engages in risky behavior? Does shading the truth *really* matter to her—and consequently to her unborn baby? Of course!

But the consequences go even further. There are over 25 major sexually transmitted diseases in the United States. With many of them condoms make virtually no difference.

Physician Robert C. Noble writes in *Newsweek*:

I can't say I'm comforted reading a government pamphlet called "Condoms and Sexually Transmitted Diseases Especially AIDS." "Condoms are not 100 percent safe," it says, "but if used properly will reduce the risk of sexually transmitted diseases, including AIDS." *Reduce* the risk of a disease that is 100 percent fatal? That's all that's available between us and death? How much do condoms reduce the risk? They don't say. So much for Safe Sex.[42]

In fact, all latex condoms have microscopic holes that are *fifty times larger* than the HIV virus. The oil-based lubricants used with condoms can also damage them. If a condom is too old, or has been exposed to heat or cold, it may be less effective.[43]

What comfort is the lie of "safe sex" to the young man who contracts gonorrhea or to the young woman who develops herpes or to the newborn who is born with AIDS? Telling incomplete "truths" can change a life—or cause death. It is vital that we know and tell the absolute truth.

The Problem with Absolute Truth

Most Americans believe in absolute truth, right? Wrong! Truth has been a major casualty in our modern culture. In a study by George Barna of Americans between ages 26 and 44, only 20 percent of those surveyed strongly disagreed with the statement: "There is no such thing as absolute truth; different people can define truth in different ways and still be correct."[44] Shockingly, only 27 percent of those who described themselves as born-again Christians strongly disagreed! Fifty-two percent actually agreed at least somewhat with the statement![45]

If we look at the phrase "there is no absolute truth," it is logically inconsistent. It states an absolute truth about absolute truth while claiming there is no absolute truth! Many philosophers in the West today recognize that moral relativism is an intellectually bankrupt theory despite popular culture's acceptance. However,

> The phrase "there is no absolute truth," is logically inconsistent.

the baffling dilemma for those philosophers who do not believe in the existence of God is identifying any rationally credible source for moral absolutes and moral obligation.

The whole idea that truth is relative contradicts God's Word. Second Timothy 3:16

says, "All Scripture is inspired by God and is useful to teach us what is true and to make us realize what is wrong in our lives. It straightens us out and teaches us to do what is right." For example, the Bible teaches that homosexuality is wrong. Every clear reference to homosexual behavior in the Bible is negative. No exceptions. If you disagree, then try to find one clear reference to homosexual behavior in the Bible that is positive. I challenge you to find even one.[46] Yet I often read about situations like the school board in Massachusetts which voted unanimously to teach pre-schoolers (ages 3–5) about homosexual lifestyles. Pre-schoolers! This is a symptom of a culture that has rejected absolute truth.

Many people argue that even religious people cannot agree on what is absolute truth. As Christians we say that the Bible is true. The Hindus reject that, preferring the writings, or Vedas, of their holy men. The Muslims put their faith in the Koran, claiming Mohammed received it as a prophet of God. The Mormons are convinced that Joseph Smith got his messages straight from God.

To make the situation more confusing, other people claim to have received absolute truth. More than a million people purchased the bestseller *Conversations with God, Books 1 and 2*, which the author, Neale Donald Walsch, insists were dictated to him by God. Listen to the "absolute truth" that Walsch's god advocates: "I do not love 'good' more than I love 'bad.' Hitler went to heaven. When you understand this, you will understand God."

In his column in *The Wall Street Journal*, Charles Colson writes, "Mr. Walsch's God liberates us from traditional authorities—rabbis, ministers, parents, the Bible... He confidently attempts—in dialogue form, with his own questions and comments and God's replies and explanations—to repeal or modify every known religious truth and propound his own version of God's message as authoritative."[47]

A famous New Age believer made a statement in a television interview with Kathie Lee Gifford that everyone goes to Paradise after they die. Then with a question uncharacteristic of the media, Kathie Lee, asked, "Are you saying you believe that the same thing happens to Hitler as to Mother Teresa?" The New Ager stuttered and stumbled and had no reply. Kathie Lee's poignant question demonstrated the ludicrous nature of those who reject truth.

What Is Absolute Truth?

If you were asked to describe absolute truth, what would you say? By what standard can we measure truth to determine if it is truth? If you do not believe there is such a thing as absolute truth, how do you find anything to be true and trustworthy? Following are three qualities of absolute truth.

Absolute truth is internally consistent.

No matter which way you approach a true statement, it remains unassailably true. When we say that our God is absolutely truthful, we mean above everything else that He is internally consistent in His character and being. Proverbs 30:5 says, "Every word of God proves true." In fact, the Hebrew word for *truth* means conformance to a standard—God's standards.

Internal consistency of character is vital to all of God's attributes. If you can prove that God is not truthful in any aspect of who He is and how He acts, then His other qualities have no validity. If He were not absolutely consistent, then God's unlimited power, for example, could be compromised by His love. He would be like a powerful president of a country who fails to take action against evil because he lets his emotions, his wrong understanding of love, negate his power.

> The idea that truth is relative contradicts God's Word.

Absolute truth is true for all people in all places at all times.

Not everything qualifies as absolute truth. For example, if you said, "Today, the interest rate for home mortgages is at 6.5 percent," that could be true for you living in America. But for someone living in Brazil, the interest rate might be 50-plus percent. And a month from now, the interest rate for you could change to 8 percent. Because interest rates fluctuate, the percentage rate is not true for all people in all places at all times. The rate is not an absolute truth.

On the other hand, if you say, "Adultery is always wrong," you would be stating an absolute truth (Exodus 20:14). Whether you live in Bangladesh, Japan, or the United States, adultery is still wrong. Adultery was just as wrong a thousand years ago as it is today. Adultery is wrong for the wife living with the alcoholic husband, or the business or military person separated from a spouse by extended travel.

Absolute truth has its source in our holy God.

No human can think up or discover a new truth. Truth has always existed in God's nature; He is the author of truth.

We must always measure our beliefs by the truth in God's Word. Since He is the author of truth and since absolute truth resides in Him, He is the only One who can guide us to absolute truth. With Him, we see truth face to face. Any other guide will only lead us into confusion and deception.

Moses said, "God is not a man, that He should lie, nor a son of man, that He should change His mind. Does He Speak and then not act? Does He promise and not fulfill?" (Numbers 23:19, NIV). Whatever God says is absolutely right. Whatever He promises will always be fulfilled.

> By what standard can we measure truth to determine if it is truth?

Nothing Can Change God's Absolute Truth

Have you ever heard the phrase, "written in stone"? This usually refers to some statement that cannot be changed. The phrase comes from the Old Testament account of when God gave the Ten Commandments. About two months after the Israelites had left their slavery in Egypt, they reached Mount Sinai where God revealed Himself to the people. God's holiness and power were very evident:

All Mount Sinai was covered with smoke because the LORD had descended on it in the form of fire. The smoke billowed into the sky like smoke from a furnace, and the whole mountain shook with a violent earthquake. (Exodus 19:18)

Moses went up the mountaintop into a cloud that looked like a devouring fire and stayed forty days and nights. During that time God wrote the Ten Commandments with His own finger on tablets of stone. God required His people to obey these timeless gems of absolute truth.

Meanwhile, the people, under the leadership of Moses' brother, Aaron, began to think that Moses would never return. So Aaron built them a golden calf to take God's place.

Aware of the peoples' disobedience, God told Moses to go back down the mountain. As Moses strode downward clutching the stone tablets, he heard noises like the sounds of celebration. When he got near, he saw God's people worshiping a golden calf. The people who had promised to obey all of God's laws had already broken one of the Ten Commandments. In anguish and anger over the sight, Moses hurled the tablets to the ground, shattering them.

Then God said to Moses: "Prepare two stone tablets like the first ones. I will write on them the same words that were on the tablets you smashed" (Exodus 34:1). Once more Moses climbed that cloud-covered mountain; once more God etched the Ten Commandments into stone with His finger.

Do you see the picture of absolute truth in this account? God wrote the commandments in stone. No one can erase or alter them; they are absolute truth. Moses, in his anger, shattered the stone tablets. As humans we can break God's commandments, but we cannot change them. The broken laws are not any less true. Once shattered, God just wrote them on stone once more. Nothing we can do will ever change God's absolute truth.

God's Absolute Truth Lasts Forever

A woman received directions to a home for a baby shower, complete with the street name and the house number. But she never found the correct house and went home embarrassed. The next day she discovered some pranksters had switched several street signs in the area. She failed to reach her destination *even though she had true directions.*

If you have ever had an experience like that, you may be skeptical whenever you receive directions to an unfamiliar setting. That is how many people approach what God has said. They are not at all sure that His truth is absolutely accurate or applies to modern life. *Maybe He has forgotten about a turn, a detour, or a switched street sign,* they think. *Times change, so how can we rely on truth given centuries ago?*

Because God knows the end from the beginning, not one of His statements ever turns out to be a misdirection. He does not shade the truth or leave out an essential part. His absolute truth applies to every situation in history.

I encourage you to read Psalm 119, one of the greatest chapters in the Bible, about the endurance and truth of God's Word. Verse 160 says, "All Your words are true; all Your just laws will stand forever." Not only is God's truth absolute, but it lasts forever! We can count on it for eternity.

> As humans we can break God's commandments, but we cannot change them.

How God Reveals His Absolute Truth to Us

God wants us to know the absolute truth, so He has taken the initiative to show us truth in several ways: in His Word, the Bible; by the life, death, and resurrection of His Son; and through His Holy Spirit.

God recorded truth for us in the Bible.

The Bible is God's absolute truth in written form. Jesus tells us, "Your word is truth" (John 17:17, NIV). We can read it, memorize it, and meditate on it. God uses the Bible to reveal truth about Himself, ourselves, and about life (2 Timothy 3:16). There is no way anyone can live a holy, satisfying, fulfilled life without spending regular time in the Word of God.

It has been my practice for years to read through the Bible each year. My most important priority every morning is to read God's Word, even before I eat breakfast. Somehow the time I spend with God in the morning is more than compensated in the way the rest of the day unfolds.

God manifested truth to us through the life, death, and resurrection of Jesus Christ.

Truth is not just a concept, it is embodied in a person—Jesus Christ. While many people claim to *know* the truth, only Jesus could honestly claim to *be* the truth. Jesus explains, "I am the way, the truth, and the life. No one can come to the Father except through Me" (John 14:6).

John Wesley writes, "The word of His truth and wisdom is more ardent and more light-giving than the rays of the sun, and sinks down into the depths of heart and mind." The words of God put into human form by Jesus purify us when we let them sink into our hearts.

God guides us into truth through the working of the Holy Spirit.

As Christians, we have the Holy Spirit living within us. One of His primary responsibilities is to reveal truth to us. Jesus calls Him "the Spirit of truth" (John 14:16,17, NIV). The Holy Spirit is Christ's representative who communicates directly with us, illuminating God's truth, and giving us the power to obey that truth. In fact, when we worship God, we are to worship Him in spirit and in truth (John 4:24).

I often use the illustration that the Holy Spirit represents one wing of an airplane and the Word of God represents the other. Our Lord Jesus Christ is the pilot. No airplane will fly with just one wing. If we do not rely on the Holy Spirit to guide us and also saturate ourselves with God's truth—His holy, inspired, inerrant truth—then our holy life will not fly. We must also allow Jesus to be the navigator of our plans, desires, wills, and emotions, for He is the truth.

We do not need to be confused about what is right or wrong—we can look to God's Word. We cannot complain that we do not have an example of how to put God's truth into practice—we have the truth in the flesh, Jesus Christ. And we cannot excuse ourselves from knowing and following God's truth—we have the power of the Holy Spirit who leads us into all truth. God gave us His Truth in the Bible, lived it in Jesus Christ, and empowers us to follow it by His Holy Spirit.

In the next chapter we will explore how God's Truth sets us free spiritually and emotionally.

Talk About It: I AM Absolute Truth

"So God has given both His promise and His oath. These two things
are unchangeable because it is impossible for God to lie."
(Hebrews 6:18)

1. When it comes to truth, many people reject absolute truth. If you have your "truth" and I have my "truth," what does that imply about the reliability of truth?

2. What are three essential qualities of absolute truth? How do you respond to those qualities?

3. Read Numbers 23:19. List some of the reasons people are tempted to bend the truth or even lie. Based on what you know about God, do any of these reasons tempt God to lie? Why or why not?

4. Is it important for you to know that God never lies? If so, why?

5. Some things scientists believed to be true ten years ago have been proved incorrect by more recent discoveries. Scientists were not necessarily lying; they just did not have all the information. Now consider God's holiness, power, love and ever-present nature. How do these attributes make it impossible for God to ever mislead us?

6. Since God cannot lie to you, how do you respond to statements in the Bible that you do not like? Explain.

7. On a scale of 1–10, how would you rate your heart's desire to follow what God says is true? (1=I don't care; 10=I am totally committed)

8. How does your answer reflect your relationship with God?

FOCUS ON GOD

On an index card or your favorite electronic device, write the following statement and verse, or just take a picture of it:

**God, because You are absolute truth,
I will believe what You say and live accordingly.**

"You will know the truth,
and the truth will set you free." (John 8:32)

Look at it when you get up, when you go to bed, and at least once during the day as a way of intentionally shifting your focus from yourself to God. During one of those times each day, take a few minutes to think about the positive benefits in your life of God's truthfulness.

CHAPTER 15

My Truth Sets You Free

On February 3, 1998, Karla Faye Tucker died. She had known the date of her death since December because she was scheduled to be executed in a Texas prison for the double murders she had committed.

Karla Faye Tucker was the first woman since the Civil War to be executed in the Texas prison system. In 1983 after three days of non-stop drug taking, she and Daniel Garrett broke into a Houston apartment and killed Dean and Deborah Thornton. Karla Faye was the one who swung the pickax. If anyone deserved a sentence of death, she did.

But something miraculous happened to Karla Faye during her fourteen years on death row. Soon after her arrest, she learned the truth that God loves even the vilest sinner and that He pardons completely the person who asks Him for forgiveness. Karla Faye said in an interview a month before her execution, "I asked [God] to forgive me and I knew I needed forgiveness. And I knew I had done something really horrible. But I think right at that moment what mostly hit me was His love. His love. It just surrounded me."[48] In that moment, the murderer became a child of God.

Although she would never again set foot outside a prison, God's truth had made her free. George Sechrist, who represented Karla Faye in her appeal process, saw her change as she grew in her faith. He says, "I've represented a number of folks on death row. All of them certainly are deserving of their day in court, regardless of what they've done, but I've never seen anyone who has genuinely transformed in any way as she has. And, quite frankly, I doubt I'll ever see it again!"[49]

Karla spoke about the power of the Holy Spirit to change a life ruined by sin. Her words were broadcast over radio and television to millions.

No one can commit a sin so rotten that God cannot transform that life into one which brings glory to Him. Although Karla reaped the consequences of her crime with the death penalty, she also influenced thousands of others for Christ with her story before she died.

Every day, we make decisions based on beliefs and values that we assume are true. Too often, we later discover our beliefs were an illusion of truth projected by our corrupt society. As John the apostle explains, "They are from the world and therefore speak from the viewpoint of the world, and the world listens to them" (1 John 4:5, NIV). The world's viewpoint is based on wrong values and misguided purposes, not absolute truth, and its ideas fluctuate with the time, the person, and the culture. Eventually, the world's viewpoint enslaves us to sin. But as we read in John 8:32, God's truth sets us free.

> Every day, we make decisions based on beliefs we assume are true.

God's liberating truth is our anchor point for life. Solomon writes, "Truth stands the test of time; lies are soon exposed" (Proverbs 12:19). God's truth has endured for thousands of years. Man's "truth" has not. And since God's truth lasts for eternity, its power to free us from sin will never diminish.

We Can Trust God's Word

Most of us have at least one friend we consider very honest. When we ask that person for his opinion, we find out what he really thinks. If we ask him to take care of something important for us, he will be open about whether or not he can complete the job. We would not consider him a faithful friend if there were areas of his life where he acted dishonestly.

That is even more true of our holy God. We can trust His Word—completely and implicitly. The psalmist writes, "All Your commands are true. Long ago I learned from Your statutes that You established them to last forever" (Psalm 119:151,152, NIV). It would violate God's truthfulness if His Word could not be trusted.

During the first centuries of the Church, false teachers tried to argue that the Bible was not completely truthful. The apostle Paul clearly defended the Bible's reliability (2 Timothy 3:16). He proclaimed that all Scripture is God's truth! That assurance is what gave Paul such incredible confidence as he traveled about the Roman Empire proclaiming the Good News of Jesus' death and resurrection. His life of service through incredible pressures and persecutions is proof that God's Word has power to sustain us.

We can absolutely trust God's Word—to the last period on the last page. After more than fifty years of studying the Bible, I am convinced beyond any shadow of doubt that it is the holy, inspired, and inerrant Word of God. During these years, I have anchored my life of service to Jesus Christ on a God who is faithful and stands behind His holy Word. God has never failed me, and He never will.

God's Promises Are True

If God's Word can be trusted, we can be sure that the promises in His Word are also true. The writer to the Hebrews encourages us, "Let us hold unswervingly to the hope we profess, for He who promised is faithful" (Hebrews 10:23, NIV). God's truthful nature backs up His promises; therefore, we can immerse ourselves in His promises, applying them to our life situations. For example, consider Jesus' promises:

- "When everything is ready, I will come and get you, so that you will always be with Me where I am." (John 14:3)
- "The truth is, anyone who believes in Me will do the same works I have done, and even greater works, because I am going to be with the Father." (John 14:12)

- "I am leaving you with a gift—peace of mind and heart. And the peace I give isn't like the peace the world gives. So don't be troubled or afraid." (John 14:27)

The Bible is full of thousands of other wonderful promises from God for every imaginable occasion. They mean so much to me that years ago I wrote a devotional book called *Promises: A Daily Guide to Supernatural Living*. The promises highlighted on each of the pages are still blessing the lives of those who read them. I encourage you to read through the Old and New Testaments, highlighting the amazing promises of God. You will be greatly blessed with what you find! Memorizing them will create an invaluable source of continual encouragement.

God's Truth Exposes Deception and Ignorance

Because our secular society has rejected God's holy inspired Word as the absolute standard for truth, we have lost our reference point for reality. Now our society often defines truth based on public opinion polls. We live in a media culture of sizzle and hype which influences public thinking. Advertising hucksters and spin-doctors are constantly at work to influence our thinking about events and issues. Educational institutions promote diversified views at the expense of truth. Even many journalists are no longer satisfied with reporting the facts. Instead, they slant the news to fit their own, often anti-God, interpretation.

This is the nature of the world system controlled by Satan, who is the father of lies (John 8:44). These masters of deception, distortion, and manipulation take truth out of context or give only half-truths. Anyone who accepts this world system becomes bound up in deception, manipulation, lies, and ignorance. Many Christians, sadly, have bought into these lies.

> Why are so many guilt-ridden people filling up psychiatrists' couches?

But God's truth is a light that shows us the difference between falsehood and truth. Jesus taught, "I am the light of the world. If you follow Me, you won't be stumbling through the darkness, because you will have the light that leads to life" (John 8:12). Without His truth, we are left to grope about in spiritual darkness. But His light frees us to see and do what is right and good.

Consider some of the deceptions promoted by our culture and the contrast of God's truth, as shown in the following table. Of the six options, which of the two columns are you tempted to base your life on? Every day, each of us makes choices about what we want to do or what we perceive to be true. Only God can free us from the deceptions and distortions of the world system. He has given us the Bible as a handbook for identifying truth, and His Spirit, the Counselor of Truth, within us as our Guide.

SOCIETY'S LIE	GOD'S TRUTH
Money is the key to happiness. Wealth provides comfort and security, prestige and respectability. If you have a nice house and own the things you always wanted, you will find fulfillment in life.	"Stay away from the love of money; *be satisfied with what you have*" (Hebrews 13:5). "Seek first His kingdom and His righteousness, and all these things will be given to you as well" (Matthew 6:33, NIV). "My God will meet all your needs" (Philippians 4:19, NIV).
Think of yourself first. Otherwise, your needs will go unmet. You deserve more out of life. Go ahead, reward yourself. You owe it to yourself.	"If you try to keep your life for yourself, you will lose it. But *if you give up your life for Me, you will find true life*. And how do you benefit if you gain the whole world but lose your own soul in the process?" (Matthew 16:25,26).

SOCIETY'S LIE	GOD'S TRUTH
You have a right to satisfy your sexual appetites and passions in whatever way you want. It's nobody's business what you do as long as you are not hurting anyone. Besides, biblical standards for sexual purity are prudish and old-fashioned.	*"Run away from sexual sin!"* (1 Corinthians 6:18). "Remain faithful to one another in marriage. God will surely judge people who are immoral and those who commit adultery" (Hebrews 13:4). "Do not commit adultery" (Exodus 20:14).
It's okay to sin a little. Nobody's perfect. Loosen up and have some fun. No one will ever find out what you do. Lighten up. Get a life.	"The time is coming when everything will be revealed; all that is secret will be made public" (Luke 12:2). "Do not be deceived: God cannot be mocked. *A man reaps what he sows*" (Galatians 6:7, NIV).
You have a right to get even. You're a wimp if you let people get away with anything. If someone hurts you, hurt them back. It's an eye for an eye and a tooth for a tooth.	*"Get rid of all bitterness, rage and anger"* (Ephesians 4:31, NIV). "Do not repay anyone evil for evil… Do not take revenge" (Romans 12:17,19, NIV). "Love your enemies. Do good to those who hate you" (Luke 6:27).
Character doesn't matter. If you want to get ahead in life, tell people what they want to hear. Bend the rules to achieve your purposes because the end justifies the means. Ability is more important than conduct.	*"I the LORD search the heart and examine the mind,* to reward a man according to his conduct, according to what his deeds deserve" (Jeremiah 17:10, NIV).

Do your decisions and lifestyle demonstrate that you are listening to God through His Word and His servants? Or are you living in the darkness of the lies of society and popular culture? Like a powerful floodlight, God's truth will expose for us the foolishness and destructiveness of every myth promoted by the world.

How God's Truth Sets Us Free

God's truth frees us to live as God intended. On the other hand, Satan, the deceiver, wants us to base our lives on false assumptions. Jesus said to His followers, "You are truly My disciples if you keep obeying My teachings. And you will know the truth, and the truth will set you free" (John 8:31,32). Here are several ways God's truth sets us free.

We are free from death and eternal separation from God.

Jesus said, "I give them eternal life, and they will never perish. No one will snatch them away from Me" (John 10:28).

Paul wrote to Titus about the certainty of eternal life: "a faith and knowledge resting on the hope of eternal life, which God, who does not lie, promised before the beginning of time" (Titus 1:2, NIV). Paul knew that way back in eternity past God had promised salvation for those who believe in Him. That promise became reality in Paul's life, as it will for all of us who accept the message of Jesus' death on the cross for our sin. The Book of Hebrews assures us:

> God also bound Himself with an oath, so that those who received the promise could be perfectly sure that He would never change His mind. So God has given us both His promise and His oath. These two things are unchangeable because it is impossible for God to lie. (Hebrews 6:16–18)

That is why the hope of eternal life based on God's promises is so firmly anchored for us.

We are set free from bondage to sin and guilt.

Our society has tried to cleanse itself from guilt by removing the Ten Commandments from our public schools, buildings, and courts so that no one will be reminded of breaking them. Those who sin try to rationalize all kinds of behavior repulsive to God by blaming it on their background, circumstances, a parent or spouse. With society saying, "Don't worry, it's not your fault," why are so many guilt-ridden people filling up psychiatrists' couches? Because we are all born in bondage to sin and guilt, and only God can break those bonds. Only He can break the chains of blame shifting, bad habits, and addictions.

Nick Smith, a 17-year-old who participated in Josh McDowell's "Right from Wrong" campaign, understood this principle. By attending the meetings, he prepared himself to make godly decisions. While he was at an out-of-town track meet, he discovered several teammates glued to a less-than-wholesome movie on the HBO channel. He had two choices: to follow the biblical guidelines he had learned about keeping himself pure or to go along with his friends. Nick said, "Y'all shouldn't be watching that. It messes up your mind."[50]

One of the boys agreed with Nick and left the group. Not only did Nick resist the temptation to do something wrong, he also influenced another young man to do the same! If you turn your temptations over to God and trust in His power, He will help you step out of that pile of chains as a free man or woman.

Paul writes in Romans 6:22, "Now that you have been set free from sin and have become slaves to God, the benefit you reap leads to holiness, and the result is eternal life" (NIV). In Jesus we can live freely and joyfully.

We are set free from self-centeredness.

If you want to take a test to see how self-centered you are, note your instinctive reaction the next time you see a photograph showing a group of people including yourself. Whose face do you look at first? Your best friend's or your own? How about when you hear good news about someone close to you? Do you immediately think about how your friend is feeling or wonder why you do not get the "lucky breaks" in life?

You are not alone. We all have a self-centered nature. It's part of the human condition.

Jesus told His disciples, "If any of you wants to be My follower, you must put aside your selfish ambition, shoulder your cross, and follow Me. If you try to keep your life for yourself, you will lose it. But if you give up your life for

Me, you will find true life" (Matthew 16:24,25). Only Christ can free us to be more others-centered as we walk in the power of His Spirit. He fills us with His powerful love, which "does not demand its own way. Love is not irritable, and it keeps no record of when it has been wronged" (1 Corinthians 13:5).

We are set free from bondage to fear.

Paul informs us, "You did not receive a spirit that makes you a slave again to fear, but you received the Spirit of sonship" (Romans 8:15, NIV). Yet many Christians still live in fear because they focus on their circumstances rather than on the eternal God who loves them. It robs us of joy and limits what we can do for our Lord. But God enables us to live in freedom through the power of His Holy Spirit—if only we will trust and obey Him!

> Every day we must choose whom we will believe.

We are set free from a life of mediocrity and insignificance.

God, the creator of over 100 billion galaxies, also created us in His image and offers a wonderful plan for our lives (Jeremiah 29:11). Nothing the world offers can even come close to what God has planned. We will only be significant to the degree we are willing to follow the plan for which God has created us.

You Can Begin to Live Freely in God's Truth

Many years ago, a young missionary from Africa came to see me for counsel. He told me that he had little knowledge or experience of the Holy Spirit. He had spent several years on the mission field with no tangible results and felt like a miserable failure.

As we sat together, I explained that his ministry had been fruitless because he did not draw on the power of the Holy Spirit to help him. I further explained how important it is that we confess all known sin to God, turn from our sin, and walk in obedience to Him. Then as we surrender to the Lordship of Christ, we can by faith ask God to fill us with His Holy Spirit (Ephesians 5:18). We can claim His promise to fill us knowing that if we ask anything according to His will, He hears us (1 John 5:14,15).

In response, the man exploded in anger. He said, "I have spent my life serving God at great sacrifice. I have faced death and all kinds of persecution on the mission field. And now you offer me this simplistic solution to my problem?" He was irate and stormed out of my office.

A few days later he called me for another appointment. He said, "I don't agree with you. I believe that your explanation of the Spirit-filled life is too superficial and simple, but you obviously have a quality in your life that I don't have and I want very badly. I will ask God to show me if what you say is true."

I will never forget a letter I received from him a few weeks later. He wrote out of a joyful heart overflowing with praise and thanksgiving to God. He said, "I now understand what you have been trying to tell me. I did what you told me to do and now I want to return to the mission field and teach other defeated believers what you taught me. I've been liberated. I'm free!"

If you have never learned how to let the Spirit of God guide you every moment of every day then I suspect you are like that young missionary, working hard to serve and follow God but still feeling inadequate. You can change that today. Please see Appendix B, "How to Be Filled With the Holy Spirit," to learn the truth of how to be empowered by the Holy Spirit for fruitful service every day. In Acts 1:8 Jesus said, "But you will receive power when the Holy Spirit comes on you; and you will be My witnesses in Jerusalem, and in all Judea and Samaria, and to the ends of the earth" (NIV). Jesus made you a promise, and He would never lie to you.

The choice is ours. Every day we must choose whom we will believe, God or the World (Satan). Diligently seek God's truth, and then base your life on it because His absolute truth will set you free as you allow His Spirit to guide you. And that is the Truth.

Talk About It: My Truth Sets You Free

"You will know the truth, and the truth will set you free."

(John 8:32)

1. Read Jesus' words in John 14:6. Do you believe He was speaking the truth? Why or why not? What implications does your answer have on those who embrace other ways to God?

2. When Jesus told the Jewish religious leaders, "I tell you the truth, before Abraham was even born, I AM," they picked up stones to throw at Him (John 8:58,59).
   - Why did they react so strongly? (See Exodus 3:14.)
   - What do you think Jesus was claiming, and why did He say it this way?
   - Do you believe Jesus was telling the truth, or was He lying or just totally nuts? Explain.

3. Can Jesus be a liar and a good man? Can Jesus be a liar and the Savior?

4. Review the chart of Society's Lies and God's Truth. Can you think of other lies we believe that are contrary to God's truth? How has God's truth set you free?

5. Look up each of the following verses and answer two questions: What is God's part? What is your part?
   - Psalm 119:18
   - Psalm 119:105
   - John 16:13
   - Romans 12:2

6. Ephesians 4:15 says, "We will speak the truth in love, growing in every way more and more like Christ." Is it possible to speak the truth in love without compromising truth? What does it look like to speak the truth in love?

FOCUS ON GOD

Continue to review the statement and verse you wrote down last week, at least three times each day, allowing them to become a part of your "continuous conversation" with God.

**God, because You are absolute truth,
I will believe what You say and live accordingly.**

*"You will know the truth,
and the truth will set you free."*
(John 8:32)

This week, be intentional about speaking the truth and doing it in love.

CHAPTER 16

I AM All-Knowing

M any people consider Albert Einstein the most dazzling intellect in history. Did you know that the beginnings of his theory of relativity came from an essay he wrote when he was 16 years old? By age 26, he had published five major research papers in an important German journal. For one of those papers, he received his doctorate. The ideas he introduced in those papers were so revolutionary that they changed the way we view the scientific universe.

When Hitler and the National Socialists came to power, they denounced Einstein's work, confiscated his property, and burned his books. Soon after, he moved to America and became a US citizen. In 1939, Einstein learned that German scientists had split the uranium atom. He wrote a letter to President Franklin D. Roosevelt warning him about the German discovery, which he predicted would lead to the invention of the atomic bomb. Because of Einstein's advice, the US government established the Manhattan Project, which developed the first two atomic bombs in 1945.[51]

Einstein's ideas impacted not only the way scientists think about matter, but also the way war is waged. They even spilled over into the moral realm. To Einstein's shock, modern philosophers took his scientific theory of relativity and applied it to the moral realm as *relativism*. This philosophy destroyed society's belief in absolute truth and helped produce acceptance for situational ethics. While Einstein's discoveries about the atom have advanced the arenas of energy and medicine, they have been used to destroy morality, resulting in many shattered lives and broken families.

Knowledge is essential and can even change lives. But it is not enough to simply know facts. Knowledge in the pure sense can be used for good or for evil. Consider how the facts of computer technology have been used for both good and evil on the Internet. But this we can be sure of: God not only knows everything, He uses this knowledge for the good, including our good.

God is the only source of all knowledge, understanding, and wisdom; everything we know and understand originated with Him. As the prophet Isaiah declares:

Who has understood the mind of the LORD, or instructed Him as His counselor? Whom did the LORD consult to enlighten Him, and who taught Him the right way? Who was it that taught Him knowledge or showed Him the path of understanding? (Isaiah 40:13,14, NIV)

What great news! We do not need an intellect like Einstein's. We know Someone who knows the answers to all of life's questions. "Oh, what a wonderful God we have! How great are His riches and wisdom and knowledge!" (Romans 11:33).

The Greatest Knowledge

What a person knows can lead to riches, power, and advancement. Major corporations and companies pay consultants handsomely for their knowledge. Consider the computer industry. Fortunes are being made because people want quicker ways to find and manage information.

In 1953, there were only 100 computers in use around the world. These machines each weighed many tons and filled huge rooms. Today, there are millions of computers of all shapes and sizes on every continent.[52]

Our knowledge base now doubles every year. College graduates often discover that what they learned in their many years of study quickly becomes obsolete due to this information explosion. Every day new discoveries change what we previously accepted as factual. Yesterday's cutting-edge concepts are being replaced by today's insights. These in turn will give way to tomorrow's breakthroughs.

Yet the more we learn, the more we realize how much we still do not know. To compensate for our lack of knowledge, we are always trying to build a faster, smarter way to access knowledge. Computer technology is advancing at mind-boggling rates. At the same time, many of these scientists and experts reject the one Person who has the greatest knowledge of all. According to 1 John 3:20, "He knows everything." Our magnificent Creator God not only knows everything but also is the source of all knowledge. His knowledge is absolutely pure, totally true and accurate, and undefiled by distortions or wrong perspectives. Unlike man's knowledge, God's knowledge is never superseded or made obsolete by new discoveries.

> God's knowledge is never superseded or made obsolete by new discoveries.

Most scientists spend their lives trying to understand and solve the mysteries of life and the universe. But for our all-knowing God, there are no mysteries. He has a clear understanding of everything that baffles mankind.

Our All-Knowing God

Theologians call God's unlimited knowledge *omniscience* (all knowing). What does God's omniscience mean? More than 300 years ago, one of the 17th century's great theologians, Stephen Charnock, wrote:

> He knows what angels know, what man knows, and infinitely more; He knows Himself, His own operations, all His creatures, the notions and thoughts of them.[53]

Because God knows absolutely everything that can ever be known, He has never had to learn anything. He does not need a computer because all knowledge is instantly accessible to Him and He remembers everything at all times. He is never bewildered or confused or perplexed. He never has to figure something out; everything is always absolutely clear to Him. Nothing ever surprises God; He is always completely aware of all events because He sees everything. Nothing ever turns out differently than He expected or planned.

In this chapter, I want to highlight four areas of God's omniscience. They will help us more fully understand how much we can trust God with everything in our lives.

Only God Knows Everything About Himself

As humans, we do not understand much about ourselves. For example, has anyone ever pointed out a task you messed up and said, "You should have known better than that"? But you thought you did know what to do when you started— until you failed.

Not so with the God of the Bible. He knows His own essence and infinite perfections. He knows what is unknowable to anyone else. First Corinthians 2:11 says, "No one can know what anyone else is really thinking except that person alone, and no one can know God's thoughts except God's own Spirit."

If God did not know Himself completely, then His knowledge of everything else would be incomplete as well. We could not trust Him with our problems. Let us take this a step further. If God did not know Himself perfectly, then He would be ignorant of the full extent of His own ability; He would not know how far His power extends. That would mean He could not govern everything, for He would not know how to exercise His power. Let me give two examples of the importance of God's knowledge of Himself.

First, as humans, we do not know ourselves completely, let alone what is going on in the heart of another person. That is why many of our laws when put into practice work against what they were intended to do. For example, malpractice laws intended to help patients injured during a medical procedure can also be used by a dishonest person to cheat the system out of millions of dollars. In a similar way, if God did not fully know His own holiness, He could not fully discern the difference between evil and good. Consequently, He could not prescribe fair laws or execute justice, for He would be limited in His knowledge of a person's heart attitudes. But He does understand His holiness, so He is the perfect judge.

Second, if a king did not know his own authority or the borders and nature of his kingdom, how could he rule? His authority would suffer from serious lapses. But God does know every detail about His creatures, and His ability to rule in majesty and fairness is unequaled.

Jesus tells us, "No one really knows the Father except the Son and those to whom the Son chooses to reveal Him" (Matthew 11:27). What we know about God is possible only because He has revealed Himself through creation, the Bible, and Jesus Christ.

Only God Knows Everything About His Creation

Some people believe that our vast and orderly universe originated as a result of a massive explosion known as the "Big Bang." This theory proposes that billions of years ago, before there were stars or planets, all of the energy and matter of the universe were crammed together into a single point. Somehow, this point exploded, which caused the planets, stars, and galaxies to emerge. Yet even renowned scientists admit that no one really knows how stars originated. Abraham Loeb of the Harvard University Center for Astrophysics says, "The truth is that we don't understand star formation at a fundamental level."[54]

Where did the original matter and energy come from? What was the catalyst that caused the explosion? How could life originate from non-living, inorganic matter? And why do explosions today create only chaos and destruction instead of the order and intricate design that is present throughout the universe?

How foolish to believe that this universe created itself. Truth and knowledge about creation can only originate with God.

Only God Knows Everything That Has Ever Happened or Will Happen

Have you ever known someone who was a "know-it-all"? No matter what you say, he corrects you. If you tell a story, he has a better one. He parades his knowledge about the latest fads or news. Soon your ears tire of hearing him talk about what he knows.

Although God knows everything that has ever happened or will happen, He never comes across as a "know-it-all." He never uses His knowledge in a selfish way. Not a single event throughout all eternity has gone unnoticed by God. In the Book of Isaiah, God declares, "I am God, and there is none like Me. Only I can tell you the future before it even happens" (Isaiah 46:9,10). His omniscience is vitally important to us. As we get to know Him more intimately, we realize that we can trust Him because He does know everything we have done and will do, yet He loves us anyway.

God knows every good intention we have—as well as every temptation.

Some people are intimidated by God because He knows the end from the beginning—and everything in between. Statements like Proverbs 15:3 unnerve them: "The LORD is watching everywhere, keeping His eye on both the evil and the good." They know that He sees their sin. This truth is disturbing for a husband who secretly looks at pornographic material and the employee who steals from the job. But God who sees what is done in secret will someday reveal such behavior publicly. On the other hand, God's omniscience is comforting to those who confess their sins as they recognize them. They know their sins have been forgiven.

God Knows the Past

None of us have a perfect memory, and we sometimes forget incidents in our past that would be helpful in the future. As a result, we run into all kinds of obstacles because we did not remember the past.

Our omniscient God, however, never forgets the past. One of the marvelous facets of God's knowledge is that He knows everything that has happened in the past as though it were happening right now. He has no dark recesses in his memory where some past action lies hidden. Since He knows our past perfectly, as we submit to the Holy Spirit, He illuminates what we need to know to take proper action.

The only time God promises not to remember our past is when we seek His forgiveness. God says, "I, even I, am He who blots out your transgressions, for My own sake, and remembers your sins no more" (Isaiah 43:25, NIV). Even though He is aware of our sins, He consciously does not "remember" them after we confess them (1 John 1:9).

God Knows the Present

If God did not know all the present, then He could be deceived and misled. But God knows everything about all His creatures. The psalmist writes, "The LORD looks down from heaven and sees the whole human race. From His throne He observes all who live on the earth. He made their hearts, so He understands everything they do" (Psalm 33:13–15).

We can compare God's knowledge to a mother who knows exactly what her child has done and is doing. Mothers often intuitively discern the real motives of their children's actions. If that is true of a mother, how much more is it true of our heavenly Father! God knows every good intention we have—as well as every temptation to rebel against His commands.

This can be very encouraging. For example, during Jesus' final meal with His disciples before the crucifixion, He predicted that Peter would deny Him. Jesus said to him, "Simon, Simon, Satan has asked to sift you as wheat. But I have prayed for you, Simon, that your faith may not fail. And when you have turned back, strengthen your brothers" (Luke 22:31,32, NIV). Knowing the condition of Peter's heart and that Peter would later disciple his brothers and sisters in their faith, Jesus prayed for him even before his denial. Jesus does the same for us today.

God Knows the Future

It has been said that economists successfully predicted ten of the last three recessions. Economists, like weather forecasters, can at best make educated guesses. No one really knows what the economy will do. As someone once remarked, "If you lined up all the economists in the world one after another, you wouldn't have enough to reach a conclusion."

Now consider the foreknowledge of God. At one time, nothing existed but God, yet at any point in time, He knew the past, present, and future. He knew when He would create the universe, that Adam and Eve would sin, and that He would send a Savior.

> There is neither a thought in your mind nor a motive that God does not know.

To prove His ability to predict the future, God gave us hundreds of prophecies in the Bible. One that fascinates me is the prophecy that the Jewish people would be scattered across the globe and then called back together as a nation (Deuteronomy 30:3; Isaiah 11:11,12; Jeremiah 23:3,4; Zephaniah 3:20). The temple of Jerusalem was destroyed in AD 70 and the Jewish nation destroyed. But almost 2,000 years later, in 1948, the Jewish people reestablished their homeland in Israel. The odds against that happening after nearly two millennia are astronomical! God's prophecies are 100 percent accurate because He not only knows the future through His omniscience, but He also controls the future by His power and sovereignty.

Only God Knows Everything About Us

Occasionally when Vonette and I are talking together, one of us will say, "You read my mind; that was what I was about to tell you." Sometimes I will be silently praying about something, and she will ask me, "Have you thought about such and such?" To my amazement, that was the very thing I was praying about. How does that happen? I do not understand it, but I know that if human beings can be so in tune with one another, how much greater is God's ability to know our thoughts, discern our motives, and understand our weaknesses. There is not a thought in your mind or a motive in your heart that God does not know. That is an awesome thought! King David explains:

> Oh LORD, You have examined my heart and know everything about me. You know when I sit down or stand up. You know my every thought when far away. You chart the path ahead of me and tell me where to stop and rest. Every moment You know where I am. You know what I am going to say even before I say it, LORD. You both precede and follow me. You place Your hand of blessing on my head. Such knowledge is too wonderful for me, too great for me to know! (Psalm 139:1–6)

I encourage you to take a few moments to worship God because of His knowledge and love for us. One way to worship our incomprehensible Creator is by coming before Him in silence and awe. Shut out everything else; turn off the radio, television, electronic devices, or music, and come into His presence. Tell Him how great are His attributes and works. Then listen in quietness as His Spirit speaks and ministers to your spirit.

Talk About It: I AM All-Knowing
"In Him lie hidden all the treasures of wisdom and knowledge."
(Colossians 2:3)

1. Has anyone ever said any of the following to you:
   "If only I had known…"
   "I didn't know you could…"
   "I wish I knew how to help you…"
   Have you ever thought about what God would say to you instead:
   "I know…"
   "I know you can…"
   "I know exactly how to help you…"
   With that in mind, who do you go to first when you need wisdom? Is anything holding you back from turning to God first and trusting in His guidance?

2. Based on what you read in this chapter, how would you finish the following statements:
   Because of our human limitations and flaws, our knowledge can be____
   _____.
   Because of God's holiness, unlimited power, and eternal omnipresence, His knowledge is _____.

3. Read Romans 8:28–30. If God "foreknew" those who would love Him, what does that say about the extent of God's knowledge in relation to the past, present, and future? Do you think God simply knows the past, present, and future, or does He simultaneously exist in the past, present, and future—"*an eternal present*"? Explain.

4. Unlike Christianity, some religions believe that their god continues to grow, learn, and "evolve" over time, like humans do. If that were true, what would it imply about the extent and reliability of their god's knowledge? What implications would that have for the trustworthiness of their religion's holy book? Why?

5. Read Luke 22:33,34. Compare what Peter thought he knew about himself to what Jesus actually knew to be true of Peter.

6. Read Luke 22:54–62. Like Peter, have you ever done something hurtful that you thought you would never do? Do you find Peter's story encouraging? Why?

7. How do you feel about the statement "There is not a thought in your mind or a motive in your heart that God does not know":

___Uncomfortable ___Exposed ___Reassured ___Guilty
___Afraid ___Relieved ___Angry ___Other

Explain why you feel that way. Does the fact that God is also loving, merciful, and unchanging affect your answer?

FOCUS ON GOD

On an index card or your favorite electronic device, write the following statement and verse, or just take a picture of it:

**God, because You know everything,
I will come to You with all my questions, concerns, and worries.**

"In Him lie hidden all the treasures of wisdom and knowledge."
(Colossians 2:3)

Look at it when you get up, when you go to bed, and at least once during the day as a way of intentionally shifting your focus from yourself to God. During one of those times each day, take a few minutes to reflect on the positive benefits in your life of God's omniscience.

In preparation for next week, read Genesis chapters 37, 39–41, the story of a man named Joseph. Briefly jot down the major events in Joseph's life as you read, and include the verse references. Bring your notes with you next week.

CHAPTER 17

I Know Everything About You

S hortly after I became a Christian, a friend invited me to a celebration hosted by a man who headed one of the largest oil companies in the world at the time. As I went through the reception line, I knew I was just another nobody to this man. But afterward, the Holy Spirit began to impress upon me that I needed to talk to him about his soul. I obediently called his office, and to my surprise, he agreed to meet with me.

When I arrived for my appointment, I passed by all the various people who screen his visitors and walked into his office. He sat behind a big, mahogany desk in a high-back chair, not a sheet of paper on his desk. "What can I do for you?" he asked.

"Well, sir," I said, "I asked you for fifteen minutes of your time. I don't want to impose. I have come to talk to you about your relationship with Jesus Christ."

Suddenly, he began to cry. As he was sobbing, he told me his story. He became a Christian when he was eight years old, but after attending college and getting involved in business, he turned away from God. He said, "I haven't been to church in thirty years. I have made such a mess out of my life. Some think that I am at the top of the ladder of success, but I feel like a great failure. I seem to have everything, but I have lost my family and everything dear to me."

Before I met with him, I had no way of knowing where this man was spiritually or what he was going through, but God did. As I responded to the Holy Spirit's leading, God opened the door so that this man's life could be turned around. He spontaneously volunteered, "I will be in church on Sunday."

Only God knows us perfectly and intimately. He understands our desires, motives, and thoughts. Nothing about us escapes His notice. In fact, God knows infinitely more about us than we will ever know about ourselves. God also knows what is going on in the lives of the people with whom we come into contact every day. He knows their struggles and has the answer to their problems.

> As our Creator, God custom-designed us for a unique purpose.

God not only knows all about us, but He will never forget us. He even keeps an account of the number of hairs on our heads (Matthew 10:30). God promises through Isaiah:

Can a mother forget the baby at her breast and have no compassion on the child she has borne? Though she may forget, I will not forget you! See, I have engraved you on the palms of My hands. (Isaiah 49:15,16, NIV)

The reference to the engraving on the palms of God's hands is a prophecy about the death of Christ on the cross when the Roman soldiers drove nails through His hands. Christ submitted to death because of His love for us; the nail holes are eternal reminders of that love. No wonder we can have assurance that God will never forget about us!

Consider a few things that demonstrate how well God knows you.

God Knows How You Are Designed

Do you ever feel that your parents do not listen to you, your boss does not respect you, or your coworkers in the church, even the pastor, do not understand you? How devastating to realize that almost no one knows what you are like inside or the dreams you dream. Take heart. Remember that God knows how we are formed (Psalm 103:14). As our Creator, He custom-designed us for a unique purpose.

David declared that the steps of a godly person are directed by the LORD (Psalm 37:23). That means He will guide us as we live our lives for Him. God even "understands how weak we are; He knows we are only dust" (Psalm 103:14).

This assurance was evident in the experience of a pastor of a small church. He became so discouraged that he was ready to give up the ministry. A friend invited him to a prayer summit of pastors. When he got there, he confessed to his group, "I've been so defeated that I don't even think God knows where I am." But God did know where he was. The next day, the other pastors stood in a circle around him and prayed for him, and he had such an overpowering sense of God's presence that he went home walking on air. God knew exactly what this pastor needed to be renewed in his heart and mind. He will help each of us in similar ways because He designed us and knows exactly what we need at every moment.

God Knows Everything About Your Past

God is aware of everything every person has ever done—both good and bad. God told Jeremiah, "The human heart is most deceitful and desperately wicked. Who really knows how bad it is? But I know! I, the LORD, search all hearts and examine secret motives. I give all people their due rewards, according to what their actions deserve" (Jeremiah 17:9,10).

In man's system of justice, accused murderers are brought to trial, then prosecutors use every possible tactic to get the accused convicted. On the other side, defense attorneys use every possible tactic to get the jurors to believe their client is innocent, no matter what the evidence says. Jurors are often swayed by the skill of the attorneys rather than by the facts.

However, our all-knowing God accurately judges not only the actions of people but also the intents of their heart, no matter what excuses they give, no matter how long they seem to get away with their sins. In the next chapter we will learn more about God's justice in greater depth. But let me ask you: What is your reaction to a God who knows every sin you have ever committed? Do you fear your future is doomed because of your past? He has not left us in a hopeless condition.

God loves you unconditionally in spite of your past sin. He will forgive you when you sincerely confess it to Him. We never have to fear that He will discover something in our past that will change His mind about loving us.

God Knows Everything You Face in the Present

When we face challenges or difficulties, the fact that God knows all things is encouraging. Pastor David Jeremiah tells his congregation:

> Our God knows what we are going through. He knows every minute of our pain and suffering. He not only knows what we feel, He also knows why we feel what we feel. He knows how it happened, and how long it's going to last and how intense it is. He knows every emotion associated with it; and when you are going through such difficult times, all you can do sometimes is look and say, "Father, you know…you know."[55]

Whatever your circumstances, whatever your need, God understands and will go through it with you. He knows about your hurt, rejection, and pressures. Your feelings and struggles are not unknown to Him, but He also knows the purposes for your trials. He wants to help you accomplish those purposes and to experience His joy through them. In Him there is hope for a way out and a better tomorrow.

God Knows the Future He Wants for You

Amy Carmichael was one of the most beloved missionaries during the end of the 19th and beginning of the 20th centuries. She served God in India for fifty-five years. Sherwood Eddy wrote, "Amy Wilson Carmichael was the most Christlike character I ever met, and…her life was the most fragrant, the most joyfully sacrificial, that I ever knew."[56]

When she was growing up in Ireland, she desperately wanted blue eyes. With the faith of a child, she truly believed that God would change her brown eyes to blue if she asked Him. One night, she prayed fervently for blue eyes, then confidently went to bed. When she awoke the next morning, she ran to the mirror. Her same brown eyes were reflected in the glass. How disappointed she was!

Later during her years in India, she became aware of the tragic plight of many girls from poor families who were sold to Hindu temples as prostitutes. Amy began rescuing these young girls and bringing them to her home in Dohnavur to raise them and teach them how much God loves them. She would stain her white skin with coffee grounds and dress in Indian clothing so she could sneak into the temples unnoticed. One day as she dressed, she realized that her disguise worked only because she had brown eyes. Blue eyes would have been a dead giveaway! At that moment, she realized that one of the reasons God said no to her prayer as a child was because He had a plan for her future that involved the lives of hundreds of other precious little ones. God had known her future—even when she was a little girl half a world away.

In Ephesians 2:10, Paul tells us, "He has created us anew in Christ Jesus, so that we can do the good things He planned for us long ago." God knew what He had planned for our lives before we were even conceived. He understands our capabilities, opportunities, and life mission. We can trust Him with every moment of our future.

God Knows Which Choices Will Lead to His Best for You

As you were sitting in the classroom in high school or college, you probably thought many times, *I don't see any purpose in all the stuff I'm having to learn.* Or maybe you have a friend who is a sports trivia addict who can spew out an incredible number of statistics on players who were active in the '40s and '50s. What purpose is his knowledge, except to amaze his friends?

God uses His omniscience for more than categorizing information. Peter tells the crowd that Jesus "was handed over to you by God's set purpose and foreknowledge" (Acts 2:23). What was the purpose of this foreknowledge? To establish a way for us to have an intimate relationship with God through His Son, Jesus Christ, whose death and resurrection would result in victory over Satan and eternal death. His purpose was our freedom.

God knew that once you chose to become His child, you would become "holy and blameless" before Him (Ephesians 1:4, NIV).

> Believers often deprive themselves of God's solutions.

Unfortunately, sometimes we think we know better than God does and do not listen to Him. How many times have you gotten impatient with the way your life is going and wanted to go directly from point A to point C? But it is not just getting to the destination that is important. God knows that by taking us through point B, the process of the journey will change us so we will be the kind of people we need to be when we arrive at our destination.

In Jeremiah 29:11, God promises, "I know the plans I have for you," declares the LORD, "plans to prosper you and not to harm you, plans to give you hope and a future" (NIV). Following His plan leads to the best choices for our lives—right now, in the future, and for eternity.

God Knows You Need Wisdom

Because God's Spirit resides within us, we can rely on Him as our Teacher, Counselor, and Guide into all truth. He is willing to share His great knowledge with us. God promises:

> If you need wisdom—if you want to know what God wants you to do— ask Him, and He will gladly tell you. He will not resent your asking. But when you ask Him, be sure that you really expect Him to answer, for a doubtful mind is as unsettled as a wave of the sea that is driven and tossed by the wind. (James 1:5,6)

God is never surprised when we have problems, and He is always with us to help us. But believers often deprive themselves of God's solutions because they do not take time to study His Word (Hosea 4:6). Or they may know the Word but not want to obey it or meet the conditions of God's promises. Thus they do not receive full benefit from God's omniscience.

Solomon writes, "Trust in the LORD with all your heart; do not depend on your own understanding. Seek His will in all you do, and He will direct your paths" (Proverbs 3:5,6). But God's help does not guarantee us a life free of trials and tribulations. In fact, James 1:2–4 and Romans 5:3,4 inform us that God uses our adversity, heartache, testings, and persecutions to bless us.

Trusting God does not eliminate temptation either. Remember how we read earlier, "No temptation has seized you except what is common to man. And God is faithful; He will not let you be tempted beyond what you can bear. But when you are tempted, He will also provide a way out so that you can stand up under it" (1 Corinthians 10:13, NIV). We sometimes wish we knew what that way out would be. Yet when we accept the fact that the God who knows the end from the beginning is providing the way out, we can relax. He has the power to make us victorious.

God knows all about you and loves you unconditionally. I encourage you—yes, I plead with you—to open your heart to Him and determine to walk with Him regardless of the cost. Remind yourself every day of the truth that He knows everything. You will never again feel the same way about your daily personal fellowship with our wonderful God.

In the next chapter, we will explore one of God's attributes that flows from His omniscience—His justice. Since He already knows everything, He can always render a just decision. Combine that with His holiness (His purity and perfection) and He is able to render perfect justice every time.

Talk About It: I Know Everything About You
"Trust in the Lord with all your heart; do not depend on your own understanding. Seek His will in all you do, and He will show you which path to take."
(Proverbs 3:5,6)

1. Have you ever been thankful God answered your prayer with a "No" or "Wait"? Why?

2. Go through Genesis chapters 37, 39–41 and concisely summarize each major event. For example:

   Genesis 37:5–11 <u>Joseph dreams of becoming a ruler</u>

3. In those passages, what skills and character qualities was God teaching Joseph that he was going to need in order to be successful later?

4. Read Genesis 45:3–8. How did Joseph end up viewing both his circumstances and God?

5. Has it ever felt like just as things were looking up in your life, something bad happened? How did it affect your relationship with God?

6. How would you rate your degree of trust and reliance on God's wisdom and knowledge in your life? (1=Not at all; 10=Completely trust His wisdom) Why?

7. Read James 1:5,6. What does God promise? What is His warning? What are some things we are tempted to put our faith in rather than God's wisdom? Why is that?

FOCUS ON GOD

Continue to review the statement and verse you wrote down last week, at least three times each day, to remind yourself that God already knows the answer to all your questions, concerns, and worries.

God, because You know everything,
I will come to You with all my questions, concerns, and worries.

"In Him lie hidden all the treasures of wisdom and knowledge."
(Colossians 2:3)

Are you going through a challenging time and you are not sure what to do or where to turn? What steps are you willing to take this week to seek the wisdom and guidance of the God who knows everything?

In the meantime, let your "continuous conversation" with the One who knows everything about you be a continual source of rest for your soul.

CHAPTER 18

I AM Just

D o you ever wonder what happened to justice? Why is it becoming increasingly elusive? What has gone wrong with the manmade judicial system?

In one of the worst travesties in American justice, four young men from Chicago with no history of violence were convicted of kidnapping, rape, and double murder. The bullet-riddled bodies of a young couple were found on May 12, 1978. Acting on an anonymous telephone tip, the police arrested Dennis Williams, Verneal Jimerson, Kenny Adams, and Willie Rainge. News reports declared that the crime had been solved. The men were soon convicted, and two were sentenced to death row. Appeals failed; all looked hopeless.

In September 1981, a tattered envelope with a return address of the "Condemned Unit," Menard, Illinois, arrived at the offices of the *Chicago Lawyer* magazine. That letter led Rob Warden, editor and publisher of the *Chicago Lawyer*, and Dennis Protess, professor at Northwestern Medill School of Journalism, to investigate the case. They uncovered substantial evidence that exonerated the four convicts, including the first use of DNA to prove that multiple defendants were excluded as suspects in a rape case.

On July 2, 1996, more than eighteen years after the murders took place, Judge Thomas Fitzgerald ended the defendants' fight against an unjust sentence by reading, "All the convictions are vacated."[57] The four prisoners were free! The next day, the state attorney's office charged the real killers, Ira Johnson, Arthur Robinson, and Juan Rodriguez.

Justice is a pillar of any society. It vindicates the innocent and punishes the guilty. All too often, though, this standard is compromised for personal gain. Corrupt judges sometimes tilt the scales of justice; unscrupulous lawyers manipulate laws and juries; witnesses lie. Facts are often distorted to benefit the rich, famous, and powerful.

Today, people are becoming less concerned about doing what is right. In Judges 17:6, God describes it this way: "All the people did whatever seemed right in their own eyes." They bend the rules believing they will never get caught. If their transgression is discovered, they assume they will never be convicted. If they are found guilty, they can always appeal. If the appeal is denied, they will likely serve only a fraction of their sentence anyway. Since our justice system can often be manipulated, many people mistakenly believe they can also manipulate God's justice. They think that their excuses and alibis fool God. But oh how wrong they are! God told Jeremiah, "I the LORD search the heart and examine the mind, to reward a man according to his conduct, according to what his deeds deserve" (Jeremiah 17:10, NIV). You can always count on God being just, because He is perfect and holy in every way.

God Is a Perfect Judge

The Supreme Court is the highest court in our country. If we could expect justice anywhere, it should be when a case comes before these esteemed justices. Yet they are just human. Their caseload is so overwhelming that the solicitor general of the Justice Department chooses from thousands of potential cases to be brought before the court. The Supreme Court Justices are ten times more likely to hear a case if the solicitor general files it.

The staff of the solicitor general has mushroomed in recent years. They file briefs and make appearances in about 150 to 175 cases a year. But think of how many petitions are denied! There is so much paperwork in the Supreme Court system that detailed rules are applied to the way documents are filed, from the precise wording that must appear on the cover to the length of the brief.[58]

With all these constraints, most cases do not make it to the bench. Perfect justice is therefore not being rendered. It is humanly impossible.

But God does not need a brief to examine a case. He does not run out of time to consider the evidence. No research or investigation is needed in His court—He already knows it all. He knows the motives, thoughts, actions, and purpose for everything done. Our only option is to confess before a holy, omniscient, omnipresent, omnipotent, just God.

Justice is not an external system to which God tries to adhere. He did not have to go to law school to learn how to apply the law. God's justice comes out of His inner being and is based on His holiness, truthfulness, and righteousness. Moses observed, "Everything He does is just and fair. He is a faithful God who does no wrong; how just and upright He is!" (Deuteronomy 32:4). God cannot be bribed or corrupted because His judgments are grounded in integrity. Because He has all the facts at His disposal, He cannot be fooled. His decisions are always based upon absolute truth. And when God pronounces judgment, He has the power to carry out the punishment.

> Many people believe they can manipulate God's justice.

God's standard is the benchmark by which all human behavior is measured. God "always acts in a way consistent with the requirements of His character as revealed in His law. He rules His creation with honesty. He keeps His word. He renders to all His creatures their due."[59]

God's attributes assure us of justice. If He were not all-knowing, how could He know whether we sinned deliberately or manipulated the facts to serve our purposes? If He were not present everywhere at once, how could He know all the circumstances surrounding the issue before Him? If He were not all-wise, how could He carry out the judgment in a totally just way?

When Abraham learned that God planned to destroy Sodom and Gomorrah, he argued that God could not destroy the righteous with the unrighteous. He pleaded his case by saying, "Far be it from You to do such a thing—to kill the righteous with the wicked, treating the righteous and the wicked alike. Far be it from You! Will not the Judge of all the earth do right?" (Genesis 18:25, NIV). In the New Testament, James writes, "There is only one Lawgiver and Judge, the one who is able to save and destroy" (James 4:12, NIV). To get a clearer picture of God's role as the perfect Judge, let us look at a few characteristics of an effective judge.

A judge must have authority.

Our government endows judges with authority through the oath they take to execute justice. The law enforcement and prison systems back up the judge's authority. The robe that he wears and having everyone in the courtroom stand as he enters help to emphasize that authority. His gavel and his elevated seat in the courtroom show that he commands the proceedings.

> Perfect justice is humanly impossible.

God, as the Creator of the universe, has the authority to do whatever He deems best with His creation. He is the potter; we are the clay. His throne is high above us in the heavens. His pronouncements are final. There is no higher authority than God.

God will judge *every* wrong act ever committed, *every* sinful motive, *every* evil word. The sentence for these crimes is eternal separation from God. Anything less would compromise His holiness and perfection. If His holiness is compromised, then all of His other attributes are also compromised—including His love. In fact, if God ever compromised His holiness, even once, He would cease to be holy for all of eternity.

But there are those who live in safety with God. These are the ones who have accepted Christ's payment for their sin when He died on the cross. Our loving Savior, Jesus Christ, paid the sentence pronounced by the perfect Judge. God sees these "sinners saved by grace" as righteous in His courtroom. Therefore, they will live eternally in the love, peace, and joy of God's presence.

If you have any doubt about how God will judge you, see Appendix A, "Would You Like to Know God Personally?" to learn more about how Jesus paid the penalty for your sin, so your sins could be forgiven and you could have a relationship with God now and forever.

A judge must have the power to execute his authority.

Can you imagine what would happen if judges had no authority to carry out sentences? Our prisons would be empty. No criminals would be deterred for fear of what the courts would do. Murderers, rapists, robbers, and child molesters could walk the streets terrorizing law-abiding citizens.

Since God is omnipotent (all-powerful), whatever He decides to do He can carry out. He does not have to ask anyone's permission; He does not need a police force to back Him up. In His courtroom, His authority is the last word. No one can appeal His decisions. That is why He is pictured in heaven on a throne. As Sovereign of the universe, His authority and power are total and complete.

A judge must understand and know the law.

Many times, a higher court will throw out the ruling of a judge in a lower court. Why does this happen? Sometimes it is because the judge in the lower court, such as a municipal court, did not have the authority to apply the overarching laws of the state. Other times it is because a lower judge did not properly understand the law. The defendant can appeal his case to the State Supreme Court, which has greater power and can overturn the verdict.

God also follows laws—which He established. We find them in His Word as commands and rules. There is no higher law than God's laws. Not only is He the judge, He is also the lawmaker. Since God's laws are perfect, His justice is also without flaw.

> If a judge is not truthful, honest, and wise justice cannot be served.

A judge needs high moral qualities to judge fairly.

Our court system would fall apart if most judges did not have high morals, for our trials are only as good as the judges who preside over them. Unfortunately, some judges use the courtroom to advance their personal ideologies, instead of enforcing the law. Other judges take bribes because of their greed. Judge Robert Bork tells the story of Judge Martin Manton, a Court of Appeals judge who was almost nominated to the US Supreme Court:

When it became known that Manton took bribes from parties appearing before him, he claimed innocence on the interesting ground that he took bribes from both sides, decided the case on its merits, and then returned the money to the losing party. That defense caused Judge Learned Hand, perhaps the most distinguished court of appeals judge in our history, to call Manton a moral moron.[60]

Would you like to bring your case before a judge like Manton? Corrupt judges lead to injustice and unfairness. Victims do not receive proper consideration. The wronged are helpless; the wicked hold the power. If the judge is not truthful, honest, and wise in presiding over the courtroom, justice cannot be served.

A Just God Hates Sin

As the holy and righteous Sovereign of the universe, God cannot ignore or overlook any act of sin—not even one. King David writes, "God is an honest judge. He is angry with the wicked every day" (Psalm 7:11).

God's anger over sin should never be underestimated: "You spread out our sins before You—our secret sins—and You see them all. We live our lives beneath Your wrath…Who can comprehend the power of Your anger? Your wrath is as awesome as the fear You deserve" (Psalm 90:8,9,11).

You cannot grasp how deeply God loves you until you understand how profoundly He hates your sin. This is why Jesus, God's only Son, had to die in your place in order to pay the full penalty for your sin, satisfying God's perfect justice.

I urge you to live in reverential fear of God, continually searching God's Word and examining your heart for sins that you need to confess to Him. Unconfessed sin hinders your relationship with God here on earth. It makes it difficult to hear His voice and experience His presence, and impossible to be filled with His peace and joy.

One of the greatest truths I have discovered in over 50 years of walking with the Lord is a concept called "Spiritual Breathing." This process is similar to physical breathing. As we become aware of our sins, we *exhale* by confessing our sin to God (1 John 1:9). Then we *inhale* to appropriate (take in) the power of the Holy Spirit, based on God's command to be filled with the Spirit (Ephesians 5:18). We can know that God will fill, enable, and equip us because He promised to hear and answer our prayers in accordance with His perfect will (1 John 5:14,15). This spiritual principle has allowed me to walk in fellowship with God and help others come to know and serve Him. This is the privilege of every believer.

To learn more about "Spiritual Breathing" and how to be filled and empowered by the Spirit of God every moment of every day, see Appendix B, "How to Be Filled With the Holy Spirit."

God Will Eventually Punish All Sin

The Bible tells us, "God will bring every deed into judgment, including every hidden thing, whether it is good or evil" (Ecclesiastes 12:14, NIV). Yet, I am sure there have been times when you have asked, "Why are the wicked so prosperous? Why are evil people so happy?" (Jeremiah 12:1). There may be several reasons why someone appears to be getting away with wrongdoing without being punished. Here are two:

- God delays His judgment because He is patiently providing an opportunity for us to repent. But while God is waiting for repentance, the severity of future punishment is mounting if we do not repent.
- Sometimes we do not recognize God's judgment because it occurs in a way that we did not expect. The apostle Paul explains, "Do not be deceived: God cannot be mocked. A man reaps what he sows" (Galatians 6:7, NIV). The more seeds of sin a person sows, the more harm will result. Sin is like an addictive poison. If you drink a little poison you may only get sick. But if you keep on drinking poison, it will eventually kill you.

The final judgment will occur at the end of time. Are you spiritually ready for that day of judgment? We will look at what is going to happen during that awesome time later in this chapter.

God Built Natural Consequences into Sin

God does not wait until Judgment Day to settle sin accounts. He also built natural consequences into sin as a deterrent for our disobedient behavior.

I am reminded of a friend who was one of the most remarkable preachers and pulpit personalities I know. He was a pastor of a thriving church. Then one day, a prostitute came to his office seeking his counsel. He felt sorry for her and asked his wife if this prostitute could live in their home so they could rehabilitate her.

After living with them for three weeks, the prostitute told his wife that she wanted her husband. The wife just laughed in disbelief. They had a happy home and several children. He was one of the pillars in the Christian community. Yet to everyone's shock, he eventually left his family to live with this prostitute.

Many people from the Christian community pleaded with him to repent of his sinful lifestyle, but he persisted. This former pastor had several illegitimate children, and in time the prostitute deserted him for another man.

Finally, this former pastor did come back to the Lord, but he had been brought so low that despite his giftedness he could not hold a job. The last time I saw him, he was a haggard man weeping over his illegitimate children, wishing they would come to know the Lord. Finally, he went to his grave prematurely—a broken man, his life in shambles, and his family devastated.

> God cannot ignore or overlook any act of sin.

We cannot thumb our noses at God's righteous principles and not expect to experience the just consequences of our actions. A reverential fear of God will help us avoid doing anything to hinder our relationship with Him. I live daily in reverential fear of God because when we disobey Him, we open the door to greater temptations. Sin grows until it totally engulfs us in destruction.

God Will Exercise the Final Judgment

We need mention only two of God's judgments in the Old Testament—the flood in Noah's time and the destruction of Sodom and Gomorrah during Abraham's time—to recognize that many sinners receive God's judgments here on earth.

God predicts judgment for the ungodly: "It is mine to avenge; I will repay. In due time their foot will slip; their day of disaster is near and their doom rushes upon them" (Deuteronomy 32:35, NIV). Yet many live as though they will never be judged. They scoff at the idea of an eternal hell.

The final judgment has, however, been part of the biblical message for thousands of years. The Holy Spirit inspired Paul to write this ominous warning:

> Because of your stubbornness and your unrepentant heart, you are storing up wrath against yourself for the day of God's wrath, when His righteous judgment will be revealed. God "will give to each person according to what he has done." To those who by persistence in doing good seek glory, honor and immortality, He will give eternal life. But for those who are self-seeking and who reject the truth and follow evil, there will be wrath and anger. (Romans 2:5–8, NIV)

Those are hard words from a holy, just God. In Revelation, we have a visual description of that final Judgment Day of wrath:

> Then I saw a great white throne and Him who was seated on it. Earth and sky fled from His presence, and there was no place for them. And I saw the dead, great and small, standing before the throne, and books were opened. Another book was opened, which is the book of life. The dead were judged according to what they had done as recorded in the books. The sea gave up the dead that were in it, and death and Hades gave up the dead that were in them, and each person was judged according to what he had done. Then death and Hades were thrown into the lake of fire. The lake of fire is the second death. If anyone's name was not found written in the book of life, he was thrown into the lake of fire. (Revelation 20:11–15, NIV)

I never want to face that judgment seat! Thankfully, those of us who have trusted Christ will not appear before the Great White Throne judgment of unrepentant sinners. All believers will appear before Christ's judgment seat. This is a not a judgment of sin, but of how faithfully we have followed and served our Savior with the opportunities and talents He gave us. Then, we will receive rewards for what we have done for Christ in the power of the Holy Spirit. In our next chapter, we will learn more about how God's justice works on behalf of those who follow Christ.

Talk About It: I AM Just

"Everything He does is just and fair. He is a faithful God who does no wrong; how just and upright He is!"
(Deuteronomy 32:4)

1. What are strengths and weaknesses of our legal system? Do you believe justice is always served by our legal system? Why?
2. What are some reasons judges do not render perfect justice 100 percent of the time?
3. Which of God's other attributes ensure He always can and always will be perfectly just?
4. Indicate whether you agree or disagree with the following statements, and explain why.
   a. God would be unjust if He ignored or excused any of my sin.
   b. Since God is love, His love always trumps His justice when the two are in conflict.
   c. The point of Jesus' death on the cross was to demonstrate how much God loves us. But if I am a good person, accepting Jesus' sacrifice is unnecessary in order to go to heaven.
   d. Accepting Jesus' payment for my sin is a necessary first step, but then I have to be a good person to make it into heaven.
5. Why do you think it is hard for some people to accept that God's justice can only be satisfied through Jesus' payment for our sin?
6. Read James 4:12. Why do you think God says He's the only One who can judge? What is the difference between judging and speaking the truth in love?

FOCUS ON GOD

On an index card or your favorite electronic device, write the following statement and verse, or just take a picture of it:

**God, because You are just,
I know Your justice will prevail.**

"Everything He does is just and fair."
(Deuteronomy 32:4)

Look at it when you get up, when you go to bed, and at least once during the day as a way of intentionally shifting your focus from yourself to God. During one of those times each day, take a few minutes to reflect on the positive benefits in your life of God's justice.

CHAPTER 19

My Justice Works for Your Good

At every age, we recognize that many situations in life are not fair or just. If you have watched preschoolers play, you will soon hear, "That's not fair. I had it first." A high school student is killed in an accident caused by a drunk driver and the parents' question, "Where's the justice? The drunk driver has barely a scratch, and our child is dead!" A pastor faithfully serving the Lord watches his wife, the mother of their three children, die of cancer. In his despair he wonders aloud about the justice of it all.

Yet the Bible is very clear in announcing that God is just. After leading the people of Israel for forty years in the wilderness, Moses said, "Everything He does is just and fair. He is a faithful God who does no wrong; how just and upright He is!" (Deuteronomy 32:4).

There is, however, not always an immediately apparent relationship between what we have done and what happens to us. Because questions about the justice of God plague us, let us consider practical implications of the statement, "Our God is just."

God's Patience Toward Sinners

Justice delayed is often justice denied. If a defense lawyer can keep postponing a murder case, for example, evidence that is available in a speedy trial becomes useless. Witnesses may die or move away. The defense can challenge the validity of a witness's memory. Police departments misplace evidence.

What about justice for Christians? Sometimes they are unjustly targeted because of their faith. Nina Shea writes in *In the Lion's Den*, "Christians are the chief victims of this religious persecution around the world today."[61] Today hundreds of Christians will die or suffer brutality because of what they believe.

In Morocco, Rachid Cohen, a Jewish man who had received Christ as his Savior, was arrested and tortured for ten hours a day. He was burned with cigarettes, shocked in a low-voltage chair, and forced to sit in his own excrement. In China, persecutors beat, starve, and shock believers with electric probes. Thousands of stories of injustice toward believers have been documented.

Consider how God felt about the evil people living during the time of Noah. They all deserved the maximum punishment. If you had been God, how quickly would you have followed through on your threat to destroy the wicked? Would you have waited a week? A month? A year? More than five years?

Although the violation of God's justice had been described in detail, God did not act immediately. He invited Noah to build an ark to save himself, his family, and representatives of every animal group. Without modern tools, it took Noah 120 years to build that ark.[62] Did the sin of the people decrease at all during that period of divine patience? No. Even after 120 years, only Noah and his family qualified to be rescued from the destructive flood.

> All believers are saved because God delays His justice.

So why did God not act immediately after declaring that He would destroy all humans except Noah and his family? Second Peter 3:9 says, "The Lord isn't really being slow about His promise, as some people think. No, He is being patient for your sake. He does not want anyone to be destroyed, but wants everyone to repent."

All believers are saved because God delays His justice. At what age did you discover God's love and forgiveness? At 15 or 30 or 70? Whatever age you and I received God's promise of eternal life was more than enough time for God to have caused His wrath to fall on us. How many evil deeds had we committed before that day? How many people had we hurt? How many sins had we excused? None of us deserve even one day of life because of our sinful, depraved nature, so we ought to be grateful for a just God who delays punishment.

Dr. Cyril E. M. Joad, a famous skeptic, was head of the Philosophy Department at the University of London for many years. Dr. Joad and his colleagues, Julian Huxley, Bertrand Russell, H. G. Wells, and Bernard Shaw, have probably done more to undermine the faith of the collegiate world of subsequent generations than any other group. Dr. Joad believed and taught that God was an impersonal part of the cosmos and that there is no such thing as sin.

Did God strike him dead? Did He send a crippling disease? No, but before he died, Dr. Joad became convinced that the only explanation for sin was found in the Word of God—and the only solution for sin was the cross of Jesus Christ. He became a zealous follower of Jesus. No doubt many of his followers turned to faith in God through his testimony and writings. God's long-suffering and incredible patience brought this skeptic to his knees at the cross. Truly, God's delayed justice is an opportunity for His mercy to be shown to many.

God Is Aware of Injustice

In 1960, Raleigh Washington joined the army. He was quickly promoted from captain to major and then lieutenant colonel. He was well on his way to becoming a general when a group of white officers falsely accused Raleigh, who is black, of conduct unbecoming an officer.

Although none of the accusations were proven, he was given the choice of retirement in lieu of being discharged. But to get his retirement benefits, he had to admit that he was guilty. He refused. He was discharged one day short of twenty years of service, and therefore was disqualified from all of his retirement benefits. At the time, his wife was pregnant with their fifth child.

How would you have reacted? Since he had become a Christian two years earlier, Raleigh decided not to be bitter against the whites who had mistreated him. Instead, he applied to Trinity Divinity School to study to become a pastor. As a student, his income dropped by 90 percent. How he could have used that retirement income! But the Lord provided for the family's finances in exciting ways. When he graduated, the Evangelical Free Church recruited him to plant churches. Although he was their only black pastor, the white church members enthusiastically supported his church-planting efforts.

While he was planting his church, he met a Jewish lawyer named Jeff Strange, who learned about his military case. For the next nine years, Jeff worked to reverse the decision the army had made. Raleigh says, "Finally, I was reinstated for one day, so that I might retire. My retirement was made retroactive to 1980, and I received the accrued retirement benefits. In addition, they cleared my record and every document against me was destroyed. My military record was made immaculate.

"God uniquely sustained me and my wife and protected me from becoming bitter when falsely accused. Because I did not get bitter, God used whites to embrace my ministry, to support me, to befriend me. God used that time after my dismissal from the Army to teach my wife and me to walk by faith."[63]

We may encounter injustice in any place at any time. But God has His own way of righting wrongs. Even if someone deals with us unfairly, God is still in control. If you are the only Christian on a police force, in a fire station, an athletic team, or on a school faculty, you may be experiencing ribbing, even harassment for your faith. In fact, you may even be passed over for promotion or fired because of your Christian convictions. Where is justice when this happens? Why does God not act?

That is a question only God can answer, but we do know that He is aware of every injustice. Within the scope of eternity, He makes everything right.

Through the prophets in the Old Testament God demonstrated His concern for those who were mistreated, abused, and denied opportunities to participate fully in the life of the community. As a result, He often allowed foreign armies to oppress the people of Israel and Judah. Instead of seeing rich and fertile fields, choice vineyards and pleasant gardens, God saw crops of injustice, bloodshed, and oppression. He saw how the greedy landowners oppressed the poor. He saw the injustice in the courts, where the bribes of the affluent deprived the poor of justice. He witnessed the murder of innocent people (Isaiah 5:1–10).

Jesus told a story about a judge who was approached by a widow pleading, "Grant me justice against my adversary" (Luke 18:3, NIV). For some time this judge refused to respond to the widow. Finally she became so persistent that he said, "I will see that she gets justice, so that she won't eventually wear me out with her coming!" (Luke 18:5, NIV). Jesus relates this story to the suffering of the ones He loves: "Will not God bring about justice for His chosen ones, who cry out to Him day and night? Will He keep putting them off? I tell you, He will see that they get justice, and quickly" (Luke 18:7,8, NIV),

> Within the scope of eternity, God makes everything right.

Sometimes we will see almost instant justice. On other occasions, we must wait. And at times we will not receive justice until after we join our heavenly Father in His home in heaven. But we can be assured that God sees it all—and that He cares about the mistreated even more than we do.

Blessings and Judgment

When the Supreme Court was formed in the late 1700s, the first order of business was to fill in the details of the judiciary. After the lower federal courts were established and the new justices appointed, it was time to hear cases. The initial Court session began on February 1, 1790, in the Royal Exchange Building in the heart of what is now New York City's financial district. Robert Wagman writes, "When it became apparent that the five justices would have absolutely nothing to do, the session was adjourned after ten days."[64] On August 2, they met again, but once more they had nothing to do, so they adjourned for the year. It was not until February 1793 that the Court heard its first case.

Although the Supreme Court's jurisdiction was more narrow back then, can you imagine if today's Supreme Court adjourned early for a lack of cases to hear? Because of the tremendous number of cases presented to the Supreme Court today, it must limit itself to four cases per day. Each side gets one hour to present its arguments. The Justices hear cases two weeks, then recess for two weeks to allow them to write their opinions on these cases. The docket is always packed. Obviously, much has changed in two hundred years!

America has been greatly blessed because our ancestors acknowledged God's supreme sovereignty and their complete dependence on Him. They believed Psalm 33:12, "Blessed is the nation whose God is the LORD" (NIV).

Although America was never a theocracy, Christian values were cherished and publicly promoted, and laws were established that promoted biblical morality.

As we prospered we began to feel self-sufficient and to see our greatness as the product of our own abilities rather than the result of God's blessing. Abraham Lincoln said in 1863:

> We have been the recipients of the choicest bounties of Heaven; we have been preserved these many years in peace and prosperity; we have grown in numbers, wealth, and power as no other nation has ever grown. But we have forgotten God. We have vainly imagined in the deceitfulness of our hearts that all these blessings were produced by some superior wisdom and virtue of our own. Intoxicated with unbroken success, we have become too self-sufficient to feel the necessity of redeeming and preserving grace, too proud to pray to the God that made us.[65]

For the past several decades, our nation has taken drastic steps to divorce itself from God's standards of righteousness. What has happened since then? Scholastic Aptitude Test (SAT) scores have dropped dramatically. Pregnancies, rapes, aggravated assaults, and murders have increased at an alarmingly epidemic rate among our teenagers. Suicide has become the second leading cause of death among adolescents. Gangs have turned many urban schools into war zones. The US now leads the world in illegal drug use, exporting of pornography, divorce rates, abortion, and violent crime, and we lead the Western world in teenage pregnancies and illiteracy.

Thomas Jefferson wrote about the foolishness of abandoning God:

> God who gave us life gave us liberty. And can the liberties of a nation be thought secure when we have removed their only firm basis—a conviction in the minds of the people that these liberties are the gift of God? That they are not to be violated but with His wrath? Indeed, I tremble for my country when I reflect that God is just; that His justice cannot sleep forever.[66]

We are in danger of reaping God's judgment. If our country is lost, it is only because we as Christians have not obeyed our Lord's command to be salt and light to the people around us. You may be asking, "What can I do to help turn the tide of godlessness and immorality?" In 2 Chronicles 7:14, God's conditional promise begins with your willingness to humbly come before Him to admit your disobedience and indifference and seek His forgiveness. Then ask God to cleanse your heart from all wrongdoing. Pray that He will rekindle your first love for Him and once again send revival to your heart, your church and community, our nation, and our world.

Christ Will Judge Believers

Our just God is not primarily concerned with punishing disobedience, but with rewarding right behavior. Yet God will reward only those who accept Christ's penalty for sin because His payment for our sins opened the way for God to reward us for what we do for Him.

> Do you trust God's perfect justice?

Christ will evaluate each believer's life to determine rewards for faithful obedience and service or loss for disobedience. Paul explains, "We must all stand before Christ to be judged. We will each receive whatever we deserve for the good or evil we have done in our bodies" (2 Corinthians 5:10). Jesus will consider several factors when we appear before His judgment seat.

- He will judge the words we have spoken (Matthew 12:36,37).
- He will judge the deeds we have done.
- He will judge our motives (Colossians 3:23,24).
- He will judge our faithfulness (Matthew 25:21).

God will also reward those who lead others to Christ. God told Daniel:

Those who are wise will shine like the brightness of the heavens, and those who lead many to righteousness, like the stars for ever and ever. (Daniel 12:3, NIV)

Every believer should desire to hear Jesus say these words: "Well done, My good and faithful servant" (Matthew 25:21). Hebrews assures us, "God is not unjust; He will not forget your work and the love you have shown Him as you have helped His people and continue to help them" (Hebrews 6:10, NIV).

Are you living for the glory of God or for self-satisfaction? There is an incredible reward awaiting the person who seeks to glorify God. Paul is so sure of this reward that he writes:

Whatever you do, work at it with all your heart, as working for the Lord, not for men, since you know that you will receive an inheritance from the Lord as a reward. It is the Lord Christ you are serving. (Colossians 3:23,24, NIV)

Do you trust God's perfect justice? It is undergirded by His holiness, truth, and righteousness and perfectly administered through His omniscience, omnipotence, and omnipresence. He is the perfect Judge.

Talk About It: My Justice Works for Your Good
"The Lord isn't really being slow about His promise, as some people think. No, He is being patient for your sake. He does not want anyone to be destroyed, but wants everyone to repent."
(2 Peter 3:9)

1. What do you learn about the timing of God's justice in 2 Peter 3:8–10? What do you learn about the ultimate enforcement of His justice?
2. How do you respond when someone appears to "get away with" doing wrong?

3. How do you respond when someone wrongs you? Read Romans 12:19,20. If God is going to take care of it, how should that affect the way you respond? Why?

4. Read Galatians 6:7–9. In what ways could someone mock the justice of God? Can you think of a time where you, in effect, "mocked" the justice of God?

5. Justice reflects punishment owed for doing something wrong as well as rewards due for choosing to do what is right. When you think of God's justice, do you primarily think of His punishment for sin or His rewards for faithfulness? Why?

6. Read 2 Corinthians 5:10. What motivates you more: the potential of reward, honor, and joy, or the potential of loss or shame? Review your timeline from Chapter 1 and think about what motivated you most at each step along the way.

7. How do we align our hearts, mind, and actions with God's justice? (Read Philippians 4:8.)

FOCUS ON GOD

Continue to review the statement and verse you wrote down last week, at least three times each day, to remind yourself that God is just, allowing them to become a part of your "continuous conversation" with God. Ask Him to help you align your heart, mind, and actions with His justice, but leave final judgment to Him.

**God, because You are just,
I know Your justice will prevail.**

"Everything He does is just and fair."
(Deuteronomy 32:4)

CHAPTER 20

I AM Faithful

One day in Armenia in 1988, Samuel and Danielle sent their young son, Armand, off to school. Samuel squatted before his son and looked him in the eye. "Have a good day at school, and remember, no matter what, I'll always be there for you." He hugged his young son, and the boy ran off to school.

Hours later, a powerful earthquake rocked the area. Buildings crumbled; electrical power went out everywhere; people panicked. In the midst of the pandemonium, Samuel and Danielle tried to discover what happened to their son. As the day wore on, the radio announced that casualty estimates were in the thousands. People were trapped under beams and rubble in flattened buildings—even schools were destroyed.

Kissing his wife, Samuel grabbed his coat and headed for the school yard. When he reached the area, what he saw brought tears to his eyes. Armand's school was a pile of debris. Other grief-stricken parents stood nearby, weeping.

Samuel found the place where Armand's classroom used to be and began pulling a broken beam off the pile of rubble. He picked up a rock and put it to the side, then another, and another.

One of the parents looking on asked, "What are you doing?"

"Digging for my son," Samuel answered.

The man exclaimed, "You're just going to make things worse! This building is unstable," and tried to pull Samuel away from his work.

Samuel just asked, "Are you going to help me?"

The man's wife shook her head sadly, "They're dead. It's no use."

Samuel set his jaw and continued digging. As time wore on, one by one, the other parents left. Concerned, a firefighter tried to pull Samuel away from the rubble. "What are you doing?" he asked.

"Digging for my son," was the reply.

"Fires are breaking out. You're in danger. We'll take care of it."

"Will you help me?" Samuel asked without stopping his work.

The firefighter instead hurried off to a more pressing emergency, leaving Samuel still digging.

All through the night and into the next day, Samuel continued digging, his hole growing larger. Parents placed flowers and pictures of their children on the ruins. Soon, a row of photos of young, happy faces smiled up from the rubble. But Samuel just squared his shoulders and snatched up a beam. Wedging it under a stubborn boulder, he tried to pry it out of the way. Finally, the boulder gave.

A faint "Help!" came from under the rubble. Samuel stopped his work and listened. He could hear nothing. He kept digging.

The faint voice came again. "Papa?"

Samuel recognized the voice! "Armand!" He began to dig furiously. Finally, he could see his young son. "Come out, son!" he said with relief.

"No," Armand said. "Let the other kids out first, 'cause I know you'll get me."

Child after child emerged until, finally, a sputtering Armand appeared. Samuel took him in his arms.

"I told the other kids not to worry," Armand said confidently. "I told them that if you were alive, you'd save me and when you saved me, they'd be saved. You promised you'd always be there for me."

Fourteen children were saved that day because one father was faithful.[67]

How much more faithful is our heavenly Father! Whether trapped by fallen debris in an earthquake or trapped by life's hardships and struggles, we are never cut off from His love for us. As Jeremiah writes, "Because of the LORD's great love we are not consumed, for His compassions never fail. They are new every morning; great is Your faithfulness" (Lamentations 3:22,23, NIV).

The Ancient Patriarchs Trusted God's Faithfulness

There are many examples throughout Scripture of those who believed God would be faithful to keep His promises. The Old Testament highlights the lives of many of the patriarchs who trusted in God's faithfulness. They staked their lives, the lives of their loved ones, and their futures on God's word. Hebrews chapter 11 highlights many of them.

Hebrews 11:7 mentions Noah, who "built an ark to save his family from the flood. He obeyed God, who warned him about something that had never happened before." God was faithful to bring them through the flood alive.

Abraham is sometimes called the "father of the faith." Hebrews says, "It was by faith that Sarah together with Abraham was able to have a child, even though they were too old and Sarah was barren. Abraham believed that God would keep his promise" (Hebrews 11:11). Abraham believed that God would keep His commitment to provide an heir because *he considered God faithful.* In time, God did send a son, Isaac, to Abraham and Sarah. Isaac became the physical link to the Messiah, Jesus Christ.

> God's faithfulness means all His attributes work at full capacity at all times.

The most serious challenge to Abraham's trust came when God asked him to sacrifice his own son. Strengthened by his experience with God's faithfulness to His promises, Abraham bound Isaac and placed him on an altar, lifting the knife to sacrifice his son to God. Abraham believed that when God said He would provide a physical line through Isaac, God would fulfill that promise—even if it meant raising Isaac from the dead. That is when God, who is faithful, provided the ram in the thicket as a substitute for Isaac (Genesis 22:13).

About one hundred years later, Isaac blessed his son, Jacob, believing that God would be faithful to the promise He made to Abraham. His family was small, but God promised that his offspring would be as numerous as the stars in the sky or the sand on the seashore.

Approximately 500 years passed and the parents of Moses hid him for three months after he was born even though Pharaoh had commanded that all male Israelite babies be killed. They knew God had a special purpose for their son, and trusted God would be faithful to take care of him.

In the experience of the patriarchs, God did not exist in a vacuum. He was working in their behalf at each step of life's journey. Their faith flowered into heroic deeds because they trusted in an absolutely faithful God. Their God was faithful down to the smallest detail.

God's Faithfulness to Us

All of us understand a little bit of how an automobile engine functions. Pistons, fan belts, water pumps, and thousands of moving parts all whirl around within a small space, making power for us to drive our car. Each piece in the motor has a different part to play in helping the engine function as it should. If one piece gets even a fraction of an inch out of line, the engine malfunctions. At the same time, oil and coolant circulate to keep the engine running smoothly. The parts all work together harmoniously as part of the whole engine.

That is the way God's attributes function too. If you took away love, God's character would not be complete. God's love works with all other attributes, like His justice, to produce the right kind of results. We can compare God's faithfulness to the oil in the engine that keeps the internal parts running smoothly. God's faithfulness means that each attribute in His character is working at full capacity at all times. When does God's love fail? Never, because He is faithful. When is God less than holy? Never, because His character is pure and He is always faithful to who He is and what He says. Therefore, you can count on Him to keep His promises and carry out His purposes.

> God's faithfulness is not affected by anyone's lack of faith.

God's faithfulness is at the core of His nature. He is always all-knowing, all-powerful, ever-present, holy, righteous, merciful, and loving because He is faithful to His own character. He never changes any of His attributes to accommodate someone else's wishes. Paul drew on that knowledge when he wrote to the Thessalonians that they could depend on God because "the one who calls you is faithful and He will do it" (1 Thessalonians 5:24, NIV). The psalmist writes, "Your faithfulness continues through all generations; you established the earth, and it endures" (Psalm 119:90).

So when you get up in the morning and the sun is shining, thank God for His faithfulness. When you look outside and find it raining, thank God for His faithfulness in watering the earth and all the plants on it. If, as evening approaches, lightning flashes and a thunderstorm roars, thank God for His faithfulness in producing valuable nitrogen to renew the plants and trees. Truly, God's faithfulness is new every morning and refreshes us every night.

God's Faithfulness Is Not Changed by Man's Response

We tend to put conditions on our relationships. "If you look good, I will love you." "If you have lots of money, you can be part of my inner circle." "If you do this for me, I'll do that for you."

God's faithfulness, however, is unconditional. We can sometimes see that quality reflected in the godly examples of faithfulness among His people. Let me give you an example.

Dr. Robertson McQuilkin was the well-loved president of the highly respected Columbia International University. When his wife began to show symptoms of Alzheimer's disease, Dr. McQuilkin resigned his distinguished position to care for her. Such faithful commitment lifts our spirits because this kind of sacrifice is so rare. We realize that actions like these are not normal to our human nature, but that they must come from a higher source.

God's faithfulness is so much a part of who He is that He cannot become unfaithful to anyone—whether to grateful believers or to skeptics who doubt the reality of God—despite the cost. Paul assures us, "If we are faithless, He will remain faithful, for He cannot disown Himself" (2 Timothy 2:13, NIV).

God also is faithful to us when we feel we have no faith left in us. Paul writes: "What if some did not have faith? Will their lack of faith nullify God's faithfulness? Not at all! Let God be true, and every man a liar" (Romans 3:3, NIV). God's faithfulness is not affected by anyone's lack of faith.

God Keeps His Promises

It follows then, that in His faithfulness, God *always* keeps His covenants and promises—without fail. The psalmist declares: "He remembers His covenant forever, the word He commanded, for a thousand generations" (Psalm 105:8, NIV). Paul writes, "No matter how many promises God has made, they are 'Yes' in Christ. And so through Him the 'Amen' [so be it] is spoken by us to the glory of God" (2 Corinthians 1:20, NIV).

That is why we can completely trust God's Word. The writer to the Hebrews reminds us, "Let us hold unswervingly to the hope we profess, for He who promised is faithful" (Hebrews 10:23, NIV).

One way I have seen God's faithfulness over the years is that His Word produces fruit in the lives of those who love Him. As reporter Clarence W. Hall followed American troops through Okinawa in 1945, he and his Jeep driver came upon a small town that stood out as a beautiful example of a Christian community. He reported, "The old men proudly showed us their spotless homes, their terraced fields, and their prized sugar mills." The newsman saw no jails and no drunkenness, and divorce was unknown in the town.

Why was this village so unusual? An American missionary had come thirty years earlier and introduced two elderly townspeople to Christ and left them with a Japanese Bible. These new believers studied the Bible and in turn introduced their fellow villagers to Jesus.

The reporter's Jeep driver was equally amazed at the difference: "So this is what comes out of only a Bible and a couple of old guys who wanted to live like Jesus." God's faithfulness to His Word had resulted in the transformation of the whole village.

I have found God faithful to His Word on tithing and sacrificial giving. When God's Word tells me, "God loves a cheerful giver" (2 Corinthians 9:7, NIV), I believe it. When I read, "God is able to make all grace abound to you, so that in all things at all times, having all that you need, you will abound in every good work" (2 Corinthians 9:8, NIV), I believe it—and act on it. I constantly check to make sure that our tithes are paid up-to-date. I would rather live on bread and water to save money than to get behind in paying our tithes. Over the years, God has also provided me with many opportunities to give offerings above my tithe, and to help the poor, all motivated by a spirit of gratitude and compassion, never guilt or obligation. In all my years of ministry, God has always provided everything I have needed in order to do what He wanted me to do. He is faithful!

God never forgets a promise He has made. He is perfectly capable of standing behind His Word. God is ready and able to deliver all He has promised. But we must claim His generous promises!

Exercising Our Faith

I recently boarded a plane in Europe bound for the United States. A man I had never seen before, whose name I did not even know, boarded the same plane, entered the captain's cabin and seated himself at the controls. A short time later, the aircraft began to move, and soon—by some means that I do not fully understand—it left the ground. Hours later we touched down in Orlando.

Not once during our flight did it occur to me to question the man at the controls. I never even thought to ask for his pilot's license or some other identification to prove he was capable of flying that plane. I never asked him to explain to me the physical laws by which he could keep such a heavy object in the air. I have flown millions of miles to most parts of the world. On each of those flights, I have placed my faith in such a stranger, believing he was capable of taking me safely to my destination.

Every day in hundreds of similar situations, believers and nonbelievers alike exercise faith without even thinking twice. If we have such unquestioning faith in fellow human beings—who are not only fallible, but also deliberately sinful and even unfaithful at times—how much more should we put all our faith in God, whose character and capabilities for faithfulness are beyond question?

> God is reliable. He is trustworthy. He cannot be otherwise.

God is reliable. He is trustworthy. He cannot be otherwise. His faithfulness ensures that every attribute we have looked at so far is available to us. He wants us to reflect His faithfulness on earth. He is the example; we are His ambassadors to the world. Yet even though we understand this fact, in our humanity, we must grow in our Christian experience. That means exercising our faith in Him daily to build our trust in God as the Faithful One. Each time He proves Himself faithful in our life, our trust will become stronger.

What can you trust God for today that you were unable to trust Him for yesterday? What circumstances do you struggle with that you can begin turning over to Him? Exercising faith is just like exercising a muscle. The more you use it, the stronger it becomes. If you have difficulty trusting God, take a small step of faith today. Then lengthen these steps in the days to come.

In the next chapter, we will discover additional ways we can become more faithful in response to God's faithfulness to us.

Talk About It: I AM Faithful

"O Lord God of Heaven's Armies! ... You are entirely faithful."
(Psalm 89:8)

1. What are some reasons we are not always faithful to keep our promises and commitments?
2. If God's faithfulness means that each attribute in His character is working at full capacity at all times, how does that impact His other attributes? Why does that matter? What difference should it make in your life today?
3. What do you think about the fact that God's faithfulness is not affected by anyone's lack of faith? Does this mean our faith or lack of faith in God is irrelevant? Why?
4. If God's faithfulness were dependent on our faith, what implication would that have for His other attributes?
5. If you do not give back to God when your budget is tight how does that reflect your view of God's faithfulness? Why? What does that say about your view of His love, power, justice, and omniscience?

6. Read Hebrews 10:23. Is it challenging for you to trust that God is faithful to all His promises? Why or why not? What is one step you can take today to exercise your trust in God and His faithfulness?

FOCUS ON GOD

On an index card or your favorite electronic device, write the following statement and verse, or just take a picture of it:

God, because You are faithful,
I will trust You to always keep Your promises

"He who promised is faithful."
(Hebrews 10:23, NIV)

Look at it when you get up, when you go to bed, and at least once during the day as a way of intentionally shifting your focus from yourself to God. Thank Him for His faithfulness in your life each day and ask Him to help you exercise greater trust in Him this week.

This next week, each time you sit down and read a promise that God makes in the Bible, ask God the following question: "God, do you really mean it for me?" If you ask that with a sincere and open heart, God's Word will quickly grow into a great source of daily encouragement.

CHAPTER 21

You Can Trust Me

Unfaithfulness has become a hallmark of contemporary society. Too often, husbands and wives are unfaithful in keeping their marriage vows. Many excuse their self-centeredness by saying "God wants me to be happy," as though God approves of their unfaithfulness. Parents are frequently unfaithful in their commitment to the well-being of their children. Children tend to disobey their parents. Employees do not always serve their employers as they should, and some employers take advantage of those who work for them.

God is the only one we can completely trust because He has the integrity and flawless character that enables Him to be absolutely faithful to His Word and commitments. No one else can fulfill all promises as He does.

The Bible is filled with praises for the faithfulness of God. David writes, "Your unfailing love, O Lord, is as vast as the heavens; Your faithfulness reaches beyond the clouds" (Psalm 36:5). Psalm 89:8 declares, "O Lord God Almighty! Where is there anyone as mighty as you, Lord? Faithfulness is your very character."

But merely understanding God's faithfulness is only part of our responsibility as Christians. God's faithfulness is the essential foundation for building faithfulness in our lives. Let me give you an analogy that will help explain this principle.

The sun is the most important body in our sky. From it we get warmth, light, and beauty. If the sun would ever burn out, we could not survive. The moon is also a familiar sight in our sky. It has its own beauty, but it does not provide us with heat or light. All the light that comes from the moon is actually a reflection from the sun.

Almost every year, you could travel to some place in the United States to see a lunar eclipse. It usually lasts an hour or two. It is caused when the Earth moves between the moon and the sun, and the Earth's shadow falls upon the moon. Because the moon generates no light of its own, when the sun's light does not strike the surface of the moon, the moon is dark. We cannot see it.

We are like the moon. In our own strength, we cannot be faithful. At best, we are inconsistent, wavering, and selfish. Even when people who do not know God personally act in a faithful manner, it is only because they are created in God's image. They are reflecting God's quality of faithfulness. But it is only believers, walking in the power of the Holy Spirit, who can become truly faithful to God, their families, and themselves. Whenever we allow any sinful act of disobedience to break our fellowship with God, we no longer reflect His faithfulness. Our lives become like that darkened moon.

> The faithfulness of God should cause us to love Him more.

God wants us to have a better understanding of His faithfulness, which will result in a more intimate relationship with Him. We know that "God, who has called you into fellowship with His Son Jesus Christ our Lord, is faithful" (1 Corinthians 1:9, NIV). Daily, the faithfulness of God should cause us to love Him more, study His Word, share the message of salvation with others, and pray without ceasing. Such responses draw us ever deeper into our fellowship with the Savior. As we spend more time with Him, our lives begin to reflect more of His faithfulness in how we love others and in the mercy we are able to give.

Our Faithful God Has Planned a Life of Joy for Us

God's faithfulness enables us to live a life of joy and fruitfulness. Years ago, a friend told me the story of Sally, a woman whose life is a vivid illustration of the bittersweet way many Christians live.

When Sally's husband, Jeb, died years before, as far as she knew, he left only enough life insurance to pay off the mortgage. Now she was almost penniless. The house was deteriorating around her. Her car had been junked long ago when she could not keep up with the repair and insurance bills. When the electric bill got too high to pay, she made do with a camping stove and candlelight. She lived this way for years: destitute, lonely, and defeated.

One day an old acquaintance remembered her childhood friend and decided to visit. Miriam was heartbroken when she saw Sally's living conditions. She decided to stay a few days to encourage her friend. As she helped straighten up the house, Miriam made a startling discovery. Tucked away in the file drawer of Jeb's old rolltop desk was a folder labeled "For Sally." Inside, Miriam found a bank savings book and a key.

Sally discovered that the key fit a safety deposit box at the bank. Her eyes widened as she lifted the metal lid. Inside were several bundles of cash totaling $32,000, a pile of stock certificates, and three folders of rare coins. In all, Sally was worth more than $883,000! She had been living in misery and despair when more money than she would ever need had been available to her all along.

Although God has promised us all the strength and help we will ever need, many of us try to "go it alone." We seem unaware of the boundless resources God has provided in the person of the Holy Spirit and His faithfulness to bring about everything He promised to do. As a result, we live like Sally—unfulfilled, fruitless, and spiritually malnourished. Frantically hurrying about in our self-imposed spiritual poverty, we never cash the checks of joy, peace, and abundance that are in our hands. No wonder we think at times that God has abandoned us.

God has not moved away from us; we have just not taken advantage of the miraculous life He has planned for us. Our faithful God has reserved for us a life of abundance and joy; we have the key of the Spirit-filled life to give us access to all that God has provided for us. If you have never made the wonderful discovery of the Spirit-filled life, I urge you to turn to Appendix B, "How to Be Filled With the Holy Spirit," right now and discover the secret to living a faithful, fruitful, and joy-filled Christian life.

God Is Faithful During Trying Circumstances

We all experience hard times in our lives. These struggles with sickness, danger, financial problems, grief, or depression happen to each of us at times. But these only prompt us to cling ever tighter to God—not to turn away from Him, blaming Him for causing or allowing all our troubles. He does not promise to prevent problems from coming into our lives, but He does promise to go through them with us. Suffering and death are as much a part of living as eating and breathing, and we can rely on God to use these situations to build character and faith in our lives.

> No one who has called on God in faith has been refused.

God will never fail us! Moses exhorted the people of Israel, "Understand, therefore, that the LORD your God is indeed God. He is the faithful God who keeps His covenant for a thousand generations and constantly loves those who love Him and obey His commands" (Deuteronomy 7:9). The more we understand this, the less room we have in our hearts for worry.

I have found that as I rely on God's faithfulness and the promises in His Word, He has proved more than able to walk with me through every situation. Truly, He's been faithful to me!

In Pakistan during a time of great political upheaval, Vonette and I finished a series of meetings in Latbre and rushed to the train station. Although we did not know it, an angry crowd of thousands was marching on the station to destroy the train with Molotov cocktail bombs. The director of the railway line rushed us to our compartments and told us not to open our doors under any circumstances.

As I put on my pajamas for the night, a peace filled my heart. From my studies of God's Word, I knew the Lord was with Vonette and me and our party. I was confident God would protect us. It was not until we arrived in Karachi some 28 hours later that I discovered how guardian angels had indeed watched over us. The train before us had been burned when rioting students had lain on the track and refused to move. The train ran over them and, in retaliation, the mob burned the train and killed the officials.

Our train was next to arrive. The angry mob was prepared to do the same to us, but God miraculously went before us, and we arrived safely in Karachi to discover that martial law had been declared and all was peaceful. It was during this incredible, memorable train ride that I revised my book *Come Help Change the World*.

Today even more than ever, I rely on God to faithfully respond to my prayers when I pray in accordance with His Word and will. David writes of this assurance, "O LORD, hear my prayer, listen to my cry for mercy; in Your faithfulness and righteousness come to my relief" (Psalm 143:1, NIV). God does not promise to make life easy for us. But He promises to be with us in all our trying circumstances, protecting us from anything that is not in the center of His will. He will be by our side as we walk through all the difficulties and trials that come our way, giving us His peace.

God Faithfully Protects Us From Temptation

Paul wrote to the church in Corinth, "Remember that the temptations that come into your life are no different from what others experience. And God is faithful. He will keep the temptation from becoming so strong that you can't stand up against it. When you are tempted, He will show you a way out so that you will not give in to it" (1 Corinthians 10:13).

God's faithfulness is a great encouragement when we face temptation. He knows exactly the limits of what we can bear. He promises that He will not allow us to get into situations where we are overpowered by temptation.

Whenever we give in to sin, it is not because we cannot say "no." Rather, it is because our focus is on the attractiveness of the temptation, instead of on God's faithfulness to deliver us from that situation. Scripture declares, "The Lord is faithful; He will make you strong and guard you from the evil one" (2 Thessalonians 3:3). God limits Satan and his demons from tempting us beyond our ability to resist. If we trust and obey God, He always gives us a way out of any predicament without having to yield to sin.

Often, we are more afraid of offending individuals with their own worldly agenda than we are of offending our holy, righteous, loving God. The results can be catastrophic. But never forget—God is as loving and faithful as He is just. Every day try to live before Him in a spirit of reverential awe as a child who knows that God loves and cares for him.

God Forgives Us When We Are Unfaithful

When we first trusted in Christ to forgive our sin, He did so. Not one person who has called on God in faith has been refused. He has always been—and always will be—faithful to the sinner who comes to Jesus in faith.

The Holy Spirit inspired John to write, "If we confess our sins to Him, He is faithful and just to forgive us and to cleanse us from every wrong" (1 John 1:9). Since John was writing to believers, we have assurance that God has also forgiven all the sins we commit after our spiritual birth as well as the ones we had piled against our account before we received Christ as our Savior. No matter when we are unfaithful to God, He will be faithful to forgive when we ask. But on our part, we must be sincere in our repentance and not abuse God's grace.

Because we are still in these bodies of flesh, we have a tendency to sin and, ultimately, to be unfaithful. Our unfaithfulness may be motivated by fear or desire. At other times, our fleshly weakness competes with our desire to do God's will. No matter the cause, how encouraging it is to remember God's promise to be faithful to us even when we fail Him!

God Faithfully Gives Us Gifts to Serve Him

God's faithfulness continues beyond the act of giving us new life in Christ and help in times of need. Paul writes to the Corinthians:

> Therefore you do not lack any spiritual gift as you eagerly wait for our Lord Jesus Christ to be revealed. He will keep you strong to the end, so that you will be blameless on the day of our Lord Jesus Christ. God, who has called you into fellowship with His Son Jesus Christ our Lord, is faithful. (1 Corinthians 1:7,9, NIV)

Our faithful God called us into fellowship with His Son—and in that act He also committed Himself to our future. That starts with giving us everything we need for our life of worship and witness, for we "do not lack any spiritual gift." Our faithful God never gives us an assignment for which He has not prepared us and enabled us.

God leads us into work experiences and training when we are available to Him. While in his teens, a young man committed himself to serving the Lord wherever God wanted to use him. In his late teens, he began teaching a preteen Bible study class on Sunday morning and as a mission outreach Sunday afternoon. Some years later, he taught high schoolers in one church and early teens in another church. While serving the Lord in the bookstore at Moody Bible Institute in downtown Chicago, he interacted with neighborhood children who came into the store. Thus he was not surprised when he was called to write Sunday school curriculum for inner city teenagers. Later he was given an opportunity to write Bible studies for preteen boys for a national magazine. The Lord prepared him for these assignments over two decades—both by giving him a gift for writing and by providing life experiences that matured him in his service for God.

God is also faithful to give us less tangible gifts when we experience suffering, such as the pain of a child turning away from the Lord, a friend rejecting us, or the death of a loved one. In these life experiences, God gives us strength, wisdom, and peace to enable us to reflect His faithfulness through the situation.

In his letters to the early Christians, Peter wrote at length about the benefit of suffering. He concludes: "So then, those who suffer according to God's will should commit themselves to their faithful Creator and continue to do good" (1 Peter 4:19, NIV). Peter recognized that it is easy to turn inward and become bitter during times of inner pain and suffering. That is why he urges us to turn upward to our faithful Creator and commit ourselves to Him and find the purpose He has for us in these situations (Romans 5:3).

Paul reminds us in 1 Corinthians 1:8 that "He will keep you strong to the end, so that you will be blameless on the day of our Lord Jesus Christ" (NIV). That is the glorious promise of God to all who follow Him. He will keep us faithful to the end, so that we will be with Him in eternity.

No Better Way to Live

As we have seen, it is God's plan for us to become holy and advance His kingdom, and He is faithful to bring this to pass. He will leave nothing undone to bring us to a point of maturity in our Christian growth and faith. Paul declared to the Philippians, "I am sure that God, who began the good work within you, will continue His work until it is finally finished on that day when Christ Jesus comes back again" (Philippians 1:6).

In what area of your life is fear of failure beginning to plague you? Which of your relationships is in danger and you wonder who cares? What task do you face that you feel you cannot do? You can make it through anything—for our faithful God is there for you even when you do not feel like a hero of the faith. He is working in your life right now, even though you may not see Him at work or feel His presence. Let His faithfulness in the past fuel your faith and the power of His Holy Spirit fill your soul. Then you, too, can be a hero of the faith in whatever situation you face.

Once He has filled your heart with the joy of His faithfulness to you, He will strengthen you with His power. Then you will reflect His faithful nature to others. They will see the love of God shine through you as you relate to others. Your friends and relatives will notice the consistency of your standards in all areas of your life, opening up

> Let His faithfulness in the past fuel your faith today.

many opportunities to help others understand the depth of God's faithfulness. As God meets your needs, lifts you up during trying circumstances, and gives you gifts to serve Him beyond your expectations, you will be a reflection of His faithfulness.

I cannot imagine a better way to live. As we focus on the God who is faithful, we become more and more faithful in response. Only then are we equipped to truly change our corner of the world for Him!

In the next chapter we will discover another characteristic that sets Him far above anything or anyone else: His sovereignty. This attribute is the one that gives us complete hope for the future because He is in control of the entire universe—past, present, and future.

Talk About It: You Can Trust Me

"Let us hold tightly without wavering to the hope we affirm,
for God can be trusted to keep His promise."
(Hebrews 10:23)

1. Have you ever been accused of breaking a promise that you did not think you made? What happened and why?

2. Indicate whether the statements below are promises God has made (Y/N):

   _____ God will always give me the strength I need to resist temptation.

   _____ God will make me prosperous if I follow Him.

   _____ My happiness is God's top priority.

   _____ God will always be with me.

   _____ God will always protect me from harm.

3. Why is it critical for us to know what God promises and what He does not promise?

4. In each of the following verses, what does God promise? What does He not promise?

   John 14:27

   Isaiah 40:29–31

   Romans 8:28

   1 Corinthians 10:13

   Philippians 4:19

5. What does this statement mean: "We are not called to have great faith; we are called to have faith in a great God"? How could you live this out in your daily life?

6. Review your timeline, and identify or add examples of when God has demonstrated His faithfulness to you. How has that affected your trust in Him today?

7. Is there anything you think God wants you to do that would require you to take a step of faith trusting in God's faithfulness this week?

8. Where does the power to be faithful to God come from?

FOCUS ON GOD

Continue to review the statement and verse you wrote down last week, at least three times each day, to remind yourself that God is faithful, allowing them to become a part of your "continuous conversation" with God.

**God, because You are faithful,
I will trust You to always keep Your promises.**

"He who promised is faithful."
(Hebrews 10:23, NIV)

Is there something you have a hard time trusting God with? A relationship? A circumstance? A past action? Stop and think about what attribute(s) of God you are struggling to believe is true in this context. Why do you think that is? Do you believe He is always faithful to operate in the framework of all His other attributes at all times? If so, claim His faithfulness this week, confidently trusting in His promise to be faithful. Then ask Him to help you trust Him in this specific context.

"If we are unfaithful, He remains faithful, for He cannot deny who He is."
(2 Timothy 2:13)

CHAPTER 22

I AM Sovereign

P eople around the world are fascinated with royalty. Pictures of British royalty fill the tabloids and television screens. Why does their every appearance captivate our attention? Perhaps it is the grandeur in which they live.

Since we live in a democracy in a time in which sovereigns do not rule grand empires, it is hard for us to understand the depth of feeling that people have toward their kings and queens. When King Hussein of Jordan died in February 1999, his entire country mourned. Nearly a million people lined up to see the funeral procession—almost one-sixth of Jordan's population! Hundreds of Jordanians broke through the security barrier to get near the coffin. All over Jordan, black flags waved from doorposts and car antennas. The country was almost shut down for a week for official mourning.

From earliest days, kings and queens have received honor and respect. One example is in 1911 when the former Indian rulers' courts paid homage to King George V and Queen Mary of England on the Delhi plain. The royal couple sat on a dais while the princes advanced according to protocol and did their salutes. The first prince gave the king a necklace that held a ruby the size of a pigeon's egg. His Highness of Panna presented the king with a twelve-inch umbrella made from a single emerald. Dressed in gold and silver brocade, Sir Tukoji Rao of Indore came with a gold stick that had jeweled engravings and a hilt carved from a single ruby.[68]

English royalty held lavish ceremonies to establish their positions, often spending months on elaborate preparations. When Queen Elizabeth II was crowned in Westminster Abbey in London, she rode in a gold coach pulled by eight magnificent grays.

She was crowned with the large solid-gold, pearl- and ruby-studded St. Edward's Crown. The Scepter of power and justice was placed in her right hand and the Rod of equity and mercy in her left. Then the peers of her realm, including her husband, performed the Act of Homage by kneeling before her and swearing allegiance to the crown. Drums rolled, trumpets resounded, and cannons were fired in carefully orchestrated celebration.

The Greatest Sovereign

Yet there exists another Royal King whose majesty, splendor, and awesomeness are almost indescribable. Compared to Him, no other ruler or reign is even a blip on the screen of eternity. He does not need ceremony or to drape Himself in grandeur to appear more regal. Jewels and wealth mean nothing to Him. Yes, this divine Ruler is none other than the Sovereign God. His throne is far above the universe in heaven; He rules over all.

> God does not derive His right to rule from anyone or anything.

David, himself a king, asked, "Who is this King of glory?" Then he answers his own question: "The LORD, strong and mighty, the LORD, invincible in battle... The LORD Almighty—He is the King of glory" (Psalm 24:8–10, NKJV). In one of the final chapters in the Bible, John identifies Him as "KING OF KINGS AND LORD OF LORDS." John describes how he heard a loud voice of a great multitude in heaven shouting, "Hallelujah! Salvation and glory and power belong to our God... Hallelujah! For our Lord God Almighty reigns" (Revelation 19:1,6,16).

As John continues to describe his vision of God's throne, he tries to convey what cannot be adequately described in words. I want to quote a portion here:

I saw a throne in heaven and Someone sitting on it! The One sitting on the throne was as brilliant as gemstones—jasper and carnelian. And the glow of an emerald circled His throne like a rainbow. Twenty-four thrones surrounded Him, and twenty-four elders sat on them. They were all clothed in white and had gold crowns on their heads. And from the throne came flashes of lightning and the rumble of thunder… In front of the throne was a shiny sea of glass, sparkling like crystal.

In the center and around the throne were four living beings… Day after day and night after night they keep on saying,

"Holy, holy, holy is the Lord God Almighty—the One who always was, who is, and who is still to come."

Whenever the living beings give glory and honor and thanks to the One sitting on the throne, the One who lives forever and ever, the twenty-four elders fall down and worship the One who lives forever and ever. And they lay their crowns before the throne and say:

"You are worthy, O Lord our God,

to receive glory and honor and power.

For You created everything,

and it is for Your pleasure that they exist

and were created." (Revelation 4:2–11)

The throne of an earthly king or queen, however grand it may be, cannot compare to the glories of God. If we took away the royal trappings from any human sovereign, he would look just like one of us. His honor is derived from ceremonies and the homage paid him by other people, which can be removed in a moment. He may have the power of an army behind him, but in himself, he is a sinful, imperfect human just like you and me.

God's reign is different. God does not derive His right to rule from anyone or anything. No title was bestowed on Him by another, and there is no higher authority anywhere than His. The great I AM always does what He knows is best and answers to no one. His reign is so magnificent that we cannot even comprehend any part of it. Let's look at three truths about the scope of God's sovereignty.

God Sovereignly Rules the Universe

God reigns so supremely above His creation that we cannot question any of His actions. Whatever God wants to have happen will happen; His will cannot be thwarted. Daniel explains, "He determines the course of world events; He removes kings and sets others on the throne" (Daniel 2:21).

God's creative actions set the stage for His sovereignty. He was able to create because He was in absolute control of every particle of material even before He brought it into being. Once He formed something, no matter how simple or complex, He remained in absolute authority.

Jeremiah reminded God's people of how completely God is in control. Because of their disobedience, they wanted to escape the judgment of the God they had spurned. God sent Jeremiah to the house of a potter. As the potter worked on a piece of clay, he skillfully shaped it with his hands into a beautiful vessel. But when another pot he was making was marred, he tossed it aside and began a new pot. He did what seemed best to him.

> Whatever God wants to have happen will happen.

Through this illustration, God pointed out His limitless sovereignty. "O Israel, can I not do to you as this potter has done to his clay? As the clay is in the potter's hand, so are you in My hand" (Jeremiah 18:6). As Creator, God could do whatever He wanted with His creation. No matter how much the clay complained or rebelled, it was shaped by the strong hand of the potter. Centuries later, Paul points out: "Shall what is formed say to Him who formed it, 'Why did You make me like this?'" (Romans 9:20, NIV). Norman Geisler explains God's sovereignty this way:

> If it is a power that you can manipulate, it is not God. If it is a power that created the universe that chooses to express itself one way this time, and another way at another time, for our good and His glory, then it is God.

God Sovereignly Works Through His Laws of Nature

Stephen Charnock writes, "We cannot suppose God a Creator, without supposing a sovereign dominion in Him."[69] God dominates nature to accomplish His purposes:

> He directs the snow to fall on the earth and tells the rain to pour down… God's breath sends the ice, freezing wide expanses of water. He loads the clouds with moisture, and they flash with His lightning. The clouds turn around and around under His direction. They do whatever He commands throughout the earth. He causes things to happen on earth, either as a punishment or as a sign of His unfailing love." (Job 37:6,10–13)

God established the scientific laws that regulate the universe; only He can overrule their effect. For God, miracles are "routine."

I am amazed when I hear from Christians who doubt God's supernatural intervention in their lives. God did mighty miracles through Noah, Moses, and other Old Testament characters. He spoke through the prophets. He personally invaded our time and space in the form of His Son. Jesus performed miracles, died for our sins, rose from the grave, and ascended bodily into heaven. His resurrection is the greatest miracle of all. Now His Spirit lives in the hearts of millions of believers around the world. We sometimes take these miracles for granted.

God still suspends His natural laws today. I love the story told by former Campus Crusade staff members Dick and Carolyn Edic:

> In 1967, …300 staff and 300 selected students converged on the [University of California] Berkeley campus for a week of intense evangelism in every facet of the campus. We would meet as a group every morning for prayer, Bible study, and challenge before going out with our particular assignment on campus. Our plan was to culminate the week with a large rally in the Greek Outdoor Theatre with Billy Graham as the speaker. The Amphitheatre held about 8,000 people.

Friday morning, we met as a group… It was raining very heavily, so we feared that the heavy rain would prevent our final evangelistic outreach with Billy Graham. So we got on our knees as a group and prayed… asking God to stop the rain and prepare the way for the outreach.

When we finished praying at about 11:30 a.m., …the sun was shining! By meeting time, the seats had dried enough to attract 8,000 students… After the rally, at about 2 p.m., it started raining again!

This was the highlight of an exciting week of outreach to a tough crowd. During that week, 23,000 of the 27,000 students received a direct witness of the Lord Jesus Christ personally, in small groups, or in the mass meetings. We saw miraculous answers to prayer that demonstrated God's power to change lives and control the weather.[70]

Yet sometimes God chooses to let it rain and to work despite floods or sloshing through mud as at Campus Crusade for Christ's EXPLO '72 which drew 100,000 students to Dallas for a week of training, and EXPLO '74 in Seoul, Korea, which drew a million people every evening for a week. God is in the business of turning tragedy into triumph and sorrow into joy—at His choosing.

God Sovereignly Fulfills His Eternal Master Plan

God actively directs His creation toward a predetermined conclusion. Therefore, He controls all other authorities. The psalmist wrote, "It is God who judges: He brings one down, He exalts another" (Psalm 75:7, NIV).

The Bible records that God chose to use King Nebuchadnezzar as His instrument of judgment upon Judah's wicked kings and rebellious people (2 Kings 24:1–4). Nebuchadnezzar's armies seemed unstoppable as they captured a vast empire including Jerusalem and took most of Judah's residents into captivity in Babylon. However, when Nebuchadnezzar began to boast about what *he* had accomplished, God removed him from his throne for seven years until he humbled himself.

Seventy years later, in keeping with God's prophecy that He would bring His captive people back to Judah, God raised up another king. As prophesied,

Cyrus sent the captives back to Jerusalem to rebuild the city (Isaiah 45:13). This was all a part of God's magnificent plan to eventually send His Son, the Messiah, who would be born of a Jewish girl living near Jerusalem, bringing God's eternal kingdom to earth—turning sinners into children of God.

Responding to the Reign of the King of Kings

We do not live under the jurisdiction of a dictatorial ruler who is out to deprive us of all the fun and happiness in life. The King of kings and Lord of lords has our best interest at heart at all times. He orchestrates events to enable us to praise Him and glorify His name. When times get tough, we can remind ourselves of the conditions under which He reigns. The following paragraphs describe several ways in which He reigns in our lives.

God reigns through His omniscient wisdom.

As a young businessman I made great plans for my business and my future. I had carefully considered what I wanted out of life and what I would have to do to achieve my objectives. Then I met the Son of God! As I discovered the attributes of God—His love, holiness, wisdom, sovereignty, power—I began to realize I could trust His wisdom much more than I could trust my own intelligence.

God's sovereignty operates through righteousness.

In the 20th century, many men have held tremendous power and used it for evil: Stalin, Hitler, Mao Tse Tung, and Pol Pot, the vicious head of the Khmer Rouge in Cambodia. These few men, responsible for the deaths of tens of millions of innocent people, reigned in unrighteousness. But God sits on a throne of righteousness because He is holy. We never need to fear that He will act out of evil intentions. Submitting to His sovereignty will always be best for us.

God's sovereignty reveals His goodness.

Because God is good, He is a gracious Sovereign and obliging Benefactor rather than an arbitrary tyrant. The writer to the Hebrews encourages us to "come boldly to the throne of our gracious God" because we have a High Priest who "understands our weaknesses, for He faced all the same temptations we do, yet

He did not sin" (Hebrews 4:15,16). God has bridged the gap of understanding between us and Him. We can count on His goodness when He deals with us.

The Most Astounding Contrast

Can you imagine Queen Elizabeth II giving up her crown to live as a pauper? Putting aside her jewels and dressing in rags? That is unthinkable.

But that is exactly what God did. Reread the description of His throne at the beginning of this chapter. What majesty, perfection, honor, and glory envelops our great God and Savior! Heaven is a place of such beauty and peace, where no sin mars the atmosphere. Pain and hurt are unknown. Angels and all other beings continually praise God.

When God's Son, Jesus Christ, was voluntarily born in a humble manger in Bethlehem, the only people who worshiped Him were lowly shepherds. The stable must have been drafty and not very private. What kind of place was this for the Sovereign of the universe? Where were His crown and His scepter?

Jesus did not live like a king either. He became tired and hungry, was ridiculed, beaten, spit upon, humiliated. The soldiers ripped off His clothes, and He was taken to court before a cruel ruler named Herod. The crowd shouted that they wanted Him killed. All His friends ran away, afraid for their own lives. Then He was cruelly nailed to a cross in front of a jeering crowd. He could have shaken the world in defiance, but all He said was, "Forgive these people, because they don't know what they are doing" (Luke 23:34).

Jesus did this because God loves us so much. His love motivated Him to communicate His love and salvation to us. To do this effectively, He had to become one of us—to walk, talk, eat, and look like us. Just the thought of our sovereign God putting aside His magnificent glory brings me to tears. How can we ever reach the depths of that love? How could we ever fear putting our lives into His hands?

The Great Puzzle of Life

Submitting to God's sovereignty can be compared to putting together a billion-piece picture puzzle. History is like that giant picture. Only by looking at the photograph on the box cover can you see what everything will look like once all the pieces are in place.

Now imagine that you are given one piece of the puzzle. This is where you fit into God's great plan for the universe. What can you do with this piece? You have never seen the picture on the outside of the box. All you know is that your piece has a little dark color here and a few bright spots there. So you run around trying to match what you are doing with someone else's puzzle piece. The chances of finding one other person who has a piece that matches yours is almost zero.

> "If it is a power that you can manipulate, it is not God." — Norm Geisler

Therefore, there is no way you could ever understand what the completed picture will look like.

From a human standpoint, it is impossible to understand the many uncertainties in life. But if you let God direct you, He will help you put your puzzle piece in the right place. He is big enough to see the whole picture; He created it.

Embracing God's Majesty

Part of our problem with accepting God's authority and honoring Him is that we have lost our concept of majesty. With little sense of the majesty of God, we have trouble submitting to His sovereignty and worshiping Him. Worship is not about making us feel good; the focus of worship is about embracing who God really is with all our heart, mind, and soul. For most Christians, true worship is not something they practice very often or well. A. W. Tozer explains our dilemma:

> The modern Christian has lost a sense of worship along with the concept of majesty [of God], and of course, reverence as well. He has lost his ability to withdraw inwardly and commune in the secret place with God in the shrine of his own hidden spirit. It is this that makes Christianity, and we have all but lost it. Added numbers, yes, but lost fear. Multiplied schools, yes, but lost awareness of the invisible. Tons of literature being poured out, of course, but no consciousness of the divine Presence. Better communication, certainly, but nothing to communicate.

Evangelistic organizations, yes, but the concept of majesty and worship and reverence has almost left us.[71]

Understanding God's sovereignty causes us to focus on Him, not ourselves. Our response is to fall at His feet and give Him everything we are and own. If the royalty of England kneels before Queen Elizabeth II and pledge to submit to her reign, how much more important is it for us to kneel before God's throne and surrender ourselves to Him?

I urge you to embrace God's sovereignty right now by humbling yourself before Him. Totally and irrevocably submit to His lordship of your life. Worship Him by committing everything you own and desire to Him.

Think of your life as a house with many rooms. Go through each "room" and surrender both the room and the contents to Him. If you have a closet full of fears, let Him control that part of your life. Invite Him into the room where you hide your insecurities and hurts. Let Him take down that monument of pride to your own abilities and talents that you have displayed in your living room. Ask Him to control your checkbook and bank account.

Everything you "lose" by serving Him He will replace with something so much better. He controls the universe; He will enrich your life with joy, peace, fulfillment, satisfaction, and rewards far beyond your wildest imagination!

Talk About It: I AM Sovereign

"All honor and glory to God forever and ever! He is the eternal King, the unseen One who never dies; He alone is God. Amen."
(1 Timothy 1:17)

1. What does the Bible mean when it says God is sovereign?
2. How does God's sovereignty differ from that of a human king or queen? Why is that important to keep in mind?
3. God is either in control or He is not. If God were not completely sovereign over His creation, how would that affect His other attributes, and how would that impact your life?

4. How do we try to control God, and what does that indicate about our trust in His sovereignty?

5. Read Jeremiah 18:1–6. In the analogy of the potter and the clay, who is in control? Who is not in control? How do you feel about being clay in God's hands?

6. What did you learn about God's sovereignty from the puzzle analogy?

7. Read Romans 8:39. If God were *not* sovereign, what implication would that have on this promise?

FOCUS ON GOD

On an index card or your favorite electronic device, write the following statement and verse, or just take a picture of it:

**God, because You are sovereign,
I will joyfully submit to Your will.**

*"All honor and glory to God forever and ever!
He is the eternal King...; He alone is God."*
(1 Timothy 1:17)

Look at it when you get up, when you go to bed, and at least once during the day as a way of intentionally shifting your focus from yourself to God. Thank God that He is in control no matter what.

CHAPTER 23

I Have It All Under Control

As members of a democratic society rife with individualism, Americans have difficulty understanding God as an absolute ruler. Did we not reject living under a sovereign ruler when the American Colonies revolted against the king of England? Why should we be subject to anyone now? Yes, we Americans love our independence and freedom.

We do pay homage to our superstar heroes, especially in entertainment and sports, but only as long as they produce astonishing performances for us. Other great champions quickly replace them.

With the decline in the belief of absolute truth, we tend to argue and debate from emotion rather than reason. "How does that make you feel?" has replaced, "What do you think about that?" The long-held conviction in the Church that the chief end of mankind is to glorify God has been supplanted by the belief that the chief end of God is to make us happy. We compromise God's moral standards and consider it a virtue.

But we cannot argue, debate, or negotiate with God, the King of the universe. If He is truly the Lord of our lives, and we are His true disciples, we say, "Yes, Lord!" Saying "No, Lord" is a contradiction of terms for the true disciple of Jesus Christ.

Please, fellow believers, do not follow the teaching of some who say that if you have enough faith in God, or if you repeat the name of Jesus, or quote a formula of phrases or Scripture verses, then you will get all your prayers answered with a "yes." We cannot force God to do things our way. God alone is sovereign. He loves us but He does not share His sovereignty with us. Sometimes in His wisdom and sovereign plan, His answer to our prayers is "no" or "wait." Our position is to trust, believe, and obey, not to demand.

Choice Versus Obedience

Does that mean we have no say with our sovereign God? Of course not! He does not consider us His puppets or slaves. He made us as free moral agents with minds, wills, and emotions. He will not force His love and plans upon us against our wills. Within the context of His master plan, God gives us the freedom to choose. This is a hard concept to grasp. Let me explain with an illustration. A few days ago, I flew to Dallas. I had complete freedom to get up and walk around on that jetliner. I could go get a magazine or talk to my fellow passengers. I could take a nap or make a telephone call. I had complete freedom—within limits. However, I could not alter the plane's course. That plane was going to Dallas!

> We cannot argue, debate, or negotiate with God.

Our relationship with God is like that. We are not robots mechanically programmed to follow His decrees. God has a course for us that has been charted before the beginning of time. God assures us in His Word: "My purpose will stand, and I will do all that I please" (Isaiah 46:10, NIV). His master plan for history will be accomplished, whether we choose to work with Him or follow our own stubborn way. Although He allows us to choose and suffer the consequences of our choices, He never relinquishes control of the plans to accomplish His purposes. God turns the pages of history; we do not. As you read the following truths about God's sovereignty, ask God to show you how you can restore a sense of His majesty in your life and what He wants you to do to obey Him.

God Sovereignly Directs People, Circumstances, and Events

When you read the newspaper or look at events around you, do you sometimes wonder who is in control? More and more Christians see themselves as victims of a wicked society. Many feel overwhelmed by circumstances and struggle with hopelessness, defeat, and discouragement. But God has not abandoned them.

I can clearly see how God's sovereignty has been at work throughout my life. When my mother was carrying me, she almost died many times. During that time, she asked God to spare her life. "Lord, if you will just give me time, and allow me to give birth to this little child, I will dedicate him or her to you." Not only did she survive, but she lived to be 93 years old and her godly example and powerful prayers were the greatest influence on my life. She dedicated me to the Lord and faithfully prayed that God's will would be done in my life.

After completing my college degree, I spent one year on the faculty at Oklahoma State University Extension. Then I left Oklahoma to seek my fortune in California. Although my mother was still praying for me, I had no interest in the things of God. I wanted to be a successful businessman, a man of influence and significance. I was a self-made, happy pagan.

The first day I arrived in California, I picked up a hitchhiker who invited me to dinner at his friend's house. I agreed and, as it turned out, his friend was Dawson Trotman, founder of the Navigators Ministry. After dinner, they said, "We're going to a birthday party. Would you like to come?" That celebration was in the home of America's top radio evangelist, Charles E. Fuller.

I am still awed by the fact that through God's sovereignty, I spent my first night in California in the homes of two of the most famous Christian leaders of the 20th century. That did not just happen by chance. God was orchestrating events in my life—even though I was not a follower of Jesus—in gracious answer to my saintly mother's prayers.

God is sovereignly involved in directing each of our lives. Proverbs states, "Many are the plans in a man's heart, but it is the LORD's purpose that prevails" (Proverbs 19:21, NIV). God carefully supervises all that happens. No event escapes His notice. No person is beyond His influence. No circumstance exists outside His control.

There Is No Room for Luck in God's Sovereign Plans

"Good luck," I heard a man recently say. What about luck? Anyone who understands the Bible and God's revelation of Himself knows that there is no such thing as luck or chance, which implies a capriciousness of nature and the universe. When we use the word "luck," we express our unbelief or a lack of knowledge of God's attributes. If God is completely in control of the universe, luck cannot exist.

As believers, we live by faith in God and His Word and in the power of the Holy Spirit, not by luck or superstition. He also wants us to consciously acknowledge His sovereign control in the affairs of our lives. This means making our life's plans—from our simplest decisions to our career choices or our retirement plans—follow God's will. In the New Testament, James explains the attitudes that please or displease God:

Now listen, you who say, "Today or tomorrow we will go to this or that city, spend a year there, carry on business and make money." Why, you do not even know what will happen tomorrow. What is your life? You are a mist that appears for a little while and then vanishes. Instead, you ought to say, "If it is the Lord's will, we will live and do this or that." As it is, you boast and brag. All such boasting is evil. (James 4:13–16, NIV)

God has a much greater agenda than ours. As we make plans through the power of His Holy Spirit, we must allow God to change those plans at a moment's notice. We must seriously seek the will of God rather than our own will—and trust all our circumstances to His control.

God Uses Bad Things for Good Purposes

You may have wondered, *If God is in complete control of everything, why does He allow (or cause) birth defects, famines, and war? Why does He permit sin, evil, and suffering?* God's very nature opposes these things. It was not His desire for Adam and Eve, the first humans, to sin and bring sickness, disease, and death upon mankind (Romans 5:12–21). God created a perfect world, but mankind chose to sin, and the penalty for sin was death—physical and spiritual. This curse of death has affected all of creation, not just humans, and all the bad things that exist are due to living in a world under judgment, a fallen world.

Part of Adam and Eve's punishment was pain and suffering, fighting against nature for food, and struggling to make a living before finally dying (Genesis 3:16–19).

> Within the context of His master plan, God gives us the freedom to choose.

God does not initiate, cause, or authorize sin, or tempt anyone to sin. Yet He tolerates evil for a season to fulfill His righteous plans for people to respond by their own free will to His love. Because God is always in control and He loves us, we know that He allows troubles, illness, accidents, adversity, and similar problems to come into our lives for a good reason—it is never just by chance or by accident.

Our disappointments are often God's appointments. He is far more concerned about the quality of our eternal future than He is about our present comfort and temporary happiness. In fact, difficulties and suffering are tools with which He shapes us into the image of Jesus Christ. It is never fun to be enrolled in the academy of adversity, but unless God takes us through the curriculum of trials, we will never become the quality person He wants us to be. Adversity is the touchstone of character.

Romans 8 promises, "God causes everything to work together for the good of those who love God and are called according to His purpose for them" (Romans 8:28). God uses even the most disastrous situations for our good.

In the summer of 1976, thirty-five female Campus Crusade staff leaders—including my wife, Vonette—gathered in Colorado for a retreat. That night, they were trapped in the Big Thompson Canyon flood.

At about 1:30 in the morning, I was awakened and informed of the flood and of the rescue of one of the women, who was now in the hospital. About an hour later, another staff member was brought to the hospital by helicopter. By this time, we had good reason to believe that several of the women had drowned.

I did not know if Vonette was safe, struggling for her life in the floodwaters, or dead. But I had incredible peace because I knew that God is sovereign and ever-present. So even though I had no idea where Vonette was and could not help her, I knew God was with her and the other women. Because He is all-powerful, God could save all the women whose lives were in danger. But God is also all-knowing. If it was best for Vonette to be taken home to heaven, I could completely trust my loving Father to do the right thing.

Soon I sadly learned that seven of our staff women perished during the flood. I knew that each of these women was rejoicing in the presence of her Savior. I also learned that Vonette and twenty-seven other staff women had escaped the raging water.

In the weeks that followed, we mourned for those dear friends we had lost. But we also felt led by God to make their last moments on earth a tribute to our sovereign God. With full approval of the grieving families, friends of Campus Crusade ministry placed full-page ads in most newspapers across the country featuring pictures of the seven women who died. The headline read, "These seven women lost their lives in the Colorado flood, but they are alive and they have a message for you." The advertisement gave readers an opportunity to read the gospel and trust in Jesus Christ as their Savior.

Approximately 150 million people read those ads. The response was phenomenal. Only God knows the full extent of what happened, but many thousands wrote to say that they had received Christ that week as a result of the tragic deaths of those seven women. A foreign ambassador told us that his life was changed by the ad, and he later helped open the door for ministry in his country, which had previously been closed to the gospel.

We can give all our worries and cares to God, knowing that He cares about what happens to us (1 Peter 5:7). When tragedy strikes, take comfort in the fact that no difficulty will ever come into your life without God's permission. Knowing this truth does not make adversity pleasant, but it gives us hope that the result will be worth whatever pain we endure.

God Overrules the Evil Intentions of People

What about the intentions of evil people? Is God's hand present when they devise evil against us? Throughout the Bible we see incidents of God intervening to thwart the evil intents of humans.

Sometimes it seems as if following God's will makes us more vulnerable to the evil intentions of others. That simply is not true. Yes, since Lucifer rebelled against God, and Adam and Eve sinned in the Garden of Eden, wars have existed between God and Satan, good and evil, light and darkness. God still has His plan, and He will execute it. We just cannot always see it.

As a 19-year-old, Bruce Olsson went into the jungles on the border of Colombia and Venezuela to bring the gospel to the Bari people. God protected him from these aboriginal people who had never let a white man into their territory, and as they came to love him and his Lord, they affectionately called him *bruchko*. Then in 1988 Bruce was captured by Colombian guerrillas and held secretly in the jungle. It looked as if his ministry had been disrupted and maybe even ended.

Once the Colombian armed forces realized that the guerrillas had kidnapped Bruce, they tried to enlist the Baris, once a fierce, warlike tribe, to help rescue their beloved *bruchko*. The Baris refused, saying, "Violence only engenders violence."

Meanwhile, things were happening in the jungle. After five months in captivity, Bruce had so gained the confidence of the guerrillas that they gave him a Bible. Eventually he was able to hold Bible studies with his captors. During nine months of captivity, including one firing squad escape, Bruce led about half the guerrillas assigned to him to faith in Christ. He was so successful that the guerrilla leaders finally released him.

As the years passed after the kidnapping, these Christian guerrillas won others to faith in Christ. Finally, the entire Christian group broke away from the larger guerrilla group and surrendered themselves to the Colombian government. On April 6, 1994, Bruce Olsson wrote in a letter:

Resurrection Sunday also meant "conversion" to a great many members of the former guerrilla forces. In their camps [during my captivity] I witnessed more than a hundred breaks before the Lord in repentant tears, attentive to His Word and surrender their lives to the lordship of Jesus Christ. This action is prelude to the celebration of the 9th of April [when]…descendants from the "Armed Forces for National Liberation" (ELN) and "Armed Forces for Colombian Revolution" (FARC), representing about half of the violent revolutionary forces in Colombia, will reincorporate themselves into national life at the surrendering of their arms and signature of the negotiated "Peace Plan."

God in His sovereignty protected Bruce despite the evil intentions of guerrilla leaders—and turned the whole incident into a great victory for Jesus Christ. Bruce writes, "The Bari had no doubt in God's sovereignty and trusted in His intervention in the lives and affairs of His creation. The relinquishing of arms [by the guerrillas] in the presence of Bari leaders was significant. It was vindication of the Bari's endurance and persuasion." God was sovereign through the actions of Bruce, the Bari, *and* the guerrillas! Does that give you hope in a situation you may face right now? God will sovereignly use you, too, as you follow His will.

Our Redemption and God's Sovereignty

The entire gospel is a declaration of God's sovereign pleasure concerning Christ. Writing to the Ephesians, Paul explained:

> God's secret plan has now been revealed to us; it is a plan centered on Christ, designed long ago according to His good pleasure. And this is His plan: At the right time He will bring everything together under the authority of Christ—everything in heaven and on earth. (Ephesians 1:9,10)

Satan plotted to defeat God's purpose by arranging circumstances so that the Son of God would be crucified. His plots were successful—at first sight. Consider all the evil intentions of men that God used to bring about our redemption:

- The religious leaders plotted to kill Jesus. They succeeded in their malicious intent.
- The court crowd asked Pilate to release Barabbas rather than Jesus. Pilate agreed to their hate-filled request.
- The soldiers beat Jesus and crowned Him with a crown of thorns. They were following the evil orders of their superiors.

- The rabble in front of the cross ridiculed Jesus as He was dying. Their purpose was to make Him look weak and insignificant. And they surely did.
- The government assigned soldiers to guard Jesus' tomb to thwart any claims that He had risen from the dead. They were successful for two days.

Today we know that all these evil intents were integral parts of God's plan. Jesus was just one man standing against the evil intentions of His physical world, and the spiritual world too, but His power was greater than anything anyone could throw at Him. We have available to us that same power, because as believers, the Holy Spirit lives within us. He will comfort us during times of trial, give us wisdom to accomplish God's will, and help us glorify God through every situation.

> Our disappointments are often God's appointments.

Do you feel as privileged as I do to be part of God's eternal plan, knowing that God has revealed to us His sovereign will for the grand scale of history? In fact, our sovereign God will ensure that grand finale! Jesus Christ, the Lamb of God, who seemed to be the "victim" of evil intentions, will reign supreme forever and ever. One more passage from John's Revelation gives us the panorama of the grand finale that will take place in the City of God:

All the nations will bring their glory and honor into the city. Nothing evil will be allowed to enter—no one who practices shameful idolatry and dishonesty—but only those whose names are written in the Lamb's Book of Life.

And the angel showed me a pure river with the water of life, clear as crystal, flowing down from the throne of God and of the Lamb, coursing down the center of the main street. On each side of the river grew a tree of life, bearing twelve crops of fruit, with a fresh crop each month. The leaves were used for medicine to heal the nations.

No longer will anything be cursed. For the throne of God and of the Lamb will be there, and His servants will worship Him. And they will see His face, and His name will be written on their foreheads. And there will be no night there—no need for lamps or sun—for the Lord God will shine on them. And they will reign forever and ever. (Revelation 21:26–22:5)

When we choose to submit to God's majesty and sovereignty, we are on the winning side. We will reign with the only One who is worthy of worship and who will be our comfort, guide, and friend throughout eternity! What a Savior! I can hardly wait for that moment!

I urge you to allow God to direct your life by surrendering your decisions, trials, hurts, and pain to Him. Give Him your joys, your accomplishments, your treasures. After all, if Indian princes chose to honor the king of England with their most precious and costly possessions, how much more should we honor God with every part of our lives! Unlike an earthly king, God will take what we give to Him and multiply blessings in our lives. We do not give up anything but pride, sin, and temporal possessions; He gives us back eternal life, joy, spiritual riches, and an eternal reign with Him! What a good God!

In the next chapter we will turn our attention to one of His moral attributes—His righteousness. As we learn more about God's righteousness, we will be increasingly confident that we can put our complete faith in Him.

Talk About It: I Have It All Under Control
"But the LORD's plans stand forever; His intentions can never be shaken."
(Psalm 33:11)

1. We all tend to say "Good luck!" or "That was really bad luck," but do you actually believe in luck? Why or why not?
2. Read John 3:16. What is God's ultimate purpose? Do our choices in life make any difference?
3. List some reasons why God allows adversity in our lives.

4. Who is in control of your daily decisions? On a scale of 1–5, indicate to what degree you have relinquished control to God in each of the following areas of your life.

   (1 indicates not at all; 5 indicates completely)

   ____ Who controls my bank account?

   ____ Who controls my credit cards?

   ____ Who controls my schedule?

   ____ Who controls my relationships?

   ____ Who controls my eating habits?

   ____ Who controls my thought life?

   ____ Who controls my TV remote?

   ____ Who controls how I use my phone?

   ____ Who controls the words that come out of my mouth?

   ____ Who controls how I treat others?

5. Read Ephesians 2:10. Do you believe that God's plan for your life is better than your own plan? Explain.

6. According to Romans 8:28, what is God's part and what is our part? Who will, and who will not, receive the promised benefits in this verse?

7. If God is sovereign, what affect should that have on how, when, and where you worship Him?

FOCUS ON GOD

Continue to review the statement and verse you wrote down last week, at least three times each day, to remind yourself that God has it all under control. Ask Him to help you do your part and then rest in the fact that He is sovereign in all things.

**God, because You are sovereign,
I will joyfully submit to Your will.**

*"All honor and glory to God forever and ever!
He is the eternal King...; He alone is God."*
(1 Timothy 1:17)

Each time you read your Bible this week, think about the passages in light of God's sovereignty. Worship Him and give Him thanks that He is in control and you are not.

CHAPTER 24

I AM Righteous

How can there be so many different views about what is right and what is wrong? Why are moral issues no longer seen as black or white but rather as varying shades of gray? Why do the standards of morality constantly change within modern society?

Today the distinction between right and wrong is becoming increasingly blurred in the name of tolerance. Like ancient Israel, everyone does "what is right in his own eyes." People passionately defend their sinful actions. What is right has become a matter of interpretation by the individual, the community, or the courts. However, this view is absolutely wrong because it assumes that public opinion, legislation, or the courts provide the ultimate criterion for determining what is right. But our sovereign God sets the standards for His creation. Unlike ever-changing human opinions about right and wrong, His standards never change; they are timeless. And our American society, like many western nations, was built on the unchanging biblical principles of right and wrong.

Our culture understands how important it is to be "right" about certain things. Permit me to give you several examples.

An architect building a hundred-story skyscraper takes immense precautions to have the building's foundation perfectly level. If the footings are off even a fraction of an inch, there are tremendous consequences. The farther up he builds on an unleveled foundation, the more unstable the skyscraper becomes.

Scientists at Mission Control in Houston also know the importance of being "right" when bringing a spaceship back to Earth. If the angle of reentry into the Earth's atmosphere is off just a little, the spaceship will either encounter too much friction and burn up before it reaches the ground, or bounce off the atmosphere back into space.

Last, consider speed skaters in a race. Two lanes circle the track. The skaters not only race each other but must stay in their own lane. A skater who crosses the line into the other lane is disqualified and loses the race.

> Why do the standards of morality constantly change within modern society?

Although most people understand the importance of laying the "right" foundation, having the "right" reentry angle, or staying in the "right" lane, they have problems understanding the "rightness" of moral laws. When it comes to stealing, for example, most people divide stealing into categories like "borrowing," petty theft, robbery, and embezzlement. They feel that some categories are okay, such as taking a few supplies from their employer or school, or keeping the excess when a cashier gives them too much change. But to them it would be wrong to break into someone's home or rob a bank. Moral laws, they believe, are not as rigid as other laws. Therefore, we can bend them a little without incurring any penalty. But that is contrary to how God sees His righteous laws.

God Is Always Right

God's righteous role as Creator is evident all around us. Everything He created functions according to the laws applying to its creation. All His natural laws perform the way He intends for the good of His creation. Look at the way a coastal marsh works. Each day, tides bring fresh nutrients for the millions of tiny plants that grow in the soil and water. At high tide, all kinds of shellfish dine on these tiny plants. Fish such as spotted sea trout spawn in the calm water and the tiny hatchlings feed in their own little marshy nursery. Ducks, geese, and other birds build nests to raise their young. A stew of vegetation provides a smorgasbord for the ducklings and goslings. Natural laws and processes work together as a system to benefit all of God's creation.

It is easy to recognize how God created nature in its right order. But it is far less common to understand that God has created the moral realm to function in its right order, too.

In fact, as humans we often purposefully overlook one wrong to right another. In recent years, juries have declared a defendant "not guilty" of a crime despite evidence that clearly convicts him. Through their actions, jury members hope to make a statement about some other moral wrong connected with the crime. Many experts believe the jury in the O. J. Simpson murder trial did this to right the wrong of minorities often not getting equal justice in the court system. But ignoring one wrong to address another wrong will not make things right. We just end up with two wrongs—and no right.

As humans, we sometimes fail to do what is right in our daily lives. Have you ever said to yourself, "I know the right thing to do, but if I do what is right, I will mess up my situation"? Perhaps you are in a college class when someone advocates an immoral viewpoint. You do not challenge the speaker's opinion because you do not want to be viewed as a moral extremist. Standing up for what is morally right might cause you to be ridiculed, lose friends, receive a lower grade from the professor, or lose your job. As fallen human beings, we have a hard time even understanding perfect righteousness much less living righteous lives.

> God's standards never change.

Only God is righteous because He is holy. He has never acted unrighteously, never had an evil thought, never rationalized a questionable act to make something else seem right.

What Is Righteousness?

We learned previously that God is holy. But His holiness and His righteousness are not the same. Holiness is "a condition of purity or freedom from sin."[72] God's righteousness is "the quality or attribute of God by virtue of which He does that which is right or in accordance with His own nature, will, and law."[73]

In other words, holiness describes God's nature; righteousness describes how God acts according to His holiness. God's laws are holy because they come from His nature. God's standards for enforcing His laws are always righteous.

Let me give an example of one law. God says, "Do not commit adultery." That simple statement arises out of God's holiness. He can never be disloyal when He has made a commitment; it is against His nature. In the Old Testament, God made covenants or promises to His people. He made a covenant with Noah that He would never again destroy the earth with a flood. The rainbow in the sky is the evidence of His covenant. Over the many centuries since the flood, God has acted rightly regarding this covenant. That follow-through with His holy covenant shows His righteousness.

In the same way, when we stand before a minister and promise to love our spouse and be faithful to him or her the rest of our lives, we are making a covenant that reflects God's holiness. We act righteously when we keep that commitment or covenant.

But do not imagine that righteousness is reaching a standard like climbing a ladder to a higher level. That is what most people think when they consider righteous acts. "If I tell the truth more times than I tell lies, I'll be more righteous." "If I make up for the money I stole from my employer, then I'll be okay."

No one can work up to righteousness because it begins as purity. A white lie is still a lie. Stealing a pen from your employer is still stealing. Speeding is still breaking the law. Righteousness comes from holiness; it does not reach up to holiness.

Holiness sets the standard. Righteousness fulfills that standard.

God Is the Source of All Righteousness

How righteous is God? Everything God does is perfectly right in every way. David tells us, "The LORD is righteous in all His ways and loving toward all He has made" (Psalm 145:17, NIV). For God, righteousness is not an external standard that He must adhere to; righteousness is part of His very nature. It emanates from His inner being. As a result, whatever God wills is perfectly right. It is impossible for God to do anything wrong.

All righteousness within the entire universe has its origin in Him. The psalmist exclaims, "Your righteousness reaches to the skies, O God, You who have done great things. Who, O God, is like You?" (Psalm 71:19, NIV). Every action God has ever taken or will take is righteous. As a judge, He has never made a wrong determination. He has never had to reverse a decision when He learned more facts. His moral directives do not change over time as He acquires more knowledge because He already knows everything. As Job discovered, no one can question His judgment in all His actions.

Heaven is filled with God's righteousness. "Righteousness and justice are the foundation of His throne" (Psalm 97:2). Because God is righteous, He wants righteousness to fill His universe.

God as Righteous Judge

When you walk into a courtroom and face the judge, you may wonder, "Who gave this judge the power to decide between right and wrong? Who gave the judge the moral and legal authority to pronounce what is righteous behavior and what is grievous misbehavior deserving punishment?"

In America, whether judges are elected directly by the people or appointed by the politicians we elect, they ultimately owe their power to us, the people. However, these judges are subject to human passions and ideas, and can misuse their power. A New England judge was removed after a grand jury indicted him for forcing young men to have sex with him in his private chambers—in return for dismissing their cases. An Illinois judge was removed for "fixing" speeding tickets in return for illegal bribes.

But when we discuss the righteousness of God, we are not talking about an appointed or elected judge, prone to weaknesses and hidden personal agendas or ideologies. An infinite and powerful God does not need anyone to elect or appoint Him, to give Him righteousness. He was righteous before the beginning of time and always will be.

God told Jeremiah, "I am the LORD, who exercises kindness, justice and righteousness on earth, for in these I delight" (Jeremiah 9:24, NIV). He is the standard by which every evaluation of righteousness must be compared. If God were not inherently holy and just, He could not act righteously.

God's Laws Define Righteous Behavior

Just like us, human judges may be caught up in the culture, swayed by their own personalities and ideologies, and limited to the evidence presented in court, which may not accurately portray the truth.

The *Dred Scott v. Sanford* Supreme Court case in 1857 shows how little righteousness we really have as humans. The case began when Henry Blow filed a suit trying to free a slave, Dred Scott, who worked for him. The problem, however, was that Henry did not own Mr. Scott; a Mrs. Emerson did. Although she lived in New York and Dred Scott lived in Missouri, she would not give him his freedom.

The case wound its way from the lower courts to the Supreme Court. By the time the Supreme Court Justices heard the case, the abolition movement in the US had grown strong. Abolitionists wanted slavery outlawed in all new territories and states. Southern slave owners were desperate to keep their legal right to own slaves.

The Supreme Court could not make up its mind. It heard oral arguments twice, then the Justices recessed for two months. They were so divided on the issue that they did not even meet during that time. Finally, each Justice wrote his own opinion. Seven of them ruled that Dred Scott was still a slave, while two ruled that he was free. Since the Supreme Court ruled that slavery could not be prohibited in new territories, only a constitutional amendment could outlaw the expansion of slavery. It took the Civil War and the 14th Amendment to overturn it.

A more recent miscarriage of justice was the *Roe v. Wade* decision in 1973 in which the Supreme Court mandated that abortion be made legal in all 50 states. Violating God's law by killing helpless babies still in their mother's womb is certainly not righteous. Yet the Court approved of this travesty, concluding the unborn baby is somehow not a "person" and therefore not entitled to protection under the law. There have been many occasions when I have very ardently considered chaining myself to the Supreme Court until *Roe v. Wade* is overturned. I am praying that the Supreme Court will, one day soon, reverse its decision in *Roe v. Wade*. As our own Civil War and ancient Israel's history so powerfully demonstrate, we ignore God's laws to our own peril.

God does not struggle with right and wrong. The psalmist declares, "Righteous are You, O Lord, and Your laws are right" (Psalm 119:137, NIV). His laws reflect His own righteous nature and the moral perfection of His character. Cultural bias, ideology, a lack of knowledge, or any other factor does not alter His rulings.

God's spiritual laws are every bit as absolute as His physical laws. If we break God's natural laws, we pay the consequences. For example, if you jump off of the Empire State Building in New York City, the law of gravity will guarantee your death. Likewise, if you lock yourself in a garage and breathe carbon monoxide instead of the oxygen that your body needs, you will die.

> Holiness describes God's nature; righteousness describes how God acts.

God's spiritual laws are no less binding. As the perfect Judge and Lawgiver, God is also the law enforcer. His laws lay out the responsibilities for which He holds us accountable. They are a yardstick by which God measures our righteousness. When His righteous laws are broken, punishment must always follow.

You may wonder why God is so exacting about His spiritual laws. He did not make rules just for the "fun of it." His righteous laws focus on standards for acting rightly toward one another.

Consequently, God's spiritual laws are the pillars for justice and morality within any nation. To restate this fact, the laws of a nation are just only to the degree that they conform to the laws of God. When national leaders reject and disobey God, they cut their nation loose from the anchor of morality—the foundation of justice—and set it adrift in an ocean of moral relativity. Without God they lose their moral compass and doom their society to injustice, dishonesty, and depravity.

We Cannot Meet God's Righteous Standard

Ever since Adam and Eve first disobeyed God, every person has been born with a sinful nature that insists on exerting self-will, even against the Creator. Isaiah describes our dilemma: "How can people like us be saved? We are all infected and impure with sin. When we proudly display our righteous deeds, we find they are but filthy rags. Like autumn leaves, we wither and fall. And our sins, like the wind, sweep us away" (Isaiah 64:5,6).

Imagine a contest between an Olympic gold medal winner and me to see who can jump across the Grand Canyon, which is miles wide and deep. Who do you think would win that match? While I am sure the Olympian would jump far beyond me, he would still fall short of the other side. We would both plummet to our deaths.

That is similar to our attempts to be righteous. Even when we try our very hardest, we still fall far short of God's perfect standard. Because of our sinful nature, it is impossible for us to live the righteous life God demands. As we read earlier, if we are ever to be acceptable to God, He has to intervene on our behalf.

Faith Is the Key to Righteousness

We can be righteous only when God's righteousness is imputed, or freely given to us as we place our faith in God's only Son, Jesus Christ. Abraham was an Old Testament illustration of this truth, which was not fully revealed until Jesus came some 2,000 years later. Genesis 15:6 explains, "[Abraham] believed the LORD, and He credited it to him as righteousness" (NIV). This "righteousness" is sometimes referred to as "right standing" with God; in other words, God considers us right with Him. Abraham came into right standing with God because Abraham believed Him!

Since God's standards for morality and virtue are 100 percent perfect and we are imperfect and inadequate, we can only be righteous as a gift from God. Through our faith in His Son, He "credits" His own righteousness to our account.

In the New Testament, Paul referred to this passage about Abraham and then gave us the wonderful news that "the words 'it was credited to him' were written not for him alone, but also for us, to whom God will credit righteousness— for us who believe in Him who raised Jesus our Lord from the dead" (Romans 4:23,24, NIV). This is one of the most wonderful truths in the universe: God declares us righteous by faith, and sees us as having the righteousness of His own

Son! This is grace, or unmerited favor—a free gift purchased for us by our Lord Jesus Christ through His death on the cross.

What is our worshipful response to the knowledge that God gives us righteousness because of His Son? The Bible contains many examples of prayers that we can offer up to God. One such prayer was written by Paul and is found in 1 Thessalonians: "Now may the God of peace make you holy in every way, and may your whole spirit and soul and body be kept blameless until that day when our Lord Jesus Christ comes again. God, who calls you, is faithful; He will do this" (1 Thessalonians 5:23,24).

Make this prayer the cry of your heart. God will respond by touching your heart, spirit, soul, and body. Because He is faithful, we can be assured that He will answer this prayer and make us righteous in His sight.

Talk About It: I AM Righteous
"Righteous are You, O LORD, and Your laws are right."
(Psalm 119:137, NIV)

1. Do you believe there is anything that is always right or always wrong—no exceptions?
2. If God does not exist, where do moral absolutes come from? What in the universe obligates us to behave a certain way? What obligates us not to harm our neighbor or to always tell the truth?
3. If your starting point for morality is "survival of the fittest" how can you build a moral system that protects the weak or requires you to "love your neighbor" (or at least not "judge" your neighbor)?
4. How would you describe God's righteousness?
5. Why is God the only one truly qualified to set the standard for what is right and wrong?
6. Read Psalm 97:2. God's justice and righteousness are often spoken of together; why do you think that is?
7. If God were not righteous, what implications would it have on His other attributes?

FOCUS ON GOD

On an index card or your favorite electronic device, write the following statement and verse, or just take a picture of it:

**God, because You are righteous,
I will live by Your standards, not the world's.**

"You are righteous, LORD, and Your laws are right."
(Psalm 119:137, NIV)

Look at it when you get up, when you go to bed, and at least once during the day as a way of intentionally shifting your focus from yourself to God. Thank God daily that because He is righteous, He has made you righteous through your faith in Christ and will help you make right choices this week as you focus on Him.

CHAPTER 25

I Help You Make Right Choices

We live in a world where many believe that the end justifies the means. They say it is acceptable to compromise God's standards to get ahead. But the fact is we always lose when we violate God's standards of righteousness. On the other hand, it is not always easy to do what is right.

I think of a situation in which we found ourselves as a ministry when we moved our headquarters from San Bernardino, California, to Orlando, Florida. We had been unable to lease or sell some of our property in San Bernardino. The buildings remained empty, yet every month we still had to make our mortgage payments.

I was counseled by some successful Christian businessmen to default the payments and allow the bank to repossess the property. After all, many businesses had done this during the economic downturn. Financially, we would be far better off, but that would be wrong since we had signed a contract with the bank. We purposed to trust God to help us pay the bills and sell the property in a way that would bring honor and glory to Him. Some would say, "Boy, that's stupid." But we had given our word. Five years passed before we finally sold the property.

Although making those payments was a financial hardship, God has greatly blessed the ministry. Contributions have dramatically increased year after year.

I believe God has blessed us because we run Campus Crusade for Christ in His way. We depend on Him to help us pay our bills.

It has been said, "It is never right to do wrong in order to get a chance to do right." In other words, if we had defaulted on our agreement, we could have saved a lot of money every year. Think of all that the ministry could have done with that money—but we would have violated our word and our contract. That would not have honored God. Living righteously often means making sacrifices and saying no to desires that do not bring honor to God. We cannot live this way in our own strength.

Let us look at a few action points that will help us do what is right no matter what.

Depend on God's Righteousness Rather Than Our Efforts

We are so fortunate that "the LORD is gracious and righteous; our God is full of compassion" (Psalm 116:5, NIV). Otherwise we would be doomed by our lack of righteousness. Our righteousness does not depend on what we do, but on whom we place our faith. Paul explains:

> We are made right in God's sight when we trust in Jesus Christ to take away our sins. And we all can be saved in this same way, no matter who we are or what we have done. For all have sinned; all fall short of God's glorious standard. Yet now God in His gracious kindness declares us not guilty. He has done this through Christ Jesus, who has freed us by taking away our sins. For God sent Jesus to take the punishment for our sins and to satisfy God's anger against us. We are made right with God when we believe that Jesus shed His blood, sacrificing His life for us. (Romans 3:22–25)

There was not anything we could do to earn this gift of grace. We accepted it by faith. Now God no longer sees our sinfulness, but only the righteousness of Christ which covers us.

When we put our faith in Christ, we received a new nature—one of holiness and righteousness. Christ wants us to display His righteousness in our new life.

We are commanded: "Throw off your old evil nature and your former way of life, which is rotten through and through, full of lust and deception. Instead, there must be a spiritual renewal of your thoughts and attitudes. You must display a new nature because you are a new person, created in God's likeness—righteous, holy, and true" (Ephesians 4:22–24).

> Righteousness does not depend on what we do, but in whom we place our faith.

Yet we are all tempted to achieve righteousness under our own power. That never works. We cannot live righteously without the enabling of the Holy Spirit, and His power is released through our faith. For example, if a person has a problem with swearing, he could try his hardest to quit using foul language. For the most part, he would be able to control his tongue, but when someone cuts him off on the freeway or breaks in front of him in a line, his mouth curses before he even realizes what he is saying. All his efforts to control this reaction come up short.

The secret to changing bad habits like cursing is to turn the problem over to God. By faith, admit that you are helpless to change your bad habit. By faith ask His Spirit to give you righteous language to replace the filthy language. As you walk in the Spirit moment by moment, day by day, your heart is better prepared to act righteously the next time someone angers you. When this happens, take a deep breath and start praising God for something good in the situation. Trust God to take over and work out the problem rather than relying on your own strength to change.

Seek God First and Turn Away from Worldly Attachments

The only way we can live a life of faith is by submitting our will to the Holy Spirit moment by moment and depending on Him to empower us. When doing this, Jesus instructs us to "seek first His kingdom and His righteousness" (Matthew 6:33, NIV). As a result, we will enjoy the rewards of righteous living and agree with David, "Surely, O LORD, You bless the righteous; You surround them with Your favor as with a shield" (Psalm 5:12, NIV).

A friend of mine lived in a palatial home in El Paso, Texas. He was a very successful manufacturer who had accumulated considerable wealth. Following his retirement he ministered weekly to the poor people across the border in Juarez, Mexico.

However, in the process, one woman greatly ministered to him. She lived in a little hut with a dirt floor. Her earthly possessions were a small stove, a pot, a pan, a plate, a knife, fork, and spoon, and one change of clothes. Every time she saw him she would tell him, "God is so good to me, He is so wonderful and faithful to me." This successful businessman loved God, but this godly woman was far happier than he was. Through her, he discovered that joy and fulfillment are not found in material possessions, but in a close relationship with God and in obedience to His commands.

> We cannot live righteously without the enabling of the Holy Spirit.

Seeking God first will lead to a new perspective on life. Old, worldly attachments will seem insignificant and God's blessings will be apparent in righteous living. I challenge you to rearrange your priorities, schedule, and finances to put God first and follow His "right" plan for your life.

Adjust Your Life to God's Standards

We have discussed confessing sin when our lives take a turn from God's perfect standard, but God wants us to do more than that. Henry Blackaby and Claude King explain in their book *Experiencing God*, "God wants you to have no hindrances to a love relationship with Him in your life. Once God has spoken to you through His Word, how you respond is crucial. You must adjust your life to the truth."[74]

Some years ago, a Christian man from a Middle Eastern nation attended a Campus Crusade conference in another country. While there, he felt God calling him to join our staff. That decision meant much more sacrifice to him than it does to someone who joins our staff in the United States. Because of Muslim persecution in his country, his decision to follow the Lord in ministry could result in harm to him and even death—and the same consequences for his family. But he felt sure that God wanted him to tell his countrymen about the love of God as revealed through Jesus Christ our Lord.

After the conference ended, he went home and told his wife what God was leading him to do. Her reaction was amazing. She said, "If God wants you to join Campus Crusade for Christ, then I agree with your decision. I am willing to follow your decision."

She realized the ramifications that this change meant for her and her family. In fact, today she and her husband are exiles from their homeland because of their witness for Christ. But she adjusted her plans to fit into God's plans for their lives—and she and her husband saw tremendous fruit in their country before their exile. God continues to use them mightily in their new assignment.

This also means adjusting your life in areas in which you have been disobeying Him. If you are not sharing your faith, you begin witnessing to others. If you read questionable—even pornographic—books or magazines, or watch such videos, get rid of the objectionable materials at once. If you need an accountability partner to help you, find one today. Don't wait. Start spending more time reading God's Word or other materials that edify your spirit, instead. If you are not spending enough time with your family, readjust your schedule.

Adjusting your standards may also mean making changes in your life that fit God's leading. If God directs you to change careers, you take the necessary steps to do what He asks. If you feel the Holy Spirit guiding you to help with the preschoolers in Sunday school, you willingly give up that Sunday morning class that you enjoy. If a need arises for someone to work with boys at church one night a week and God is nudging you to help, you must be willing to do whatever it takes to be available. If He leads you to share His good news in other countries and cultures, you must step out in faith and respond. Knowing God's truth and holiness always leads to righteous action. But the rewards, friends, for you and those you serve are exciting and fulfilling.

Be an Advocate for Righteousness Where You Live

As disciples of Jesus Christ, we are to live righteous lives. But how does righteousness impact the course of a nation? The Bible declares, "Righteousness exalts a nation, but sin is a disgrace to any people" (Proverbs 14:34).

In the Book of Deuteronomy, God promised to bless the nation of Israel for obedience, but He also warned of judgment upon His people if His laws were disregarded. Second Chronicles 7:14 gives this wonderful promise: "If My people who are called by My name will humble themselves and pray and seek My face and turn from their wicked ways, I will hear from heaven and will forgive their sins and heal their land."

America has a unique heritage—one rooted in a dependence on God and His biblical principles. The scriptural principles for a godly nation were well understood by the pilgrims. Their purpose, as stated in the Mayflower Compact, was to plant colonies "for the glory of God, and advancement of the Christian faith."[75] Ninety-nine percent of the colonial population professed to be Christians and most of our founding fathers were true followers of our Lord Jesus Christ. Early in the 19th century, the French philosopher and historian Alexis de Tocqueville did a study of democracy in our country and came to this conclusion:

> I sought for the greatness and genius of America in her commodious harbors and her ample rivers, and it was not there. I sought for the greatness and genius of America in her fertile fields and boundless forests, and it was not there. I sought for the greatness and genius of America in her rich mines and her vast world commerce, and it was not there. I sought for the greatness and genius of America in her public school system and her institutions of learning, and it was not there. Not until I went to the churches of America and heard her pulpits aflame with righteousness did I understand the secret of her genius and power. America is great because America is good, and if America ever ceases to be good, America will cease to be great.[76]

For many decades after our country's founding, American leaders advocated God's righteousness in government.

- George Washington said, "It is impossible to rightly govern the world without God and the Bible."[77]
- John Adams, the second president and co-drafter of the Declaration of Independence, said, "Our Constitution was made only for a moral

and religious people, it is wholly inadequate to the government of any other."[78]

- Noah Webster believed, "The Christian religion is the most important and one of the first things in which all children, under a free government, ought to be instructed."[79]

- Nearly all of the first 119 colleges and universities of our nation, including Harvard, Yale, Princeton, Dartmouth, William and Mary, and Columbia, were founded primarily to train young scholars in the knowledge of God and the Bible.

- Abraham Lincoln said, "But for the Bible we would not know right from wrong."[80]

- The first US Supreme Court Chief Justice John Jay said, "Providence has given to our people the choice of their rulers, and it is the duty, as well as the privilege and interest of our Christian nation to select and prefer Christians for their rulers."[81]

- In 1892, the US Supreme Court made the following ruling: "No purpose of action against religion can be imputed to any legislation, state or national, because this is a religious people... This is a Christian nation."[82] That court ruling cited 87 different historical precedents.

Then at the turn of the 20th century, a bloodless revolution began to change our nation. Unrighteous philosophies such as relativism and evolution spread throughout mainstream America. Without a single previous precedent, the Supreme Court in 1947 declared the "separation of Church and State." This action was widely interpreted as separation of godly principles from public life. In 1962 and 1963, the Supreme Court declared school prayer to be unconstitutional and Bible reading was outlawed from our schools. Within a decade, the Supreme Court made it lawful to kill our unborn children yet unlawful to display the Ten Commandments in public schools. As a result, God's righteous foundation in America is systematically being destroyed. As the foundation crumbles, so does

> Whose standards of "right" will you follow? God's or man's?

the nation. It is obvious from every social indicator that the secular and humanistic system has failed.

As believers, we dare not continue to be silent. For many years, I have had a deep burden for our country's moral condition. I steadfastly believe that if Christians will stand firm on the righteous standards of God's law, we can turn our country back to its godly heritage. We must hold fast to the righteous standards set forth by the sovereign Creator and Ruler of the universe in our own lives and be advocates for His standards in our culture.

Regardless of the beliefs and behavior of a nation, ultimately God will hold every person accountable. Whose standards of "right" will you follow: God's or man's? What we do in our personal lives and how we serve as an advocate of God's righteousness to our neighborhoods, cities, states, and country will help change the world for Christ.

Every day I review and meditate on the Ten Commandments. I urge you to keep the Ten Commandments clearly in mind by writing them on a card and displaying them in your car, on your refrigerator, or at your desk. As we will see in the next chapter, the God who penned the Ten Commandments is the same yesterday, today, and forever. How comforting!

Talk About It: I Help You Make Right Choices
"The LORD is gracious and righteous; our God is full of compassion."
(Psalm 116:5, NIV)

1. Do you agree or disagree with the statement "We always lose when we violate God's standard of righteousness"? Explain.
2. Saying that God's laws take the fun out of life is like saying traffic laws take the fun out of driving. Both statements miss the real point. List three ways God's laws are like traffic laws.
   What is the purpose of God's laws?
3. What do people usually mean when they say, "It's just business"? Have you ever had to choose between what is right and what is culturally acceptable? What did you do? In light of what you now know about God, would you make that same decision today or a different one? Why?

4. What is meant by the saying, "Garbage in, garbage out"? How does that apply to becoming more righteous? What do you think this means in your daily life if you want to adjust your life to God's standards?

5. The Christian life is not simply adherence to a code of conduct, but a relationship with the living God. How do His laws help cultivate our relationship with Him?

6. As followers of Jesus, what are some of the potential consequences of upholding God's righteousness in modern culture?

7. Proverbs 14:34 states, "Righteousness exalts a nation, but sin is a disgrace to any people" (NIV). What is one thing you can do to help our nation turn away from its sin and move toward righteousness?

FOCUS ON GOD

Continue to review the statement and verse you wrote down last week, at least three times each day, to remind yourself that because God is righteous, you can reflect His righteousness.

**God, because You are righteous,
I will live by Your standards, not the world's.**

"You are righteous, LORD, and Your laws are right."
(Psalm 119:137, NIV)

This week, focus on things that will build your relationship with God knowing that righteous living will be the fruit that will eventually begin to grow from your relationship.

CHAPTER 26

I AM Unchanging

About 4,500 years ago, Pharaoh Khafre carved the Sphinx from limestone bedrock. Since then, this 66-foot statue of a man's head with a lion's body has stood in the Egyptian desert. For thousands of years, it has remained unchanged.

Or has it? Actually, this monument has undergone many changes. Khafre never finished the statue in his lifetime. For about a thousand years, it was abandoned to the Egyptian sands. In 1400 BC, Thutmose IV uncovered the statue and painted it blue, yellow, and red and erected a statue of his father in front of the Sphinx's chest. Then another great pharaoh, Ramses II, extensively reworked the Sphinx in 1279 BC. After that, the Egyptian sands once again began filling up around the gigantic face and body. Wind began to erode what the Pharaohs had done.

As early as the 15th century AD, an Arab historian wrote that the Sphinx's face was disfigured. In 1818, a Genoese sea captain cleared away the debris from the statue's chest and uncovered an ancient chapel in front of it. He also discovered fragments of the Sphinx's stone beard, which are now in the British Museum. In the early 1900s, a French engineer cleared the Sphinx down to its base and shored up the weathered headdress with stone. During the 1980s, large slabs were added to try to stop the erosion. Still, in 1988, part of the right shoulder fell off.

The Sphinx is eroding even faster today. During the last decade, repairs are once again being made to the ancient statue. The large slabs added in the 1980s are being replaced by more natural-looking stone. Many plans for helping save the Sphinx from greater deterioration are being suggested.[83]

The real fact of life on earth is change. Since the fall of Adam when sin was introduced, change has been a part of human life. The moment we are born, we begin to age. We grow, develop, and deteriorate. No matter what modern science does to slow down this process, it continues on without stopping. Our great monuments like the Sphinx are not really a testimony to our power to create something unchanging, but merely to our best efforts to delay the deterioration and ravages of time.

Our only hope in this life lies in one fact: God never changes. He is the constant that we can count on while everything else around us deteriorates.

The Unchanging Nature of God

One fascinating fact about many of the religions of the world is the unpredictable character of their gods. New Agers believe that everything is god and god is everything. The source of authority or "truth," they say, is what you experience. Shirley MacLaine, proponent of New Age religion, says, "My own out-of-body experience…served to validate the answers to many questions—the surest knowledge being derived from experience."[84] In other words, you may believe one thing to be true today, but then an experience tomorrow will change that truth. And what you believe to be true will not be true for me. For New Agers, truth changes.

But we learned that God's truth never changes. It is the same today as it has always been.

Buddhists believe that salvation is in karma. Kenneth Latourette, a leading church historian, explains this Buddhist belief: "Karma may be described as the sum of an individual's thoughts and actions in all his previous incarnations. In

> God's unchanging nature applies to all of His attributes.

each incarnation, he modifies his karma for either good or bad… The ultimate aim is not only to improve one's karma, but to do more, namely, to escape from the endless series of changes, the appalling eternal succession of births and rebirths. This would be salvation."[85]

How different this is from God's simple, unchanging plan of salvation! With God's plan, we know where we stand, what we must do, and the result—an eternal, unalterable place in the family of God.

Animists and idol worshipers have developed their understanding of how their gods work from accumulated folklore. Their gods are so capricious that they must constantly be appeased with sacrifices and a variety of rituals so they will not change the rules of the game. But we can read God's rules in His never-changing Word.

The God of the Bible is the only unchanging Supreme Being. He has never altered one bit of His character or His purpose. That is what I love about our wonderful and marvelous God. I have known Him personally since 1944, and today He is just the same in His holiness and love, His grace and mercy as He was when I first turned my life over to Him. Theologians call this consistency and dependability God's *immutability*.

When I get up in the morning to pray, His response will not be different from when I pray to Him at bedtime. When I confront a difficult situation, I have calmness of heart because I know His unchanging Holy Spirit is present to guide me.

Mormons believe God was once a man like us. Joseph Smith, the founder of Mormonism said, "God himself was once as we are now, and is an exalted man." If Joseph Smith was right then not only has God changed radically, but he can never be eternal, infinite, all-powerful, all-knowing, or even perfectly just.

The Bible presents the God we worship as One who is the same from eternity to eternity. The writer of the Book of Hebrews compares the immutability of God to His changing creation: "They will perish, but You remain; they will all wear out like a garment. You will roll them up like a robe; like a garment they will be changed. But You remain the same, and Your years will never end" (Hebrews 1:11,12, NIV). He never changes in His essential being, never varies how He reacts to sinful man, to man's repentance, or to man's worship. Sin and unbelief always displease Him; obedience and faith always warm His heart.

God's Name Indicates His Unchangeable Nature

In the beginning of this book, we discovered God's most holy name, I AM. Through this name, God introduced the concept that He is unchangeable from eternity past to eternity future. He identifies Himself with that incredible statement: "I AM WHO I AM. This is what you are to say to the Israelites: 'I AM has sent me to you'" (Exodus 3:14, NIV). The use of the present tense in I AM means that the God who met Adam and Eve in the Garden of Eden was the same God who met Abraham and Sarah and gave them a son—and He is the same God who acts on our behalf today.

God's unchanging nature applies to all of His attributes as well. We are exceedingly glad that His love, grace, and mercy are unchanging. We appreciate the fact that His holiness cannot change. Emotions or circumstances do not affect God. He "does not change like shifting shadows" (James 1:17, NIV).

The fact that we can depend on God's immutability is tremendously reassuring for us today. We must admit that at times we violate one of God's unchanging attributes, such as His holiness. But we know that when we repent, His unchanging grace brings us forgiveness and favor (1 John 1:9). We can proclaim God's message of love and forgiveness without fear that God will change the rules the next day.

God Does Not Grow or Develop

When you look at a newborn baby, you realize the tremendous amount of growing and learning that little person has to do. He cannot talk, walk, or reason. His body does not have the ability to sing, scratch his back, or throw a ball. His mind cannot tell you what he is feeling or remember what a tree feels like. He must go through all the stages of maturity—toddlerhood, childhood, puberty, adulthood, middle age, old age. In each stage, he will learn many new things.

God has never had to grow or change or develop. He was never like us. He has always been infinite. Although Jesus did grow in His physical body, He has always known everything and been able to do everything. He laid aside His divine majesty and assumed human nature in the form of a servant (Philippians 2:7,8).

Therefore, God has never had to learn anything—He has always been omniscient. God has never had to develop talents or skills—He has always been able to do everything. He has never needed to mature—He has always been perfect in all of His attributes.

God is also not moody, like we are. When I come before Him in prayer, I do not have to worry that He has just heard prayers of someone who really made Him angry and will take His anger out on me. He does not get tired, and He is not too busy to listen to my concerns. As the faithful Father, He is always there when we need Him. He is not more loving one day because He feels good and more judgmental the next because He wakes up on the wrong side of the bed. Because God's attributes always exist in fullness and in cooperation with each other, God's purposes, motives, thoughts, and actions are forever the same.

God's Word Never Changes

If God's character does not change, then it follows that His Word does not change either. If His purposes do not change, then the instructions He gives to us do not change.

Isaiah 40:6–8 records that "people are like the grass that dies away. Their beauty fades as quickly as the beauty of flowers in a field. The grass withers, and the flowers fade beneath the breath of the LORD. And so it is with people. The grass withers, and the flowers fade, but the word of our God stands forever."

Let us take a look at how true that is. The first verse in the Bible, Genesis 1:1, reads: "In the beginning God…" In Revelation 22:13, the last book of the Bible, Jesus says, "I am the Alpha and Omega, the First and the Last, the Beginning and the End."

Salvation has never changed in God's Word. When God referred to Abraham, He said, "Abram believed the LORD, and the LORD declared him righteous because of his faith" (Genesis 15:6). In the New Testament centuries later, Romans 3:27,28 says, "Can we boast, then, that we have done anything to be accepted by God? No, because our acquittal is not based on our good deeds.

It is based on our faith. So we are made right with God through faith and not by obeying the law."

The principles throughout the Old and New Testaments are the same. God deals with each of us in the same way, with the same love and graciousness.

Immutability Includes Variety

A common, misinformed picture of heaven today is of saints floating around on clouds playing harps—for eternity. Nothing disturbs their little bit of heaven, as they presumably stay right where they are—forever! Is that your picture of heaven? Does the fact that God never changes bore you?

When we speak of God's immutability, we are not speaking of a lack of variety. They are two separate things. Look at God's creation. An elephant and a mosquito both have four legs and an appendage on the front of their faces. But who would describe an elephant and a mosquito as alike? How about a mouse and a whale? They both have tails, pointed noses, and sleek bodies. But, oh, the differences!

Immutability and creativity are not the same either. Although God never changes, He is all-creative. Just think about how many different personalities He has created throughout the world. No person is just like another. How about the many different kinds of plants He has made— from a pear cactus flower to an orchid; from a giant redwood to a delicate bluebell; from moss to seaweed. There is no end to God's creativity.

> Although God never changes, there is no end to God's creativity.

What does not change are the principles and the character that underlie the variety and creativity. God's plans for us are always to conform us to the image of His Son. He changes the way He works out His plan to fit our personalities, our circumstances, and our needs.

Sometimes, however, the unchanging nature of God's work is plain to see. Do you remember the story of Paul and Silas in prison for proclaiming God's message? Their preaching and that of other Christians produced phenomenal growth during the days of the early Church. It also produced persecution for the sake of Christ, which is why Paul and Silas were in prison. While they were praying and singing hymns at midnight, a great earthquake shook the prison's foundations. All the doors flew open and the chains fell off every prisoner.

In those days, if a Roman jailer lost his prisoners, the law required a sentence of death. The Roman jailer awoke, assumed all the prisoners had run away, and was going to commit suicide. Paul shouted, "Don't do it. We're all here!" The jailer, when he saw that the prisoners had not escaped, fell on his knees before Paul and Silas and asked how he could be saved.

Paul and Silas shared the Word of God with him, and he and his entire household believed in our Lord. The next day, the city officials released Paul and Silas.

Centuries later, the pattern repeated. In the 1930s, missionaries planted the Word of God in the southwestern mountains of Ethiopia. When World War II erupted and the missionaries were forced to leave, they left a church of only 48 believers. But in five years of foreign occupation in their land, the Ethiopian church grew to 10,000!

Raymond Davis, who worked in the interior of Ethiopia, tells of a miraculous story of God's work among the Wallamo people. The Christians had been horribly persecuted for proclaiming God's message, but their congregation had grown to more than a thousand. The government forced them to tear down their precious church building, which they had built with such sacrifice of labor and materials.

Later, they dared to rebuild their church building. Consequently, several of the church leaders, including a man named Toro, were taken to the marketplace, stripped, and beaten. Then they were thrown into jail where their jailers taunted them for believing in God. Davis writes:

> Sometime later, a group of the believers in prison were praying together when a terrible rain and thunderstorm came up. Toro says he doesn't remember the lightning ever being fiercer or the thunder claps louder. While they were praying and singing, the wind blew with such terrific force that the entire iron roof of the prison was torn completely off. The torrents of rain pouring down onto the exposed mud walls made them crumble and melt. The prisoners were free!

Many of the non-Christian prisoners fled. The terrified jailers, convinced that the storm was the direct intervention of God on behalf of the Christian prisoners, came to Toro pleading that he pray to God to withhold His anger and fury—and they would be released. The jailers kept their word.[86]

Of course, not every person imprisoned for his faith is freed by an act of God, but these two incidents show that God is still at work as He was in the lives of the first-century believers. He never changes! You can count on Him!

Praising God for His Unchanging Nature

When you fly from Chicago to Los Angeles on some airlines you will fly over one section of the Grand Canyon. If you happen to fly over it during the late afternoon, the canyon's shadows help you see its incredible depth and breadth. But the fact remains—you are seeing only a segment of it, for it runs 277 miles. Now imagine yourself circling the Earth in the International Space Station and you come over the Grand Canyon. How much of it will you see now? All of it in one glance.

> God never changes!
> You can count on Him!

When we look at life on Earth, we see only a minute sliver of it, one minuscule slice of eternity. But God sees all of eternity at once, the end from the beginning. That is why we need God's perspective on the events of life—He sees it in ways we do not. As a result He can take corrective action to keep us from wandering off course or hurting ourselves as we march through life's parade of circumstances and events.

What a great God we have! We can trust Him to not turn against us, for His love is unchanging. We can trust Him for life after death, for He is eternal. That is why the writer of Hebrews could say: "Jesus Christ is the same yesterday, today, and forever" (Hebrews 13:8).

That is the God we worship and adore—and serve unconditionally. It is the God we proclaim to the entire world without ceasing, for He is worthy not only of our worship but also our obedience to His Great Commission to go and to love.

St. John Chrysostom, a third-century church leader, wrote of His Lord and Savior:

> It is fitting and right to sing of you, to praise you, to thank you, to adore you in all places of your dominion. For you are the ineffable God, inconceivable, invisible, incomprehensible, existing forever and yet ever the same, you and your only-begotten Son and your Holy Spirit. You brought us into being out of nothingness, and when we had fallen, you raised us up again. You have not ceased doing everything to lead us to heaven and to bestow upon us your future and your only-begotten Son and your Holy Spirit. You do this for all the benefits of which we know, for those of which we are ignorant, and for those that are manifest to us and those that lie concealed.[87]

I urge you to take time to enjoy the wonder of God's attributes. As you learn more facts about His greatness, thank Him, glorify Him, and praise Him for all He means to you. Let the Holy Spirit fill your mind with His love and grace, and touch your deepest feelings with His comfort and gentleness. The more you worship and meditate on His character, the more you will become like Him. The more you focus on His attributes, the more you will reflect His nature. Worship Him through giving, serving, praising, singing, and giving thanks. That is the sure road to developing an intimate relationship with God!

Talk About It: I AM Unchanging

"Whatever is good and perfect is a gift coming down to us from God our Father, who created all the lights in the heavens. He never changes or casts a shifting shadow."
(James 1:17)

1. What are some reasons things change? In nature? In relationships? In science? In government?

2. Some religions teach that God grows and changes over time—just like us. Can you think of three reasons why that is a major problem?

3. Choose two or three of God's other attributes. How would they be affected if God were not unchanging?

4. God gave Himself the name "I AM," which signifies He is eternally present, unbound by time. How does His name also indicate His unchanging nature?

5. Although nature changes and is full of surprises, the laws that govern nature never change. How does that contrast clearly reflect the difference between God's immutability (He never changes) and His creativity? Why is it an important distinction? How would this reassure people who are afraid heaven will be boring?

6. Read Isaiah 40:7,8 and Matthew 24:35. What do they tell us about God's Word? How should this truth affect the way you read and follow God's Word (the Bible)?

FOCUS ON GOD

On an index card or your favorite electronic device, write the following statement and verse, or just take a picture of it:

**God, because You are unchanging,
I know my future is secure.**

"He never changes or casts a shifting shadow."
(James 1:17)

Look at it when you get up, when you go to bed, and at least once during the day as a way of intentionally shifting your focus from yourself to God. This week, reflect on the things in your life that are changing and then thank God that He is the same yesterday, today, and forever.

CHAPTER 27

You Can Always Count on Me

D o you ever wish time would stand still? Has your neighborhood changed, or a loved one grown distant or passed away? Have dear friends moved away?

One of the hardest changes for a parent is when children grow up, move away, and become independent. I remember the day that Vonette and I helped our older son, Zac, settle into his dorm room at Life Bible College in Los Angeles. Later we helped our younger son, Brad, pack his car to leave home and drive across the country to Washington, DC, to work for Senator William Armstrong from Colorado.

Before each of our sons left home, we got down on our knees together to thank God for him and pray for his safety. When we rose, we embraced and expressed our love. Of course, as parents, we always had a few last-minute instructions. My eyes misted as I silently thanked God for each of my boys.

As Brad drove away toward Washington, DC, Vonette and I waved valiantly. I forced a smile and stemmed my tears. *My little boy isn't little anymore*, I thought as his car disappeared around a bend. *He's on his own now.*

I treasure the heartwarming memories of Zac and Brad when they were young and in our home. Vonette and I will always love our sons, and look forward to spending time with them whenever possible. Today we still miss them as much as when they left home. As many of you know, the "empty nest" syndrome that comes when your last child leaves home is very real.

But our boys are independent adults now. They do not need us like they did when they were young. Of course, I would not wish for them to come back because they have lives, families, and ministries of their own. Some of the memories of separations are erased with our delight in visiting with our grandchildren. Yet we will never forget the emotionally difficult change we experienced when each of our sons left home.

Today, we live in a time of hyper-change. Fashions and trends change weekly; people relocate frequently; technological advances quickly make the past obsolete. A way of life that was once familiar and comfortable to us rapidly fades away. This change produces a great deal of stress. As we search for stability, we wonder if there is any permanence anymore. Is there some anchor that will hold us so we will not be swept away by the waves of change washing over society?

There are several reasons we are drawn into the undercurrents of change. For one, sin and our fallen nature promote a process of decay and deterioration. Things get progressively worse when left to themselves. You can understand that if you have ever had to maintain an old house. The water heater needs replacing; the screen door comes off its hinges; the roof leaks.

Another reason we change is because we experience pressure from others or from our circumstances. We change well-laid plans because of illness or because a family member is in crisis and needs help. An airline goes on strike so our flight is canceled. All kinds of events make us modify what we want to do.

A third reason is because of boredom. We do not want every day to be exactly the same as the last. A little spice and variety make life more enjoyable.

Also, technological achievements and other kinds of improvements stimulate change. Computers have dramatically altered the way we do things. Seldom do we mail a package of important papers. Now we can e-mail a file or fax the pages immediately. Everyone expects instant turnaround time.

But the influences that cause change in our lives have no effect on God. Let us look at several benefits we enjoy because God never changes.

God's Unchanging Nature Provides Stability

A story is told of a shipwrecked sailor who clung to a rock in great danger until the tide went down. Later a friend asked him, "Didn't you shake with fear when you were hanging on the rock?"

He simply replied, "Yes, but the rock didn't."

> Life and its uncertainties may shake us, but God does not move.

Life and its uncertainties may shake us, but God—who is the Rock of Ages—does not move. If we cling to Him, His strength sustains us.

Since God never changes (James 1:17), God's character is constant. Unlike us, He does not compromise or change His values. He cannot be manipulated or persuaded to go against His word. He does not have a Dr. Jekyll and Mr. Hyde personality where He will comfort us one moment and snap at us the next.

God's Unchanging Purpose Gives Us Eternal Significance

Psalm 33 states, "The LORD's plans stand firm forever; His intentions can never be shaken" (Psalm 33:11). God's plan existed at the beginning of creation and remains the same today. It unfolds in phases and stages, which may give us the impression of change, but His original design has always been consistent. God's purposes for us are fulfilled within the framework of time and history.

The nation of Israel is the clearest example of this truth. The Lord declared to the people of Israel, "Everything I plan will come to pass, for I do whatever I wish... I have said I would do it, and I will" (Isaiah 46:10,11). From the day God placed Adam and Eve in the Garden of Eden, God's hand has been leading and guiding His people.

And we are part of His plan! We share His purpose. Paul wrote to the believers in Ephesus, "For we are God's masterpiece. He has created us anew in Christ Jesus, so that we can do the good things He planned for us long ago" (Ephesians 2:10). We no longer need to feel as if we are unimportant in the cosmos. As God's people, we are His loved ones whom He has planned from the beginning to bless and to live with forever!

God's Unchangeable Ways Assure Us of Unwavering Guidance

In the early 1960s, President Kennedy challenged NASA to send a man to the moon. The man in charge of that seemingly impossible assignment was a marvelous Christian and a dear friend. He told me that they had nothing to build on except the unchanging laws of God's creation. Imagine the frustration had God's laws of science, physics, and creation not been dependable. That is where the scientists started, and sure enough—the impossible mission happened on schedule!

Just as the natural laws of the universe never change, God's principles for life never change. David writes, "As for God, His way is perfect. All the Lord's promises prove true" (Psalm 18:30). Following His guidelines, given in Scripture, will produce fruitful lives. Not only that, He assures us that His Holy Spirit living inside us will complete what God has begun in our lives. As I look back over the events of my life, I can clearly see how God has guided me in ways that produced what He intended even when it was impossible for me to accomplish. All He required was my availability and willingness to do what He asked of me.

> Just as natural laws never change, God's principles for life never change.

For example, in 1945, as a new Christian I had a dream to produce a film about the life of our Lord. I was hoping to finance the film with the profits from my business. I was long on zeal, but short on practical knowledge.

At that time, our ministry did not have the funds to produce such an ambitious project. Yet for more than 33 years, our board of directors, the staff, and I discussed the need for a film on the life of Christ which could be used as an evangelistic tool. We reviewed more than thirty films, but most of them were not scripturally accurate. We even seriously considered buying the rights to one of these films and reworking it to make it biblically accurate. But we were never able to raise the huge amount of money for the production costs. Yet I still believed that God wanted me to complete this project.

Then in 1976, I met John Heyman, a movie producer who had produced more than thirty feature-length films. I introduced John to Paul Eshleman, our US Field Ministry director who later headed the *JESUS* film project. A few months later, Bunker and Carolyn Hunt, long-time friends and generous supporters of the ministry, provided financing for the film. God began to fulfill the dream that He had placed in my heart over three prior decades.

Accuracy and authenticity were crucial as a team of researchers painstakingly produced a 318-page document giving the biblical, theological, historical, and archeological background of every scene as presented by the Gospel of Luke. During the filming in Israel, John Heyman demanded excellence. For example, he once stopped the cameras when he noticed a ripple-soled tennis shoe print in the dust. But excellence was what we needed to produce a film that could touch the world.

We prayed that the *JESUS* film would become a mighty evangelistic instrument to introduce millions to God. When the filming and production were completed, *JESUS* opened in America in the fall of 1979 in Warner Brothers theaters. By the end of the commercial run a year later, more than four million people had seen the film. From the beginning, however, we planned that *JESUS* would go beyond American shores. We developed a strategy to bring the film to urban centers, rural areas, islands, mountaintop villages, and countries where electricity is a rarity.

To date, more than two thousand *JESUS* film teams have been sent to remote villages and great metropolitan areas. You can imagine the excitement when a team begins to set up its equipment in places where people have never had the opportunity to view a movie, particularly in their own language.

As of April 1, 1999, *more than 2 billion people in almost 500 languages in 225 countries have viewed JESUS*. Hundreds of millions have responded with salvation decisions. God has used our thousands of staff and volunteers, almost a thousand mission organizations, and tens of thousands of local churches of many denominations to introduce people to Jesus through this film.

God demonstrated His unchanging faithfulness when He began to work in me through a vision to fulfill His purposes (Philippians 2:13). Then 33 years later He brought together the resources and personnel to make the dream come true. If you have been a follower of Jesus for very long I am sure you can point to many instances where God's guidance, true to the unchanging principles of His Word, made a huge difference in your life and ministry and the lives of others. We can depend on His guidance every day of our lives if we continue to trust and obey Him.

God's Unchanging Word Equips Us With Timeless Truth

God does not change what He says based on opinion polls, focus groups, or cultural currents. His words and commands are timeless. They are valid throughout all eternity. They apply to every culture, race, and nationality.

That is why the Bible has remained relevant throughout the ages and to all civilizations. What God says is always pertinent. It never becomes obsolete. His timeless truth is the surest foundation for anything we attempt.

Almost to a man, the founding fathers of our nation sought to serve and glorify Jesus Christ with their lives. One study found that of 15,000 writings by the founding fathers included in newspaper articles, pamphlets, books, monographs, and other documents, 94 percent of all quotes either directly or indirectly cited the Bible.[88] Fifty-two of the 55 framers of the Constitution were avowed biblical Christians. They were inspired by God to dedicate this new republic for His honor and glory. Even the curriculum of the institutions of higher learning used the Bible as a textbook. The efforts of our founding fathers produced miraculous results. The United States Constitution is currently the oldest operating document of any government in the world. Every other nation on earth has instituted a new form of government since our founding documents were written. The US Constitution is unlike any other political instrument because the liberties it guarantees are greater than the liberties granted to the citizens of any other nation. And all this resulted from God's unchanging principles, which provided the timeless truths for our governing documents.

> This life on earth is but a prelude to eternity.

Abraham Lincoln, our 16th President and the man who guided our country through a civil war, stated, "I believe the Bible is the best gift God has given to man. All the good Savior gave to the world was communicated through this Book."[89]

Former President Ronald Reagan, a devout believer from his youth, declared on numerous occasions that if only the American people would "live closer to the Ten Commandments and the Golden Rule," the problems we face would be solved.[90] As you know, the Ten Commandments and the Golden Rule are basic principles from God's Word. Tragically, we are now reaping the consequences of a society that has abandoned biblical truth. Yet as we each base our lives on His Word, we will see the joy and blessing that come from living according to God's unchanging truth.

God's Unchanging Commitment Guarantees Us Everlasting Security

Recently, I stood at the grave sites of two dear friends, and as I reflected on their lives, I realized that the most important moment we can experience is our death. When we breathe our last earthly air and take our first breath of the celestial, we transition into the presence of God! This life on earth is but a prelude to eternity. My friends had no fear of crossing over, for they knew the reality of God's unwavering faithfulness to them.

Hebrews states, "God also bound Himself with an oath, so that those who received the promise could be perfectly sure that He would never change His mind" (Hebrews 6:17). We who have given ourselves to God through the death and resurrection of Jesus Christ have received eternal life. God is committed to our redemption, our Christian walk, and our eternal destiny. God's unchanging nature assures us that we will indeed live with Him forever as He promised. God's commitment is as strong as He is constant. No one and nothing can violate His promise: "[The Holy Spirit's] presence within us is God's guarantee that He really will give us all that He promised" (Ephesians 1:14, TLB). We can bank our entire future on His unchanging character. What a sure anchor for our faith!

Perhaps you are thinking: *If God never changes, what is the purpose of prayer and other communication with God?* I want to caution you about using God's immutability as an excuse not to pray or to ask Him to intervene in your daily life. Although He will never change His plans, Scriptures abound that show how God alters His temporary purposes in response to our faith and actions.

For example, He reverses His judgment because of sincere repentance of sinners (Jonah 3:4–10). At other times, He responds to the needs of human beings or the fervent prayer of the righteous (Numbers 14:1–20; 2 Kings 20:1–6; Luke 18:1–8). This is one of the mysteries of God's nature. We know that God never changes, and yet He relates to us and gives us our free will. When we pray and ask Him to intervene in our lives, He does so—when it is in line with His will. He works through us as we walk and talk with Him. So I encourage you to take comfort in the fact that God never changes; but realize that when we seek His face in repentance, we can expect Him to respond to our prayers and deal with our sin.

Now that we have discovered many facets of God's character, how will our knowledge affect our lives? Intimacy with God requires changes on our part. It also means that we will give God the praise, honor, and adoration He deserves. Only by deepening your view of who God really is, and intentionally changing your focus from your circumstances to the great I AM, can you can begin to experience the joy, peace, security. and fruitfulness He promised.

Talk About It: You Can Always Count on Me
"Jesus Christ is the same yesterday, today, and forever."
(Hebrews 13:8)

1. How does the fact that God never changes make you feel? Why?
2. Review your timeline from Chapter 1. How have you changed over the years? Do you see evidence of God's unchanging nature reflected in your experiences? If so, how?
3. Reflect on the story of the shipwrecked sailor clinging to the rock. Can you relate to his story? How has God's unchanging character been your rock in the storms of life?
4. How can you be sure He will be your rock in future storms?
5. Do you agree/disagree with this statement: "We can bank our entire future on His unchanging character." What implications does your answer have on your daily life?
6. How should the fact that God never changes impact your prayer life?

7. What is the connection between God's unchanging nature and your ability to experience the peace and joy He promises to everyone who trusts in Jesus?

8. In the areas listed below, identify any you can relate to. What attribute of God would help you most in that circumstance? If there is an attribute of God you are struggling to believe is true in that circumstance, how would embracing God's unchanging nature help?

Addictions	Broken relationships	Jealousy
Poor self-image	Critical attitude	Sexual temptations
Fear	Worry	Suffering
Abuse	Rejection	Financial crisis
Illness	Other people's choices	Questioning God

FOCUS ON GOD

Continue to review the statement and verse you wrote down last week, at least three times each day, to remind yourself that your future is secure because God never changes.

**God, because You are unchanging,
I know my future is secure.**

"He never changes or casts a shifting shadow."
(James 1:17)

Read "The Great Stone Face," a classic short story by Nathaniel Hawthorne, which you can download for free.[91] When you have finished, answer this question: "If I want to become more like Christ, what is the one thing I must do?"

CHAPTER 28

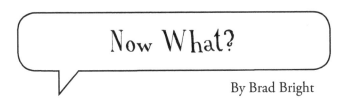

Now What?

By Brad Bright

A s the youngest son of Bill Bright, I saw my dad live out what you have just read in this book. It was an amazing privilege. His life was undeniable evidence of the life-changing power of knowing the Creator God. For me, the most convincing proof that the God of the Bible is real was my dad's life.

Shortly after I graduated from college, I was sitting with my dad in his office while a reporter from a popular Christian magazine interviewed him.

It was pretty much the usual questions until the reporter asked, "What is a problem you face that the average Joe Christian can relate to?" My dad replied, "I don't have any problems."

The reporter, completely unconvinced, retorted, "Let's not over-spiritualize this. We all have problems." He continued to ask the same question seven times, seven different ways, trying to get my dad to admit he had problems.

Finally my dad leaned forward, looked him in the eye and said, "You need to understand, I am a slave of Jesus. It is not the slave's responsibility to be successful. The slave is not responsible for the outcome. The only responsibility of the slave is to do what the Master asks him to do. That is why I do not have problems; I only have opportunities to see the Master work."

It was an "Aha!" moment that I have never forgotten. For the first time in my life I understood the real "genius" of my dad—it was his view of God! He really believed to the core of his being what he had just said to the reporter.

Do you have problems or do you have opportunities to see God work?

It explained why he could calmly walk through incredibly stressful situations that would break other men. Whether staring death in the eye as Burmese radicals prepared to stone him, weathering interrogations from hostile reporters, or discovering that associates he deeply trusted had deliberately betrayed him, he had learned to keep his eyes on his Master. It is why in all my years growing up I could never remember him raising his voice at me in anger—and I was a strong-willed child. It was the reason he could put his head back and fall asleep in less than two minutes regardless of his circumstances. He truly lived out the "peace of God, which transcends all understanding" (Philippians 4:7).

So here is my question for you: Do you have problems, or do you have opportunities to see God work?

My wife, Kathy, and I have personally experienced our own "opportunities" to see God work. A number of years ago Kathy was working on a project that she believed with all her heart God wanted her to do. Unfortunately, some folks in positions of authority over her disagreed and were not kind. For six months Kathy was miserable while she chafed under their leadership. She found that not only was she angry, but she had become bitter—and no matter how hard she tried, she could not get rid of the bitterness. She confessed her bitterness to God and asked Him to take control—again, and again, and again, and again. But each time, almost before she was done praying, the bitterness came flooding back.

One day while we were visiting with a few friends, Kathy opened up about her struggle and sincerely asked for prayer. She knew that God could not be pleased with the bitterness in her soul. As she poured out her heart, an idea struck me that I had never thought of before. I blurted out, "What attribute of God are you struggling to believe is true in this situation?" With eyes narrowed she fired back, "I believe all of God's attributes are true!"

But then she paused, sucked in her breath, and her eyes flew open as she said words I will never forget: "I've been believing those people have more power over God's will for my life than God does, and *that's not true!*" The moment the word "true" sprang from her lips, her eyes cleared and I could see that she was free. Free of the anger. Free of the bitterness. In that moment of clear focus, she recognized God's sovereignty even in this painful situation. He was still in control. No one could thwart God's will for her life. The bitterness and anger evaporated in an instant and *never* came back.

Does your focus need to be adjusted? What do you need to be set free from? What aspect of God's character are you not fully embracing today? Does something in your life indicate you are living in denial of who God really is?

In Matthew chapter 14, the Bible gives us a great example of the power of keeping our focus in the right place.

Jesus came walking across the turbulent Sea of Galilee in the early morning while it was still dark. From their boat His disciples saw Him, thinking He was a ghost. Once they realized it was Jesus, Peter called out, "Lord, if it is really You, command me to come to You." Jesus said, "Come." Peter jumped out of the boat and started walking on the water toward Jesus.

It's all about your focus.

Okay, stop right here; push pause. What was Peter doing? He was walking on water in defiance of the laws of nature! Not only that, but the wind was whipping up waves, battering the boat he had just exited. Normally we would assume he was in terrible danger. He wasn't; he was perfectly safe.

Now fast forward a few steps. Peter is drawing close to Jesus and suddenly begins sinking like a rock. In desperation he calls out, "Lord, save me!"

Push pause again. Here is the critical question. Which of Peter's external circumstances changed, thrusting him from complete safety into mortal danger? The answer is "none of the above." The only thing that changed was Peter's focus. As long as his focus was on Jesus, he was perfectly safe. The moment he took his eyes off Jesus, he truly faced mortal danger.

> Learning to keep your focus on God requires effort, but it pays incredible dividends.

What does this teach us about the Christian life? It's all about your focus. If your focus is on God, then you can walk through the storms of life. If your focus is on your circumstances or yourself, you will sink like a rock. Of course, in order to truly focus on God, you have to know who He really is.

Let me encourage you to do four things that can change the trajectory of your life if you will let them:

1. Commit to daily reminding yourself of God's character and attributes, sincerely asking the question, "Why does it matter?" We have created a free *Discover God Daily* electronic devotional just for you, at GodWhoRU. com, to help encourage you in this process.

2. Keep your focus on God by maintaining a continuous conversation with Him. Be intentional about keeping the conversation going. It requires effort.

3. The next time a major challenge crashes into your life, ask yourself the following question: "Do I believe this is a problem or an opportunity to see God work?" Be honest with yourself and God.

   If you realize you are viewing the situation as a problem, ask yourself one more question: "What attribute of God am I struggling to believe is true in this situation?" Now you have identified your real problem.

   Let me suggest you start memorizing verses from Scripture that will begin to build your confidence in that aspect of God's character. At the back of the book you can find scripture verses focusing on God's various attributes. And, of course, talk with God about it—a thousand times if necessary. God has all the time in the world.

4. If you have not already done so, read Appendix B, "How to Be Filled With the Holy Spirit." Have you been trying hard to please God but keep coming up short? Turn to the back of the book. It is God's Spirit who empowers us to live the Christian life each moment of each day.

Without His power it is truly impossible to please Him. Oh, and in case you missed it, let me say one more time, turn to the back of the book.

As finite humans, it is so easy for us to live in denial of who God really is. So remember, God loves you passionately, He is all-powerful, He is with you at all times, and He is still the sovereign King of the universe. Therefore, if you really believe you have a problem, there is either something you are struggling to believe is true about God, or you are focused on your circumstances instead of the King who is always with you. Learning to keep your focus on God requires effort, but it pays incredible dividends.

Now you understand why my dad said, "We can trace all our human problems to our view of God." My heart's prayer for you is that you can begin to see God the way Bill Bright saw God. If you do, the relationship you will have with your Creator will be more than you could ever ask or imagine.

"Now all glory to God, who is able, through His mighty power at work within us, to accomplish infinitely more than we might ask or think" (Ephesians 3:20).

Welcome to life's greatest adventure!

GodWhoRU.com

Would You Like to Know God Personally?

The following four principles will help you discover how to know God personally and experience the abundant life He promised.

1 *God loves you and created you to know Him personally.*

God's Love

"God so loved the world that He gave His one and only Son, that whoever believes in Him shall not perish but have eternal life" (John 3:16, NIV).

God's Plan

[Christ speaking] "I came that they might have life, and might have it abundantly" [that it might be full and meaningful] (John 10:10).

…What prevents us from knowing God personally?

2 *Man is sinful and separated from God, so we cannot know Him personally and experience His love and plan.*

Man Is Sinful

"All have sinned and fall short of the glory of God" (Romans 3:23).

Man was created to have fellowship with God; but, because of his own stubborn self-will, he chose to go his own independent way and fellowship with God was broken. This self-will, characterized by an attitude of active rebellion or passive indifference, is an evidence of what the Bible calls sin.

Man Is Separated

"The wages of sin is death" [spiritual separation from God] (Romans 6:23).

This diagram illustrates that God is holy and man is sinful. A great gulf separates the two. The arrows illustrate that man is continually trying to reach God and the abundant life through his own efforts, such as a good life, philosophy, or religion—but he inevitably fails.

The third law explains the only way to bridge this gulf…

3 *Jesus Christ is God's only provision for our sin. Through Him alone we can know God personally and experience God's love and plan.*

He Died In Our Place

"God demonstrates His own love toward us, in that while we were yet sinners, Christ died for us" (Romans 5:8).

He Is the Only Way to God

"Jesus said to him, 'I am the way, and the truth, and the life; no one comes to the Father but through Me'" (John 14:6).

This diagram illustrates that God has bridged the gulf that separates us from

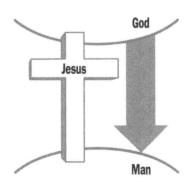

Him by sending His Son, Jesus Christ, to die on the cross in our place to pay the penalty for our sins.

It is not enough just to know these three truths…

4 *We must individually receive Jesus Christ as Savior and Lord; then we can know God personally and experience His love and plan.*

We Must Receive Christ

"As many as received Him, to them He gave the right to become children of God, even to those who believe in His name" (John 1:12).

We Receive Christ Through Faith

"By grace you have been saved through faith; and that not of yourselves, it is the gift of God; not as a result of works, that no one should boast" (Ephesians 2:8,9).

When We Receive Christ, We Experience a New Birth

(Read John 3:1–8.)

We Receive Christ By Personal Invitation

[Christ speaking] "Behold, I stand at the door and knock; if anyone hears My voice and opens the door, I will come in to him" (Revelation 3:20).

Receiving Christ involves turning to God from self (repentance) and trusting Christ to come into our lives to forgive our sins and to make us what He wants us to be. Just to agree intellectually that Jesus Christ is the Son of God and that He died on the cross for our sins is not enough. Nor is it enough to have an emotional experience. We receive Jesus Christ by faith, as an act of the will.

These two circles represent two kinds of lives:

Self-Directed Life
S – Self is on the throne
† – Christ is outside the life
● – Interests are directed by self, often resulting in discord and frustration

Christ-Directed Life
† – Christ is in the life and on the throne
S – Self is yielding to Christ
● – Interests are directed by Christ, resulting in harmony with God's plan

Which circle best represents your life?

Which circle would you like to have represent your life?

The following explains how you can receive Christ:

You Can Receive Christ Right Now by Faith Through Prayer
(Prayer is talking with God)
God knows your heart and is not so concerned with your words as He is with the attitude of your heart. The following is a suggested prayer:

Lord Jesus, I need You. Thank You for dying on the cross for my sins. I open the door of my life and receive You as my Savior and Lord. Thank You for forgiving my sins and giving me eternal life. Take control of the throne of my life. Make me the kind of person You want me to be.

Does this prayer express the desire of your heart? If it does, I invite you to pray this prayer right now, and Christ will come into your life, as He promised.

How to Know That Christ Is in Your Life
Did you receive Christ into your life? According to His promise in Revelation 3:20, where is Christ right now in relation to you? Christ said that He would come into your life. Would He mislead you? On what authority do you know that God has answered your prayer? (The trustworthiness of God Himself and His Word.)

The Bible Promises Eternal Life to All Who Receive Christ
"God has given us eternal life, and this life is in His Son. He who has the Son has the life; he who does not have the Son of God does not have the life" (1 John 5:11,12).

Thank God often that Christ is in your life and that He will never leave you (Hebrews 13:5). You can know on the basis of His promise that Christ lives in you and that you have eternal life from the very moment you invite Him in. He will not deceive you.

An important reminder...

Do Not Depend on Feelings
The promise of God's Word, the Bible—not our feelings—is our authority. The Christian lives by faith (trust) in the trustworthiness of God Himself and His Word. This train diagram illustrates the relationship among fact (God and

His Word), faith (our trust in God and His Word), and feeling (the result of our faith and obedience). (Read John 14:21.)

The train will run with or without the caboose. However, it would be useless to attempt to pull the train by the caboose. In the same way, as Christians we do not depend on feelings or emotions, but we place our faith (trust) in the trustworthiness of God and the promises of His Word.

Now That You Have Entered into a Personal Relationship Christ

The moment you received Christ by faith, as an act of the will, many things happened, including the following:

- Christ came into your life (Revelation 3:20; Colossians 1:27).
- Your sins were forgiven (Colossians 1:14).
- You became a child of God (John 1:12).
- You received eternal life (John 5:24).
- You began the great adventure for which God created you (John 10:10).

Can you think of anything more wonderful that could happen to you than receiving Christ? Would you like to thank God in prayer right now for what He has done for you? By thanking God, you demonstrate your faith.

To enjoy your new relationship with God...

Suggestions for Christian Growth

Spiritual growth results from trusting Jesus Christ. A life of faith will enable you to trust God increasingly with every detail of your life, and to practice the following:

G   *Go* to God in prayer daily (John 15:7).

R   *Read* God's Word daily (Acts 17:11); begin with the Gospel of John.

O   *Obey* God moment by moment (John 14:21).

W   *Witness* for Christ by your life and words (Matthew 4:19; John 15:8).

T   *Trust* God for every detail of your life (1 Peter 5:7).

H   *Holy Spirit*—allow Him to control and empower your daily life and witness (Galatians 5:16,17; Acts 1:8; Ephesians 5:18).

Remember

Your walk with Christ depends on what you allow Him to do in and through you empowered by the Holy Spirit, not what you do for Him through self effort.

If you have come to know Christ personally through this presentation of the gospel or would like further help in getting to know Christ better, please visit us at BrightMedia.org and request to receive *Discover God Daily*.

Fellowship in a Good Church

God's Word instructs us not to forsake "the assembling of ourselves together" (Hebrews 10:25). If you do not belong to a church, do not wait to be invited. Take the initiative; call the pastor of a nearby church where Christ is honored and His Word is preached. Start this week, and make plans to attend regularly.

APPENDIX B

How to Be Filled With the Holy Spirit

Every day can be an exciting adventure for the Christian who knows the reality of being filled with the Holy Spirit and who lives constantly, moment by moment, under His gracious direction.

The Bible tells us that there are three kinds of people:

1. Natural Man: One who has not received Christ.

"A natural man does not accept the things of the Spirit of God; for they are foolishness to him, and he cannot understand them, because they are spiritually appraised" (1 Corinthians 2:14, NASB).

Self-Directed Life

S – Self is on the throne

† – Christ is outside the life

● – Interests are directed by self, often resulting in discord and frustration

2. **Spiritual Man:** One who is directed and empowered by the Holy Spirit. "He who is spiritual appraises all things" (1 Corinthians 2:15, NASB).

Christ-Directed Life
S – Christ is in the life and
      on the throne
† – Self is yielding to Christ
● – Interests are directed by
      Christ, resulting in harmony
      with God's plan

3. **Carnal Man:** One who has received Christ, but who lives in defeat because he trusts in his own efforts to live the Christian life.

"I, brethren, could not speak to you as to spiritual people but as to carnal, as to babes in Christ. I fed you with milk and not with solid food; for until now you were not able to receive it, and even now you are still not able; for you are still carnal. For when there are envy, strife, and divisions among you, are you not carnal and behaving like mere men?" (1 Corinthians 3:1–3).

Self-Directed Life
S – Self is on the throne
† – Christ dethroned and not
      allowed to direct the life
● – Interests are directed by
      self, often resulting in
      discord and frustration

The following are four principles for living the Spirit-filled life:

1. God has provided for us an abundant and fruitful Christian life.

"Jesus said, 'I have come that they may have life, and that they may have it more abundantly'" (John 10:10, NKJV).

"The fruit of the Spirit is love, joy, peace, patience, kindness, goodness, faithfulness, gentleness, self-control; against such things there is no law" (Galatians 5:22,23).

Read John 15:5 and Acts 1:8.

The following are some personal traits of the spiritual man that result from trusting God:

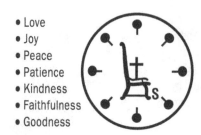

- Love
- Joy
- Peace
- Patience
- Kindness
- Faithfulness
- Goodness

- Life is Christ-centered
- Empowered by Holy Spirit
- Introduces others to Christ
- Has effective prayer life
- Understands God's Word
- Trusts God
- Obeys God

The degree to which these traits are manifested in the life depends on the extent to which the Christian trusts the Lord with every detail of his life, and on his maturity in Christ. One who is only beginning to understand the ministry of the Holy Spirit should not be discouraged if he is not as fruitful as more mature Christians who have known and experienced this truth for a longer period.

Why is it that most Christians are not experiencing the abundant life?

2. Carnal Christians cannot experience the abundant and fruitful Christian life.

The carnal man trusts in his own efforts to live the Christian life:

- He is either uninformed about, or has forgotten, God's love, forgiveness, and power (Romans 5:8–10; Hebrews 10:1–25; 1 John 1; 2:1–3; 2 Peter 1:9).
- He has an up-and-down spiritual experience.
- He wants to do what is right, but cannot.
- He fails to draw on the power of the Holy Spirit to live the Christian life (1 Corinthians 3:1–3; Romans 7:15–24; 8:7; Galatians 5:16–18).

Some or all of the following traits may characterize the carnal man—the Christian who does not fully trust God:

- Legalistic attitude
- Impure thoughts
- Jealousy
- Guilt
- Worry
- Discouragement
- Critical spirit
- Frustration

- Aimlessness
- Fear
- Ignorance of his spiritual heritage
- Unbelief
- Disobedience
- Loss of love for God and for others
- Poor prayer life
- No desire for Bible study

(The individual who professes to be a Christian but who continues to practice sin should realize that he may not be a Christian at all, according to 1 John 2:3; 3:6–9; and Ephesians 5:5.)

The third truth gives us the only solution to this problem...

3. Jesus promised the abundant and fruitful life as the result of being filled (directed and empowered) by the Holy Spirit.

The Spirit-filled life is the Christ-directed life by which Christ lives His life in and through us in the power of the Holy Spirit (John 15).

- One becomes a Christian through the ministry of the Holy Spirit (John 3:1–8.) From the moment of spiritual birth, the Christian is indwelt by the Holy Spirit at all times (John 1:12; Colossians 2:9,10; John 14:16,17).
- All Christians are indwelt by the Holy Spirit, but not all Christians are filled (directed, controlled, and empowered) by the Holy Spirit on an ongoing basis.
- The Holy Spirit is the source of the overflowing life (John 7:37–39).
- In His last command before His ascension, Christ promised the power of the Holy Spirit to enable us to be witnesses for Him (Acts 1:1–9).

How, then, can one be filled with the Holy Spirit?

4. We are filled (directed and empowered) by the Holy Spirit by faith; then we can experience the abundant and fruitful life that Christ promised to each Christian.

You can appropriate the filling of the Holy Spirit right now if you:

- Sincerely desire to be directed and empowered by the Holy Spirit (Matthew 5:6; John 7:37–39).
- Confess your sins. By faith, thank God that He has forgiven all of your sins—past, present, and future—because Christ died for you (Colossians 2:13–15).
- Present every area of your life to God (Romans 12:1,2).
- By faith claim the fullness of the Holy Spirit, according to:

His command: Be filled with the Spirit. "Do not get drunk on wine, which leads to debauchery. Instead, be filled with the Spirit" (Ephesians 5:18).

His promise: He will always answer when we pray according to His will. "This is the confidence we have in approaching God: that if we ask anything according to his will, he hears us. And if we know that He hears us—whatever we ask—we know that we have what we asked of Him" (1 John 5:14,15).

How to Pray in Faith to be Filled With the Holy Spirit

We are filled with the Holy Spirit by faith alone. However, true prayer is one way of expressing your faith. The following is a suggested prayer:

Dear Father, I need You. I acknowledge that I have been directing my own life and that, as a result, I have sinned against You. I thank You that You have forgiven my sins through Christ's death on the cross for me. I now invite Christ to again take His place on the throne of my life. Fill me with the Holy Spirit as You commanded me to be filled, and as You promised in Your Word that You would do if I asked in faith. I pray this in the name of Jesus. As an expression of my faith, I now thank You for directing my life and for filling me with the Holy Spirit.

Does this prayer express the desire of your heart? If so, bow in prayer and trust God to fill you with the Holy Spirit right now.

APPENDIX C

Attributes of God with Scripture Verses

God, because You are personal...

I will seek a deep relationship with You.

- "I have called you friends, for everything that I learned from my Father I have made known to you." (John 15:15, NIV)
- "You fathers—if your children ask for a fish, do you give them a snake instead? Of if they ask for an egg, do you give them a scorpion? Of course not! So if you sinful people know how to give good gifts to your children, how much more will your heavenly Father give the Holy Spirit to those who ask Him." (Luke 11:11–13)
- "So you have not received a spirit that makes you fearful slaves. Instead, you received God's Spirit when He adopted you as His own children. Now we call Him, 'Abba, Father.' For His Spirit joins with our spirit to affirm that we are God's children." (Romans 8:15,16)

- "Look! I stand at the door and knock. If you hear My voice and open the door, I will come in, and we will share a meal together as friends." (Revelation 3:20)
- "The Lord is a friend to those who fear Him. He teaches them His covenant." (Psalm 25:14)

God, because You are all-powerful...
I know You can help me with anything.

- "O Sovereign Lord! You made the heavens and earth by Your strong hand and powerful arm. Nothing is too hard for You!" (Jeremiah 32:17)
- "I also pray that you will understand the incredible greatness of God's power for us who believe Him. This is the same power that raised Christ from the dead." (Ephesians 1:19,20)
- *"For I can do everything through Christ, who gives me strength." (Philippians 4:13)*
- *"He gives power to the weak and strength to the powerless." (Isaiah 40:29)*
- "The eyes of the LORD search the whole earth in order to strengthen those whose hearts are fully committed to Him." (2 CHRONICLES 16:9)

God, because You are love...
I know You are unconditionally committed to my well-being.

- "We know how much God loves us, and we have put our trust in His love. God is love..." (1 John 4:16)
- "For this is how God loved the world: He gave His one and only Son, so that everyone who believes in Him will not perish but have eternal life. God sent His Son into the world not to judge the world, but to save the world through Him." (John 3:16,17)
- "Can anything ever separate us from Christ's love? Does it mean He no longer loves us if we have trouble or calamity, or are persecuted, or are hungry, or destitute, or in danger, or threatened with death? No, despite

all these things, overwhelming victory is ours through Christ, who loved us. And I am convinced that nothing can ever separate us from God's love." (Romans 8:35,37,38)

- "And may you have the power to understand, as all God's people should, how wide, how long, how high, and how deep His love is." (Ephesians 3:18)

- "We can rejoice, too, when we run into problems and trials, for we know that they help us develop endurance. And endurance develops strength of character, and character strengthens our confident hope of salvation. And this hope will not lead to disappointment. For we know how dearly God loves us, because He has given us the Holy Spirit to fill our hearts with His love." (Romans 5:3–5)

- "For the LORD is good. His unfailing love continues forever, and His faithfulness continues to each generation." (Psalm 100:5)

God, because You are holy...
I will devote myself to You in purity, worship, and service.

- "Holy, holy, holy is the LORD Almighty; the whole earth is full of His glory!" (Isaiah 6:3, NIV)

- "Who is like you among the gods, O LORD — glorious in holiness, awesome in splendor, performing great wonders?" (Exodus 15:11)

- "This is the message we heard from Jesus and now declare to you: God is light, and there is no darkness in Him at all." (1 John 1:5)

- "O God, Your ways are holy. Is there any god as mighty as You?" (Psalm 77:13)

- "For by that one offering He forever made perfect those who are being made holy." (Hebrews 10:14)

- "You must not misuse the name of the LORD your God. The Lord will not let you go unpunished if you misuse His name." (Exodus 20:7)

God, because You are everywhere all the time...
I know You are always with me.

- "Never will I leave you; never will I forsake you." (Hebrews 13:5, NIV)
- "The LORD is close to all who call on Him, yes, to all who call on Him in truth." (Psalm 145:18)
- "I can never escape from Your Spirit! I can never get away from Your presence! If I go up to heaven, You are there; if I go down to the grave, You are there. If I ride the wings of the morning, if I dwell by the farthest oceans, even there Your hand will guide me, and Your strength will support me." (Psalm 139:7–10)
- "'Am I a God who is only close at hand?' says the LORD. 'No, I am far away at the same time. Can anyone hide from Me in a secret place? Am I not everywhere in all the heavens and earth?' says the Lord." (Jeremiah 23:23,24)
- "'I have been given all authority in heaven and on earth. Therefore, go and make disciples of all the nations…And be sure of this: I am with you always, even to the end of the age.'" (Matthew 28:18–20)

God, because You are merciful…
I know that through Christ all my sins are forgiven.

- "The Lord is full of compassion and mercy." (James 5:11, NIV)
- "But God is so rich in mercy, and He loved us so much, that even though we were dead because of our sins, He gave us life when He raised Christ from the dead. (It is only by God's grace that you have been saved!)" (Ephesians 2:4,5)
- "If we confess our sins, He is faithful and just and will forgive us our sins and purify us from all unrighteousness." (1 John 1:9, NIV)
- "So let us come boldly to the throne of our gracious God. There we will receive His mercy, and we will find grace to help us when we need it most." (Hebrews 4:16)
- "He shows mercy from generation to generation to all who fear Him." (Luke 1:50)

- "The faithful love of the Lord never ends! His mercies never cease. Great is His faithfulness; His mercies begin afresh each morning." (Lamentations 3:22,23)

God, because You are absolute truth...
I will believe what You say and live accordingly.

- "You will know the truth, and the truth will set you free." (John 8:32)
- "Jesus told him, 'I am the way, the truth, and the life. No one can come to the Father except through Me.'" (John 14:6)
- "Lead me by Your truth and teach me, for You are the God who saves me. All day long I put my hope in You." (Psalm 25:5)
- "God's way is perfect. All the LORD's promises prove true." (2 Samuel 22:31)
- "Every word of God proves true. He is a shield to all who come to Him for protection. Do not add to His words, or He may rebuke you and expose you as a liar." (Proverbs 30:5,6)

God, because You know everything...
I will come to You with all my questions, concerns, and worries.

- "In Him lie hidden all the treasures of wisdom and knowledge." (Colossians 2:3)
- "Nothing in all creation is hidden from God. Everything is naked and exposed before His eyes, and He is the one to whom we are accountable." (Hebrews 4:13)
- "Oh, how great are God's riches and wisdom and knowledge! How impossible it is for us to understand His decisions and His ways! For who can know the Lord's thoughts? Who knows enough to give Him advice?" (Romans 11:33,34)
- "But true wisdom and power are found in God; counsel and understanding are His." (Job 12:13)

- "O LORD, You have examined my heart and know everything about me." (Psalm 139:1)

God, because You are just...
I know Your justice will prevail.

- He is the Rock; His deeds are perfect. Everything He does is just and fair. He is a faithful God who does no wrong; how just and upright He is!" (Deuteronomy 32:4)
- "But I, the LORD, search all hearts and examine secret motives. I give all people their due rewards, according to what their actions deserve." (Jeremiah 17:10)
- "For we must all stand before Christ to be judged. We will each receive whatever we deserve for the good or evil we have done in this earthly body." (2 Corinthians 5:10)
- "God is an honest judge. He is angry with the wicked every day. If a person does not repent, God will sharpen His sword; He will bend and string His bow." (Psalm 7:11,12)
- "For God presented Jesus as the sacrifice for sin. People are made right with God when they believe that Jesus sacrificed His life, shedding His blood. This sacrifice shows that God was being fair when He held back and did not punish those who sinned in times past, for He was looking ahead and including them in what He would do in this present time. God did this to demonstrate His righteousness, for He himself is fair and just, and He makes sinners right in His sight when they believe in Jesus." (Romans 3:25,26)

God, because You are faithful...
I will trust You to always keep Your promises.

- "Let us hold unswervingly to the hope we profess, for He who promised is faithful." (Hebrews 10:23, NIV)

- "But if we confess our sins to Him, He is faithful and just to forgive us our sins and to cleanse us from all wickedness." (1 John 1:9)
- "The LORD is trustworthy in all He promises and faithful in all He does." (Psalm 145:13, NIV)
- "O LORD God of Heaven's Armies! Where is there anyone as mighty as You, O LORD? You are entirely faithful." (Psalm 89:8)
- "For the LORD is good. His unfailing love continues forever, and His faithfulness continues to each generation." (Psalm 100:5)

God, because You are sovereign…
I will joyfully submit to Your will.

- "Now to the King eternal, immortal, invisible, the only God, be honor and glory for ever and ever. Amen." (1 Timothy 1:17, NIV)
- "And we know that God causes everything to work together for the good of those who love God and are called according to His purpose for them." (Romans 8:28)
- "For we are God's masterpiece. He has created us anew in Christ Jesus, so we can do the good things He planned for us long ago." (Ephesians 2:10)
- "But the LORD's plans stand firm forever; His intentions can never be shaken." (Psalm 33:11)
- "'My thoughts are nothing like your thoughts,' says the LORD. 'And My ways are far beyond anything you could imagine. For just as the heavens are higher than the earth, so My ways are higher than your ways and My thoughts higher than your thoughts.'" (Isaiah 55:8,9)

God, because You are righteous…
I will live by Your standards.

- "O LORD, you are righteous, and your regulations are fair." (Psalm 119:137)

- "The LORD is righteous in everything He does; He is filled with kindness." (Psalm 145:17)
- "Throw off your old sinful nature and your former way of life, which is corrupted by lust and deception. Instead, let the Spirit renew your thoughts and attitudes. Put on your new nature, created to be like God—truly righteous and holy." (Ephesians 4:22–24)
- "The eyes of the LORD watch over those who do right, and His ears are open to their prayers. But the LORD turns His face against those who do evil." (1 Peter 3:12)
- "And Abram believed the LORD, and the LORD counted him as righteous because of his faith." (Genesis 15:6)

God, because You never change...
I know my future is secure and eternal.

- "Whatever is good and perfect comes down to us from God our Father, who created all the lights in the heavens. He never changes or casts a shifting shadow." (James 1:17)
- "I am the LORD, and I do not change." (Malachi 3:6)
- "Jesus Christ is the same yesterday, today, and forever." (Hebrews 13:8)
- "Long ago You laid the foundation of the earth and made the heavens with Your hands. They will perish, but You remain forever; they will wear out like old clothing. You will change them like a garment and discard them. But You are always the same; you will live forever." (Psalm 102:25–27)
- "God is not a man, so He does not lie. He is not human, so He does not change His mind. Has He ever spoken and failed to act? Has He ever promised and not carried it through?" (Numbers 23:19)

Endnotes

1 J. B. Phillips, *Your God Is Too Small* (New York: MacMillan Publishing, 1953).

2 *Our Daily Bread*, June 11, 1995 (Grand Rapids, MI: RBC Ministries).

3 Robert Roy Britt, "Universe 156 Billion Light-years Wide," CNN.com, May 24, 2004. <cnn.com/2004/TECH/space/05/24/universe.wide/index.html>.

4 A. W. Tozer, *The Knowledge of the Holy* (San Francisco: HarperSanFrancisco, 1961).

5 "Karl Marx," *The New Encyclopedia Britannica*, vol. 23 (Chicago: Encyclopedia Britannica, Inc., 1978).

6 James M. Kittleson, "The Breakthrough," *Christian History*, Issue 34, 15.

7 Pam Beasant, *1000 Facts About Space* (New York: Kingfisher Books, 1992), 10,11.

8 Tony Evans, *Our God Is Awesome* (Chicago: Moody Press, 1994), 162.

9 David Jeremiah, *Knowing the God You Worship*, audio cassettes (San Diego: Turning Point, 1994).

10 "1969 Woodstock Festival & Concert" (www.woodstock69.com).

11 Dwight L. Moody, "The Love of God," *Classic Sermons on the Attributes of God*, compiled by Warren W. Wiersbe (Peabody, MA: Hendrickson Publishers), 1989, 12.

12 Words by Samuel Trevor Francis, 1834–1925, *O the Deep, Deep Love of Jesus*.

13 Details of the story of Vek and Samouen are found in *The Touch of Jesus* by Paul Eshleman (Orlando, FL: NewLife Publications, 1995), 149–156.

14 Ibid, 155.

15 Richard Wurmbrand, "Love Conquers Everything," *The Voice of the Martyrs*, March 1999, 10.

16 Ibid.

17 To read more about loving by faith, see my booklet *How to Love by Faith*.

18 David Jeffery, "Yellowstone: The Great Fires of 1988," *National Geographic*, February 1989, 265.

19 A. W. Tozer, *The Pursuit of God* (Camp Hill, PA: Christian Publications, 1993), 37.

20 *Nelson Study Bible*, (Nashville, TN: Thomas Nelson Publishers, 1997), 2120.

21 Stephen Charnock, *The Existence and Attributes of God* (Grand Rapids, MI: Baker Books, reprinted 1996), vol. 2, 112.

22 Louis Berkof, *Systematic Theology* (Grand Rapids, MI: Wm. B. Eerdmans Publishing Co., 1941), 73.

23 Beth Moore, *A Woman's Heart: God's Dwelling Place* (Nashville, TN: Lifeway Press, 1995), 161.

24 A. W. Tozer, *The Knowledge of the Holy* (San Francisco: HarperSanFrancisco, 1961), 75,76.

25 Bill Hybels, *The God You're Looking For* (Nashville: Thomas Nelson Publishers, 1997), 24.

26 Website of the U. S. Department of Energy, www.ornl.gov/hgmis/faq/faqs1.html.

27 In Matthew 28:18–20, Christ gave the Great Commission where He commands His followers to take His message of love and forgiveness to the entire world.

28 Brother Lawrence, *The Practice of the Presence of God* (Pittsburgh: Whitaker House, 1982), 17.

29 Ibid., 19.

30 Corrie ten Boom with John and Elizabeth Sherrill, *The Hiding Place* (Washington Depot, CT: 1971), 197.

31 Judy Nelson, "Golden Opportunities," *Worldwide Challenge*, January/February 1999, 41.

32 Brother Lawrence, *The Practice of the Presence of God* (Pittsburgh: Whitaker House, 1982), 38.

33 Ibid., 59.

34 Jim Cymbala, *Fresh Wind, Fresh Fire* (Grand Rapids, MI: Zondervan Publishing House, 1997), 56.

35 David Jeremiah, *Knowing the God You Worship*, audio cassettes, (San Diego: Turning Point, 1994).

36 David Morris, *A Lifestyle of Worship* (Ventura, CA: Renew Books, 1998), 201.

37 A. W. Tozer, *The Knowledge of the Holy* (San Francisco: HarperSanFrancisco, 1961), 92.

38 Adapted from Ed DeWeese, "The Right Man to Rob," *Worldwide Challenge*, January/February 1995, 5.

39 Josh McDowell, *The Myths of Sex Education* (San Bernardino, CA: Here's Life Publishers, 1990), 58.

40 Ibid., 59.

41 George Grant, *Grand Illusions: The Legacy of Planned Parenthood* (Brentwood, TN: Wolgemuth & Hyatt Publishers, Inc., 1988), 30. As quoted in Josh McDowell, *The Myths of Sex Education*, 60.

42 Robert C. Noble, "There Is No Safe Sex," *Newsweek*, April 1, 1991, 9.

43 Lorraine Day, M.D., "Are You Safe From AIDS? You May Be in for a Big Surprise" (www.drday.com/doctors.htm).

44 *Barna Report, 1997: American Witness* (Dallas, TX: Word Publishing, 1997).

45 George Barna, *What America Believes* (Ventura, CA: Regal Books, 1991), 84–85.

46 See Leviticus 18:22; 20:13; Romans 1:24–28; 1 Corinthians 6:9,10; 1 Timothy 1:8–10.

47 Charles Colson, "Neale Donald Walsch: The Words…" *The Wall Street Journal*, July 9, 1997, A12.

48 "Interviews from Death Row: Reporter Kathy Chiero's developing relationship with Karla," *CBN Interviews Online*, January 30, 1998, 1.

49 "New Life on Death Row: The Karla Faye Tucker Story," *CBN Interviews Online*, 1,2.

50 Lisa Master, "Houston, We Have a Problem," *Worldwide Challenge*, July/ August 1997, 24.

51 "Albert Einstein," *Compton's Encyclopedia Online* v. 3.0 (The Learning Company, Inc., 1998).

52 "Computers," *Compton's Encyclopedia Online* v. 3.0 (The Learning Company, Inc., 1998).

53 Stephen Charnock, *The Existence and Attributes of God*, Vol. 1 (Grand Rapids, MI: Baker Books, reprinted 1996), 409.

54 Cited by Marcus Chown in "Let There Be Light," *New Scientist* (vol. 157, February 7, 1998), 30. As quoted in Henry M. Morris, "The Stardust Trail," *Back to Genesis* (no. 121, January 1999), a.

55 David Jeremiah, *Knowing the God You Worship*, audio cassettes (San Diego: Turning Point, 1994).

56 Sherwood Eddy, *Pathfinders of the World Missionary Crusade* (New York: Abingdon-Cokesbury, 1945), 125. As quoted in Ruth A. Tucker, *From Jerusalem to Irian Jaya* (Grand Rapids, MI: Zondervan Publishing House, 1983), 239.

57 David Protess and Rob Warden, *A Promise of Justice* (New York: Hyperion, 1998), 222.

58 Robert J. Wagman, *The Supreme Court: A Citizen's Guide* (New York: Pharos Books, 1993), 7,11,12,16,17.

59 *Wycliffe Bible Encyclopedia* (Chicago: Moody Press) 1975, 1:981.

60 Quoted in Max Boot, *Out of Order* (New York: Basic Books, 1998), ix.

61 Judy Nelson, "The Persecuted Church," *Worldwide Challenge*, September/ October 1997, 36.

62 Some scholars believe it was closer to 75 years.

63 Raleigh Washington, "I Would Not Agree to It Because It Was Not True," *Worldwide Challenge*, March/April 1992, 24.

64 Robert J. Wagman, *The Supreme Court: A Citizen's Guide* (New York: Pharos Books, 1993), 41.

65 March 30, 1863. James D. Richardson, *A Compilation of the Messages and Papers of the Presidents*, 1789–1897 (Published by Authority of Congress, 1899), 6:164.

66 Merril D. Patterson, ed., *Jefferson Writings* (New York: Literary Classics of the United States, Inc., 1984), 289, from Jefferson's *Notes on the State of Virginia, Query XVIII*, 1781.

67 Jack Canfield (ed.), Mark Victor Hansen, *Chicken Soup for the Soul: 101 Stories to Open the Heart and Rekindle the Spirit* (Health Communications, 1995), 273,274.

68 Charles Allen and Sharada Dwivedi, *Lives of the Indian Princes* (New York: Crown Publishers, Inc., 1984), 18.

69 Stephen Charnock, *The Existence and Attributes of God* (Grand Rapids, MI: Baker Books, reprinted 1996) vol. 2, 366.

70 Dick Edic, "Miraculous Memory," *Keep In Touch*, Winter 1999, Campus Crusade for Christ Alumni Relations.

71 A. W. Tozer, *The Attributes of God* (Camp Hill, PA: Christian Publications, 1997), 181.

72 Millard J. Erickson, *Concise Dictionary of Christian Theology* (Grand Rapids, MI: Baker Book House, 1986), 75.

73 Ibid., 144.

74 Henry T. Blackaby and Claude V. King, *Experiencing God* (Nashville, TN: Broadman and Holman Publishers, 1994), 167.

75 November 11, 1620. William Bradford, *The History of Plymouth Plantation 1608–1650* (Boston, MA: Massachusetts Historical Society, 1856).

76 Quoted in *The New American*, December 12, 1986, 10.

77 Henry Halley, *Halley's Bible Handbook* (Grand Rapids, MI: Zondervan, 1965), 18.

78 October 11, 1798, in his address as President to the Military. Charles Francis Adams, ed., *The Works of John Adams–Second President of the United States* (Boston: Little, Brown, & Co., 1854), 9:229.

79 1828, in the preface to his *American Dictionary of the English Language* (San Francisco: Foundation for American Christian Education, reprinted 1967), 12.

80 September 5, 1864, addressing the Committee of Colored People from Baltimore, *Washington Chronicle*. Quoted in Stephen Abbott Northrop, D.D., *A Cloud of Witnesses* (Portland, OR: American Heritage Ministries, 1987), 285.

81 October 12, 1816, *The Correspondence and Public Papers of John Jay*, Henry P. Johnston, ed., (New York: Burt Franklin, 1970), 4:393.

82 February 29, 1892, Justice Josiah Brewer, *Church of the Holy Trinity v. United States*, 143 US 457-458, 465-471, 36L ed 226.

83 Mark Lehner, "Computer Rebuilds the Ancient Sphinx," *National Geographic*, April 1991, 32–39.

84 Shirley MacLaine, *Dancing in the Light*, 35. As quoted in Josh McDowell and Don Stewart, *Deceivers: What Cults Believe, How They Lure Their Followers* (Nashville: Thomas Nelson Publishers, 1992), 236.

85 Kenneth S. Latourette, *Introducing Buddhism* (New York: Friendship Press, 1956), 4. As quoted in Russell P. Spittler, *Cults and Isms* (Grand Rapids, MI: Baker Book House, 1962), 96.

86 Raymond Davis, *Fire on the Mountains* (Grand Rapids, MI: Zondervan Publishing House, 1975), 135,136.

87 "Adoring the Ineffable: Prayers from the Liturgy of St. John Chrysostom," *Christian History*, vol. XIII, No. 4, 38.

88 John Eidsmoe, *Christianity and the Constitution*, (Grand Rapids, MI: Baker Book House, 1987), 51,53.

89 Abraham Lincoln, September 5, 1864, in an address to the Committee of Colored People from Baltimore.

90 Ronald Reagan, Gales Quotations CD-ROM (Detroit, MI: Gale Research Inc., 1995).

91 You can find it at The Literature Network, <www.online-literature.com/ hawthorne/139/>.

CPSIA information can be obtained
at www.ICGtesting.com
Printed in the USA
JSHW022014220523
42076JS00002B/330